Teesside
Urban Legends

The best of the Boro message boards

Compiled and Edited by

Steve Goldby, Robert Nichols,
Andrew Morgan and Dave Byrne.

Copyright:
Waking Lion and Fly Me to the Moon, 2008.

Waking Lion, Suite 1, 258 Marton Road,
Middlesbrough TS4 2EZ
info@wakinglion.com
http://www.WakingLion.com

Fly Me to the Moon, Unit 7, Brentnall Centre, Brentnall Street,
Middlesbrough TS1 5AP
rob@fmttm.freeserve.co.uk
http://www.FansOnline.net/Middlesbrough

ISBN 10 0-9553363-8-4   ISBN 13 978-0-9553363-8-6

A catalogue record of this book is available from the British Library.

Designed and printed by **hpm**group, Newton Aycliffe.

Photographs:

Thank you to the Evening Gazette, Middlesbrough, for their help in supplying several photographs in this publication.

Thanks also to Blades Sports Photography and North News & Pictures.

Rock Garden photograph courtesy of John Hodgson of Tees Band Archives.

Teesside Urban Legends
is dedicated to the memory of

Tim Lloyd
The man who put Middlesbrough on the net.

Chris Cullen
(aka Littleboro)
One of the greatest Fly Me to the Moon posters.

Special thanks to all message board posters who took
part in the threads featured in this publication.
Your humour, knowledge, insights and drunken ramblings
are now recorded in print forever!

Contents

Foreword
by Emanuel Pogatetz

A dream came true the day I joined Middlesbrough. It was my long held ambition to play in the English Premier League but I knew I would face an enormous challenge. I was prepared for that and for the different way of life from my previous spells in Austria, Switzerland, Russia and Germany. What I was not prepared for was the English sense of humour, especially the Teesside version of it!

In Austria, jokes are more straightforward than they are on Teesside, so it took me some time to get used to the way that people take the mickey out of each other over here. They take the mickey out of friends, out of colleagues, out of team-mates, out of everyone! At first, I used to think people were being serious and didn't know whether to be offended, but I have grown to love the Teesside sense of humour that I now know is such a big part of what makes the people here very special.

When I was told that the fans had written a hilarious thread about me on the Fly Me to the Moon website, I immediately asked to see it. I had heard of Fly Me to the Moon and had visited the website in the past but I couldn't have imagined what the fans had created. I think 'What Happened to Pogi's Head?' is an amazing piece of humour because so many people combined to make this weird comedy. Some of the things they have written are completely bizarre and I'm not quite sure where they thought it up, but it was so typical of the people here.

I am delighted that it is now a part of this unique book, Teesside Urban Legends. If being made Boro captain is my greatest honour since moving to England, the second greatest must be having such a weird and wonderful thread written about me by the supporters. I hope it is a testament to the close relationship I have with them.

Being celebrated in this way helped form the strong bond I now feel I have with the Boro fans. When I joined Middlesbrough from Bayer Leverkusen in 2005, I could not have imagined that such a bond would exist three years down the line. Adapting to life on Teesside was initially very difficult. I had already played football in four different countries but I now had to rise to the challenge of taking on players I admired so much. I was then given the tough task of taking the left-back position off Franck Queudrue, a player I knew was extremely popular with the fans. On top of all that, I had to adapt to a way of life that was very different from anything I had experienced before – especially that unique brand of Teesside humour!

I'm proud to have overcome those challenges, to have developed into a player that is seen fit to wear the captain's armband and to have formed such a special relationship with the people of Teesside. I suppose it doesn't hurt that my particular no-nonsense playing style is one the Boro fans have always appreciated. I thank all of the supporters who have helped me along that journey, especially those who through their humour helped me become a Teesside Urban Legend of my own.

Oh, and just for the record, Kevin Davies' elbow was what really happened to Pogi's head!

Enjoy the book. I know I will!

Emanuel Pogatetz

The History Of Boro On The Web Part 1
The Early Days and FMTTM

It never ceases to amaze me just how many people switch on to the FMTTM website every day, especially considering I had to be almost dragged kicking and screaming to run the site in the first place. Then I did my best to almost delete the whole thing on at least one occasion so it really is a miracle.

Yet by 2007 FMTTM was by far and away the busiest site on the number one fans network, Rivals. In 2008 I was told that when FMTTM relaunched as part of the FansOnline.net network, it was in the top five football fan sites in the country. This is amazing when you stop to consider.

Compare our average gates at the Riverside to other top Premier League clubs (yes, I said top), or the small size of the towns of Middlesbrough and Stockton against the larger UK cities. Look at the size of our fan base outside of Teesside and abroad. On all counts we are nowhere on the radar compared to the big city clubs. Yet we love our football and are absolutely glued to football forums and websites.

The small bumbling part I've played in this process is largely thanks to inheriting an already well read and versed Boro internet community.

There was already a large community typing messages to each other at the end of the last century, four or five years before I started being involved.

The formative years were back in the mid '90s. Peter Warren of the Football Supporters Association and another big Boro fan Alex Wilson told me about some strange goings on in cyber space – whatever that was. Peter was a bit of a godsend to me when I was short of pages for the fanzine as he would turn up with loads of pages of print-outs of posts by Boro fans from around the world talking Boro.

To be honest, I didn't fully understand where he was getting it from but I was most certainly relieved when it rescued a couple of pages with deadlines looming. Moreover, it was good stuff. The internet fellows certainly knew their Boro onion bags.

Then, in a mission to deliver me from my state of ignorance, Peter asked me if I would like to experience the Boro internet presence for myself. I asked whether it would be painful in any way. When the reply was in the negative I questioned whether it would be costly and again 'no' was the answer.

So one day after work we clambered down into the bowels of a building in Teesside University. All around the circumference of the massive room people were glued to VDUs. To my mind it was like something from a James Bond set. Then again, years tend to add drama, not to mention poetic licence, to many of my memories.

I do recall a bloke in front of his computer typing something on his keyboard and then, after a gap of several minutes, there came back a reply. A reply from Hong Kong! Wow, that's clever! But hang on, couldn't they just have picked up a phone? Yes, but it would have cost an arm and a leg.

Then there was a warning that it was 5pm and America had come online so everything would slow down. I wasn't totally convinced. "It'll never catch on" I thought. Just as we were about to leave someone surfed (apparently that was the name for it) and found the last few issues of Fly Me To The Moon online. Well, cheers for asking first.

The late Tim Lloyd was the great internet pioneer of all things Boro. Tim sadly passed on well ahead of his time in his mid-30s but we will be forever indebted to him for his vision and expertise.

Ally McWilliam set up the first Boro mailing list at the request of Tim from Hong Kong. Tim took over in October 1995 as the central hub in an emailing community where messages were sent to Hong Kong for him to relay back to the whole list. When I interviewed Tim in September 1996 there were already some 300 subscribers from all over the world, including South Africa, Japan, New Zealand, Canada and USA. As I say, Tim Lloyd himself was based in the Far East. Boro's online fanbase was truly global from the very start.

As far as I'm aware a fellow called Ben Gent had the first ever Boro website and Tim Lloyd took this on as well in 1995. So thanks to pioneers like Tim, Boro was established online very early on indeed. By the time I got involved, there were already hundreds of people communicating with each other every day about Boro. They even had meetings and organised football teams and visits to Hurworth. A proper community, you might say.

Another man with a beard, Alex Wilson, designed the first Fly Me To The Moon website. It was a case of if you can't beat them, join them. Alex convinced me that if people were already sticking the fanzine on the net I might as well do it officially, unofficially. All I had to do was email Alex a few set features from every issue of the fanzine and he would do the rest. And no one charged me for doing so, which was good of them.

Then, in 2000, I got an email from London inviting me to be the Boro part of the Rivals fans' network. They actually offered to pay me a little money. No, I thought, stick to what you know with fanzines. Unofficial fan sites - what are they all about? They'll never take off.

So they emailed me again. And phoned me. And then phoned me some more. "I don't know" I thought. "I'm busy already and I've already got a website. And anyway it's boring staring at a VDU screen all day long..."

"I'll think about it" was about as committed as I got. And how lucky am I? Everywhere else in the country the Rivals crew were turning people away. Here, their combination of good cop, bad cop in the brilliantly named Ryan Herman and Dan Davies were practically battering down my door to persuade me. They obviously couldn't find anyone else at all.

It was someone I met off Tim Lloyd's Mailing List, Sal Robinson, that talked me into it. She would do all the hard stuff - or at least find people to do the tricky code business - and I could just, err... say yes.

So in the summer of 2000 we were up and running with fmttm.com. From the moment we switched the message board on, it was busy. Where on earth did everyone come from? Probably from Tim Lloyd's list for starters. It just grew and grew and grew. Suddenly it began to look like the future and, as much as it pained me to admit it, I thought that one day the paper fanzine might be a thing of the past.

We were even offered shares as stakeholders in the company. We should think of it as managing media channels for sound and pictures. It was all new and exciting. It was the future. People knew fmttm online but not fmttm fanzine. It got to areas where paper fanzines couldn't reach, to paraphrase an old advert.

Mind you, there lay a problem. Almost one year on, despite an office full of staff down in west London, there still weren't any adverts at all on the Rivals network. Then came problem number two as instead of traffic going down at the end of the first season, it went up over the summer. Tighten your belts time.

So after one season of trading we were faced with the first of several re-negotiations of our contracts - downwards. We had been just too successful we were told. It is funny looking back at how many times this happened and all the different ways bad news was dressed up. They even shifted from the good cop, bad cop to the Columbo effect.

A nationwide tour of publishers was made by a Rivals editorial double act. They won my sympathy vote as soon as I saw the plaster cast on the editor's leg. I drowned her sorrows when her assistant bought me a drink. They then gave me lots of cheery news about a brilliant future for our independent network of fans' voices. I was just getting up to leave the pub when I was stopped in my tracks. "There's just one thing." Down with the contracts again.

Anyway, life went on. Rivals was sold on, first to one company and then another. It went offshore to South Africa. It became old and almost outdated. At times it was almost in a state of permanent collapse. I had no idea who my bosses were, they gave me neither contact address nor phone number. But the cheques kept coming and somehow the world kept turning.

But then the world was turned upside down. Boro won a cup. We won the Carling Cup. Could you believe it? The website went off the scale.

Not a good time then to try to buck the trend of a lifetime and multi-task. It was whilst perching my mobile phone under my chin and talking to someone that an attempt to change an advert on the message board turned to disaster. I somehow managed to twice press the big red button marked delete and destroy the entire thing.

What had I done? I couldn't get it back. Even when calling on the services of clever people, it was beyond retrieval. All those proud posts about cup victory are now floating somewhere in the cyber ether. We'd waited 128 years and then in a moment's deleting mayhem, I had wiped the celebratory posts clean off the horizon. Oh dear. It is fair to say I had to take a bit of stick for this. People shouting at me across the street. My public shame.

Still, it was not as bad as one of the admin team who managed to remove the whole message board the morning after a night before in Europe. God knows what happened exactly but in the cold, sobering light of day, a long night of drunken ramblings did not look too clever. Rather than be ridiculed forever by friends and family, he pulled the big lever like Room 101 and consigned the whole thing to dust.

Oh, and I should mention now that without the team of trusted henchmen the various versions of the message board and websites would have gone into permanent meltdown - and me with them - many times. Thanks to mysterious names like Sal, Buddy, Piquet2, Corrupt Biggins, FW2, Regular Reader, Trod and Boro85, the wheels never quite fully came off. They knew what they were doing. Someone had to.

In December 2007, the Middlesbrough based FansOnline.net network was founded by Steve Goldby's Waking Lion Ltd and fmttm finally found a stable, permanent platform, one on which it will almost certainly reside for a long, long time to come.

Oh, I've just realised I have been rambling on for ages now. You turned these pages to read some of the amazing conversations of Boro and Boro-dom. Marvel at the magic, mayhem and madness of fellow Boro fans. I've held you back too long. It has been a privilege being involved. I say that to myself every time I am shot down in flames online. Only most days of the year then...

From the Man in the Moon

Robert Nichols
Editor, www.fmttm.boro.com

The History Of Boro On The Web Part 2
The Birth Of ComeOnBoro.com

The Internet's biggest achievement is arguably its use as a tool of mass communication. The rise of social networking sites has allowed us to get in touch with others far more easily, allowing us to share information and increase our list of personal contacts.

The setting up of websites catering to specific interests and needs has also given people easier access to like-minded people from across the globe. Hand in hand with the rise in communication came the birth of the message board culture - where devotees of a particular pastime could go online and speak to others who share the same interest.

Football is a case in point. There is nothing like it to stir the passions, to raise the emotions and to cause debate. And wherever such emotions exist, there are always people who want to vent them.

It is from here that message boards developed and from it, micro-communities. Suddenly the post-match euphoria or despair was not a solitary thing, it was a group activity and something that could be discussed and dissected. Who cares if you have never met most of these people? Who cares if they may just live round the corner or on the other side of the globe? We were all together. We all knew the dizzying highs and the painful lows of being a football supporter. At least now we were not alone.

After a short amount of time, the lure of a message board almost becomes religious, like an addictive drug fix that must be sated. Instead of popping on the board for five minutes, whole hours pass as you converse with people who have seemed like friends for years. Indeed many a job has been lost through the addictive lure that is the Internet message board as the desire to have a look at what's going on is often a temptation that is too hard to resist.

The ComeOnBoro.com message board was born from a mass-migration from the BBC 606 Middlesbrough message board in the latter half of 2004. The reasons for this were many but the main ones concerned the BBC's over-zealous moderation, the inability to swear and the fact that the forum closed down at 10pm every evening. This meant that the full terrace banter could never fully be replicated and a few had expressed their frustration about this.

The euphoria that surrounded Boro's 2004 Carling Cup success was contagious and the BBC 606 Forum was vibrant. Fuelled by this positivity, this was also the time that groups of posters first started arranging to meet up for matches. One of these meetings was for the last match of the season at Portsmouth's Fratton Park. Boro lost 5-1 and someone called Yakubu scored four for Pompey. It would turn out to be the day that ComeOnBoro.com was born.

As I headed towards London Waterloo to meet the 606 lads before our trip to the South Coast, I couldn't help but think about the pitfalls of the BBC board. They were frustrating but I could not see a way round it. I certainly never had the intention of co-founding a new Boro website.

It was at Waterloo that I met Steve Goldby and it was on the train down (and after six pints of what can only be described as fizzy piss), that we decided to set up our own website with its own message board. We also agreed that it would be unmoderated except under extreme circumstances. Thirteen days later, it went live.

The migration went easily enough, although there was a lot of initial plugging that needed to be done. Many people aren't receptive to change and many saw the negative points of 606 as being a mere irritation when compared to the many positive aspects of the forum.

You couldn't blame them. The people on the 606 board made it and to move away from that to an untried and untested alternative was seen by many as an unnecessary break. It's like living in a run-down community where everyone is offered better accommodation elsewhere. Suddenly the bad points of your current area are overlooked because at least that area is YOURS.

What altered this perception was an increase in moderation when it was suggested that only moderators themselves could start topics. Suddenly the fledging ComeOnBoro.com message board became the place of choice and, with an increasing amount of content on the main site, it became an attractive place to visit.

There have been many highlights on the COB board and there are also many interesting personalities on the forum, some well-respected, some much derided. The banter is unique and we still often meet up in the Boro (and elsewhere) socially, particularly before and after games. There are also running in-jokes and although at times it does appear to be somewhat cliquey, everyone is welcome. Even Mackems and Geordies.

The Middlesbrough message boards were my first foray into online culture and I have met many fantastic people who are still very close friends to this day. The culture surrounding the boards has also allowed Steve and I to create the biggest independent Middlesbrough Football Club fan site on the Internet and as such has provided me with a job. And all because I wanted to avoid writing my BA dissertation...

Andrew Morgan

Editor, ComeOnBoro.com

The History Of Boro On The Web Part 3
Boro United

If you had told me in May 2004 that the brand new ComeOnBoro.com website would win national newspaper awards, be hailed by industry moguls as one of the very best fan websites in the country and that I would have founded and be running a whole football fans network that would break into the top three most visited in the country within a month of launch... I may have believed it.

But that was never the intention in reality. ComeOnBoro.com was founded on a train to Portsmouth to watch Boro get thrashed 5-1 on the final day of the 2003-04 season when my soon-to-be colleague Andy Morgan slurred at me, "You can build websites - why don't we start a Boro site?"

"OK. I'll do it when I get home," said I, and that was it. ComeOnBoro.com was born. No more chat, no more meetings, just that ten-second drunken conversation.

Four seasons later and we're both full-time in an office in central Boro, with a few staff as well. And on the back of ComeOnBoro.com's success, we founded FansOnline.net, the very network which now houses the brilliant FMTTM message board.

FMTTM was always owned by some media corporation or other and we reckoned that the Boro fans would have preferred a site run by Boro fans on an independent platform based in Middlesbrough, so that is what we endeavoured to provide. And we pulled it off as well.

When Rob Nichols left the original network to reposition FMTTM on a newly formed independent network, we at ComeOnBoro.com were asked to run the Boro (FMTTM) board, which we duly did. It didn't take long to realise that despite the success of the network that housed the board, as a whole, the organisation was not running as smoothly as it should be and I knew that we could run things more professionally.

And we got an opportunity to prove that when the original network went belly-up due to a disastrous redesign that saw mass numbers from clubs in all divisions and in all areas of the country deserting their respective sites and wandering the virtual wilderness looking for a new 'home'.

The Boro fans who populated the FMTTM message board were up in arms about the old network's redesign and so we very rapidly launched a new Boro site and message board especially for them and in the style they were used to.

We hosted this new site on ComeOnBoro.com and suddenly, for the first time ever, the Boro message board was truly independent and run from within Middlesbrough. Furthermore, it was to stay that way.

The obvious thing to do was to bring Rob Nichols back into the game and we offered him the chance to manage the new site, a position which he duly accepted.

Our network, FansOnline.net, was founded in December 2007 just five short days after the launch of the new FMTTM site and message board. Just two or three hours into day one of the launch of the new FMTTM site, webzine publishers were calling from all over the country asking if we could provide them with the same facility that we had created for Middlesbrough. I just couldn't resist taking on the challenge of creating a new network and seeing how we would fare against the more established and bigger networks.

But the big problem was that we only had a short time to get the new network launched as the football message board communities that had split from the old network were fragmenting and settling into new homes, so I gave my Head of Tech, Jez Lacey, a massive challenge. Get the new network ready to be launched in five days. Together, and after five sleepless nights, we pulled it off and FansOnline.net was up and running.

FansOnline.net is now one of the top three football fans' networks in the country and the root of its success, the Middlesbrough message board, is once again known as the FMTTM board.

The FMTTM board is the fifth busiest message board in the UK and people often wonder how this can be when Middlesbrough's attendances are not amongst the best in the country.

The answer is that it's all about a sense of community and togetherness. The Boro fans have stayed loyal to the board, despite the upheaval that went on during 2007, and it is they who have created this impressive facility.

We've had several standout moments on the message boards over the last four years. Take the day after we beat FC Basel in the UEFA Cup quarter-final. Our semi-final opponents were to be Steaua Bucharest, who had beaten their city rivals Dynamo Bucharest in the previous night's other quarter-final, and we were 'visited' by Steaua fans, all keen to enquire about our club and town, as is normal on message boards.

But the civil nature of this communication very soon got out of hand when Dynamo fans found our board and started fighting (verbally) with the Steaua fans. Word spread and fans from the city's third club, Rapid Bucharest, joined in as well. So we ended up with three separate sets of Romanian fans all waging war at each other on a Boro message board. It was unusual but extremely entertaining, especially given that they couldn't spell our English swear words correctly.

Shortly after our amazing semi-final comeback against Steaua, we went to Eindhoven for the UEFA Cup final. At the final whistle, the board was once again taken over, this time by hoardes of Geordie heathens who arrived in the form of characters from TV's The Bill.

They had adopted names from the show and avatars of the show's characters as well. It was very well planned and very well executed and obviously a response to our famous 'Geordies at home, watching The Bill' song that was sung on every European night of that season.

Aside from the comedy moments, the message boards have provided a great facility for ex-pat Boro fans to stay in touch with their fellow supporters and a fantastic way for fellow supporters to discuss all things Boro, keep ahead of the news and, unfortunately, the rumours...

I am extremely proud to have played a part in the history of Boro message boarding and I am extremely proud to have played a part on this magnificent book. Both the boards and the book demonstrate the fantastic character that the people of Teesside possess and I hope that Teesside Urban Legends passes through the generations so that these wonderful moments stay alive forever.

Steve Goldby
Owner, FansOnline.net, ComeOnBoro.com

Chapter One
Middlesbrough Urban Legends

Teesside Urban Legends

TOPIC - Middlesbrough Urban Legends

Previous | Next | New Topic | Top Of Board

TOPIC

MESSAGE

POST

REGISTER

Looks like he is saying 'Where the f*s me car?'**

Eddie_Catflap 30/3 15:07

re: Middlesbrough Urban Legends

I was told the other week that Terry Scott of Terry and June and Carry On fame drove his car off the Transporter Bridge by accident in the early 70's*. And according to Google this is indeed true.

However, I cannot confirm that Mike Neville was once head butted in Billy Paul's - can anyone shed any light on this? I also read a claim that Roger Tames was pummelled outside Ayresome by a gang singing the 'Shoot' theme tune.

Yes, I'm bored today (and working from home).

* with hilarious results

Cogeur_le_Conq Posted on 30/3 15:12

re: Middlesbrough Urban Legends

Alex Higgins asked me to buy him a pint in the Wig and Pen and was bumming about the Boro playing pool for beer.

Fischer Posted on 30/3 15:17

re: Middlesbrough Urban Legends

The Terry Scott story is a belter, and absolutely true. I've had the Gazette's picture of an embarrassed looking Terry at the Transporter on my hard drive for years, just waiting for the opportunity to use it.

And now it's here. Voila...

Blogsworth Posted on 30/3 15:17

re: Middlesbrough Urban Legends

Mike Neville nutted in Billy Paul's... would loved to have seen that. In fact would have loved to have done it... smarmy twat.

London_Boro Posted on 30/3 15:18

re: Middlesbrough Urban Legends

Lol, that's the funniest piccie I've seen in ages. Thanks!!

smalltime Posted on 30/3 15:29

re: Middlesbrough Urban Legends

Weird, mate. Was talking to her indoors the other day about Terry Scott falling off the Transporter. Was told he was half caned when he did it, allegedly!

Funny pic, mind, looks like he is saying 'Where the f***s me car?'

bandito Posted on 30/3 15:30

re: Middlesbrough Urban Legends

Didn't Paul Frost get attacked on the tube going to Wembley by Chelsea fans?

Eddie_Catflap Posted on 30/3 15:41

re: Middlesbrough Urban Legends

That picture has completely made my day, thanks Fischer

That's very odd, smalltime. Quite a coincidence.

The Frosty story is true. I'm sure he mentioned it in his Gazette column.

gravy_boat Posted on 30/3 15:44

re: Middlesbrough Urban Legends

My mate saw Alex Higgins in the Arena about 7-8 years ago. He had two minders with him, and he sent one of them over to ask my mate to lend him a fag. I think he was on the pool for beer money trail at the time.

Eddie_Catflap Posted on 30/3 15:52

re: Middlesbrough Urban Legends

Another 'celeb comes to grief in Boro' story I've heard is that Bad Manners (Buster Bloodvessel et al) took a hiding after a gig at the Rock Garden, as told to me by a former regular at the Crown and Mitre. Was getting beaten up by the crowd an accepted hazard for any band playing there?

I've also heard that Higgins was living above the Dickens Inn for a while.

I know loads of useless trivia, me.

boroboy75 Posted on 30/3 15:54

re: Middlesbrough Urban Legends

I actually put my name down to play Alex Higgins, in the Dickens Inn, when he was taking on all-comers.
Couldn't be arsed hanging around all day because I knew I would've beat him anyway.

towz Posted on 30/3 15:55

re: Middlesbrough Urban Legends

I beat Andy Campbell at pool in the Rudds around Christmas time. I took a tenner off him. He was legless like.

holgate69 Posted on 30/3 16:07

re: Middlesbrough Urban Legends

I remember that pic of Terry Scott. Silly sod, he was. Also I do remember the story of Mike Neville getting thumped in Billy Paul's.

What about the story of the two apprentices getting killed at BSC? They were on conveyer belts, I seem to remember, and went into the furnace. Not sure if that was true or not but been going around for years.

towz Posted on 30/3 16:10

re: Middlesbrough Urban Legends

I also heard that Shane Ritchie got chased round Coulby Newham when attempting to do the Daz doorstep challenge.

Cobain_94 Posted on 30/3 16:11

re: Middlesbrough Urban Legends

"Was getting beaten up by the crowd, an accepted hazard for any band playing there?"

I know Adam Ant played The Rock Garden twice and got the shit kicked out of him both times.

swordtrombonefish Posted on 30/3 16:17

re: Middlesbrough Urban Legends

"What about the story of the two apprentices geting killed at BSC?"

I heard a similar story in the 1970's about a winch at Smiths Dock - the legend (if such it was) was that they had to spray the remains from the unit as there was nothing much left.

Big_Shot Posted on 30/3 16:35

re: Middlesbrough Urban Legends

Older Kray brother Charlie regularly in the Boro drinking. A mate once reckoned to have seen him in Blaises.

Eddie_Catflap Posted on 30/3 16:42

re: Middlesbrough Urban Legends

Another story had Charlie Kray getting legged by Middlesbrough 'gangsters' after the Glenn McCrory fight at Eston.

Fischer Posted on 30/3 17:04

re: Middlesbrough Urban Legends

Obligatory pointless namedrop:

I once asked Dave Vanian from The Damned if he'd heard about Adam Ant getting beaten up at the Rock Garden, and he said "No, but there's clearly some very sensible people in Middlesbrough."

Tillerman93 Posted on 30/3 18:24

re: Middlesbrough Urban Legends

Adam and the Ants were quite an edgy band when they were managed by Jordan 1977-1979, they could dish it out as well as take it.

User inserted link to interview with Kevin Mooney of Adam and the Ants which includes this quote:

"I remember one time in Middlesbrough. The skins were throwing sharpened up 50p's and Kung Fu stars, so I said, tactfully: 'If they dropped an atomic bomb on this town it would do £5 worth of damage. I've travelled all over England, I've seen every skinhead in the country and you, standing at the back, you've got the ugliest girlfriend around'. And then this big riot broke out."

Interview published on www.3ammagazine.com

wilfym Posted on 30/3 18:32

re: Middlesbrough Urban Legends

Uwe Fuchs hanging out with Jet from Gladiators? Couldn't possibly be true, could it?

borobadge Posted on 30/3 19:03

re: Middlesbrough Urban Legends

The Adam and the Ants stories are rubbish... there were no sharpened 50p or Kung Fu stars... and Adam Ant never ever got beat up @ Middlesbrough Rock Garden... not a chance...

Buster Bloodvessel didn't get chinned either... there were a few who got bottled off... and more than a few who had to stop playing and leave the stage whilst a fight had to finish... but that's a different thing all together...

Here are a few truths from the Rocky...

Pete Wylie and Wah! wouldn't play 'cos of the skinheads... so UB40 and Selector played that night instead...

O'Neill, the Undertones guitarist... played an encore wearing Park End Macca's Boro jumper and the band played "Boro boys we are here" whilst Punks, Skins and Boro fans pogoed forever...

Sting and the Police got "plastic glassed" off... for being too hippyish....

Lemmy bought me a pint when I went to see Motorhead on a Sunday night...

A girl - no names please - from Yarm slept and went off with Rusty Egan, the drummer of former Sex Pistol Glen Matlock's new band... and they were ejected from the Dragonara in the early hours following mayhem in the room...

Warsaw/Joy Division/New Order all played very early gigs there... Ian Curtis was particularly verbal with the few fans who were in the hall for Warsaw and Joy Division...

TOPIC

MESSAGE

POST

REGISTER

Bad Manners stopped playing within a 50 mile radius of Middlesbrough because of the trouble amongst the audience every time they visited the area.

In 1977 @ a pre-Boro match stripperama a 'jack' dressed in a black and white shirt caused a full scale riot inside and outside the club when she set the shirt on fire during the strip...

The Revillos (Fay Fife and co) from Edinburgh played a gig there and three of them slept on the floor at our mam's in Grove Hill, t'others had to slum it in Redcar!

Tom Robinson (a Teesside lad) played to a full house and he had the skins and punks singing acapella versions of 'If You're Glad to be Gay'... honest.

John Peel played as a DJ...

There are thousands of stories to come out of that place...

The Damned, Billy Idol and Gen X, 999, Angelic Upstarts, UK Subs, The Only Ones... there's tales of myth and mirth to be told about all of them... just remembered another... the drummer out of Culture Club Jon Moss - his band were due to play but they couldn't get the singer out of The Acklam... 'cos he was listening to Freda Payne's 'Band of Gold' on the juke box over and over and over again

Cogeur_le_Conq Posted on 30/3 19:17

re: Middlesbrough Urban Legends

Kevin Mooney's talking out of his arse on that interview.

There was no sharpened 50 pences or Kung Fu stars, just plastic glasses.

As if anyone in the Rocky could afford to lob ten bob at someone.

Adam and the Ants were very timid each time they played there, as were their fans - the Ant People.

Doug Trendle (Buster Bloodvessel) never got beat up either 'cos I was with him and his girlfriend all day. The black support band Headline got attacked by the NF mob from Stockton but that was outside when all of the anti-Nazi skins were already inside.

Bad Manners stopped playing within a 50 mile radius of Middlesbrough because of the trouble amongst the audience every time they visited the area.

I was talking to the guitarist Louie Alphonso just after the soundcheck at Whitby Spa and he asked me if many were coming down from the Boro after I'd informed him it was only 30 odd miles away.

Just as I said, "Nah, don't think so" the front doors went in and there was glass everywhere as a ruck started between the Scarborough Scooter Boys and the Rock Garden skins/punks outside about an hour before the doors opened.

TRANSITARMY Posted on 30/3 20:01

re: Middlesbrough Urban Legends

In their skinhead days, Slade (Wolves fans apparently) got beaten up after a gig at the Town Hall.

mattrich Posted on 30/3 20:15

re: Middlesbrough Urban Legends

Didn't Glenn McCrory get knocked out in the Madison and had to cancel a fight?

wilfym Posted on 30/3 20:23

re: Middlesbrough Urban Legends

Think it was his opponent in the big top at Tittybottle Park... Caesar Makitini was his name... I think.

jarazinho Posted on 30/3 23:14

re: Middlesbrough Urban Legends

Adam Ant - Rock Garden 1978... my first ever gig... he was getting pelted with all sorts!!

Eddie_Catflap Posted on 30/3 23:25

re: Middlesbrough Urban Legends

Some great debunking there by Conq and borobadge, and some good stories too.

So far we have:

Terry Scott drove off the Transporter - true, with photo evidence from Fischer.
Mike Neville headbutted in Billy Paul's - not proven but probable.
Roger Tames kicked to the tune of 'SHOOT' - unproven.
Alex Higgins playing pool for beer money and being a bum - I'm going to say that's true.
Paul Frost beaten up by Chelsea fans - true.
Bad Manners beaten up outside Rock Garden - false.
Adam and the Ants beaten up outside Rock Garden - false (despite that article).
Shane Ritchie legged around Coulby - unproven.

Towz owning Andy Campbell at pool - true.
Apprentices dying horrible death - unproven.
Charlie Kray in the Boro - unproven.
Uwe Fuchs/Jet - unproven.
Slade get kicking after Town Hall gig - unproven.
Glen McCrory or his opponent coming to grief in Maddo - unproven.

Can anyone provide some proof on any of the above?

Eddie_Catflap Posted on 30/3 23:30

re: Middlesbrough Urban Legends

A couple of more far fetched ones before I go to bed. I've heard both of these, not strictly Middlesbrough urban legends but not too far away:

There's a witches' coven out near Crathorne and somewhere out in the countryside near there is a table that they sacrifice animals on.

Several UFOs have been spotted by people parked up on Clay Bank during the middle of the night.

Cogeur_le_Conq Posted on 30/3 23:44

re: Middlesbrough Urban Legends

Charlie Kray was defo in the Boro as a guest of Spensley.

The Gazette ran a story about it.

Don't forget Jet Harris (of the Shadows) having a kid in Stockton and Engelbert Humperdinck having one in the Boro?

tonybiriyani Posted on 30/3 23:54

re: Middlesbrough Urban Legends

Wasn't it Barry Faulkner? I think it backfired on him with the council licensing committee.

red_rebel Posted on 30/3 23:59

re: Middlesbrough Urban Legends

Didn't Charlie Kray come up to show 'respect' at Lee Duffy's funeral?

Cogeur_le_Conq Posted on 31/3 0:08

re: Middlesbrough Urban Legends

Yeah, it was Faulkner.

Spensley was putting Higgins up.

Timboi Posted on 31/3 1:57

re: Middlesbrough Urban Legends

Faulkner - that name rings a bell. Doesn't he own (or at least did own) the Empire?

Revol_Tees Posted on 31/3 3:46

re: Middlesbrough Urban Legends

Speaking of the Rock Garden, what a place. I've been told a few cracking stories about that place at the height of punk/post-punk.

One of my favourites being the time Mark E. Smith allegedly sparked a riot between punks, skins and assorted others by dryly remarking: "I heard UK Subs played here last week. That must have been good."

I'm sure other factors were involved, but it's a great one-liner anyway

Smog_Monster Posted on 31/3 7:54

re: Middlesbrough Urban Legends

When I worked at the British Steel BOS plant, this heart wrenching (and totally untrue) story was doing the rounds.

A father and son were working together when the son fell into one of the ladles of molten steel. As he disintegrated from the legs up, he reached up his hand towards his father and through a haze of tears the father took a steel rod and pushed his dying child back down into the molten steel, as he thought that dying would be more preferable to living with melted legs.

Heard a similar story at BSC Stoke and Newport. NOT A FACT

boros_moggy Posted on 31/3 8:09

re: Middlesbrough Urban Legends

Certain aspects of the BSC apprentices story are true. There was definitely two lads killed after being on a conveyer belt, though they ended up in some sort of lime container and not a furnace. One lad lived in Dormanstown in one of the roads behind the Kingfisher.

PNGfulham Posted on 31/3 8:14

re: Middlesbrough Urban Legends

That guy who strapped a rocket booster onto the top of his car and ended up buried into a cliff twenty k's down the road was from Boro, wasn't he?

towz Posted on 31/3 8:29

re: Middlesbrough Urban Legends

I have several eyewitnesses for my thrashing ginger Andy Campbell at pool and my brother's mate told me the one about Shane Ritchie, so it must be true.

mattrich Posted on 31/3 9:32

re: Middlesbrough Urban Legends

Remember Faulkner looking after Kray and then the council revoking his licence because of it. He was on the front of the papers for that one. Also heard about Alex Higgins in the Dickens. I have heard the Shane Ritchie one happened in several towns/cities so don't know how true it is!

libardi Posted on 31/3 11:19

re: Middlesbrough Urban Legends

Barry Mooncult from Flowered Up, chained to a lamp post, in full flower costume, outside Alan Fearnley's. My mate saw it but with the passage of time I say I saw it.

ormesby_bank Posted on 31/3 12:10

re: Middlesbrough Urban Legends

Not sure about all the Bad Manners trouble etc... I saw them at the Kirk one time - God knows when - and it was completely riotously peaceful.

Big_Shot Posted on 31/3 12:21

re: Middlesbrough Urban Legends

I remember chatting briefly to Barry Mooncult in the Empire before Flowered Up played at the Havana which both myself and Eddie_Catflap attended. A pretty unremarkable gig apart from a couple of band members nearly coming to blows on stage.

Apparently though the next day the band caused a bit of bother in the Cleveland Centre by throwing eggs and flour at people.

Eddie_Catflap Posted on 31/3 14:44

re: Middlesbrough Urban Legends

Here's my summary so far (otherwise known as the thinking man's hoof. This thread was plummetting faster than an end of season Boro team.) If it goes now that's it - I've used up all my hoofs.

Terry Scott drove off the Transporter - true, with photo evidence from Fischer.

Mike Neville headbutted in Billy Paul's - not proven but probable.

Roger Tames kicked to the tune of 'SHOOT' - unproven.

Alex Higgins playing pool for beer money and being a bum - I'm going to say that's true.

Paul Frost beaten up by Chelsea fans - true.

Bad Manners beaten up outside Rock Garden - false.

Adam and the Ants beaten up outside Rock Garden - false.

Shane Ritchie legged around Coulby - unproven (but deserved it).

Towz owning Andy Campbell at pool - true (never doubted it!).

Apprentices dying horrible death - seems to be some basis of truth here.

Charlie Kray in the Boro - definitely up here and therefore true. No proof of the other stories though.

Uwe Fuchs/Jet - unproven.

Slade get kicking after Town Hall gig - unproven.

Glen McCrory or his opponent coming to grief in Maddo - unproven.

Witches' Coven - unproven.

You can see UFOs if you park up Clay Bank - unproven.

Jet Harris (of the Shadows) has a kid in Stockton - unproven.

Engelbert Humperdinck has a kid in Boro - unproven although I've heard this before and know who it refers to (I think).

Mark E. Smith provokes Rock Garden riot - unproven.

Father/son molten metal mercy killing - false (but a great one nonetheless).

Rocket car bloke was from Boro - false.

Barry Mooncult in flower costume chained to lamp post - I'm going to give this a qualified true. Big_Shot and I did see him in full costume but he was at liberty at the time.

The Flowered Up gig almost punch up was caused by the singer shouting "oi, sort your faacking bass out" into his mic - true.

TOPIC

MESSAGE

POST

REGISTER

Apparently the Army were on the Wilton site one day giving a recruitment drive or whatever and one of their tanks went missing.

An ICI employee was supposedly stopped in it on the way to the Half Moon in Lazenby after smashing through the perimeter fence.

Cogeur_le_Conq Posted on 31/3 15:38

re: Middlesbrough Urban Legends

A few ICI ones:

1. Cancer Castle in the middle of the Wilton site.

A big concrete block the size of a two-storey building half the size of a footie pitch.

A hazardous material that was thought to be so dangerous that they dug a big hole and buried the whole site including the bulldozers and encased it in concrete.

I have seen the block just to the right of the road as you come in from the the Grangetown gate just after the cyclohexane tanks and before you get to the power station. It doesn't serve any apparent purpose.

2. 10x more cyclohexane than Flixborough.

Those of you old enough to remember the fatal Flixborough disaster on South Humberside where the American oil fire expert Red Adair was called in to put out the fires after a massive explosion will recall that the tanks that went up were full of cyclohexane.

It is rumoured that ten times the amount that went up at Flixborough are stored just by the Grangetown entrance of ICI Wilton.

If this lot went up, it would take all of Grangetown and half of Teesside with it.

3. Pissed gadgie on a pushbike.

On a number of occasions security guards observed an ICI worker leaving the site at the end of the shift, riding his pedal iron in such an erratic manner that they assumed he had been drinking, but had turned a blind eye as was the norm in those days.

On one occasion he fell off and had great difficulty in picking up the bike.

It was only when the security guards went to help him that they discovered the frame was full of mercury that he'd been nicking on a regular basis.

4. Army Day

Apparently the Army were on the Wilton site one day giving a recruitment drive or whatever and one of their tanks went missing.

An ICI employee was supposedly stopped in it on the way to the Half Moon in Lazenby after smashing through the perimeter fence.

All the above rumours were from the period between 1978 to 1982 and could be bollox... who knows?

towz Posted on 31/3 15:43

re: Middlesbrough Urban Legends

My mate's a tiffy at Huntsman and he claims that as an initiation ceremony newly qualified apprentices used to be welded into a cylinder that was then filled with water with a small hole left in the top to breathe through. Apparently they would be left for several hours then cut out. Wouldn't fancy that!

Shaun71 Posted on 31/3 15:47

re: Middlesbrough Urban Legends

Cogeur - I'm sat about 400 or so yards from said concrete block. That rumour is totally true. Left everything in there, tables, chairs, the lot.

I've also heard the mercury bike one but couldn't confirm it.

Cogeur_le_Conq Posted on 31/3 15:50

re: Middlesbrough Urban Legends

My mate got put in a big cardboard box and the lads taped it up and stabbed it with screwdrivers and then left him in it for a few hours.

When they let him out they realised they'd pierced his skin a couple of times.

There's loads of stories about ICI inter-trade windups (e.g. welders asking you to pass a lump of red-hot metal or welding your steel toe-caps to the welding bench when you've got your welding mask on welding something else etc.)

There was loads of initiations going on when I was an apprentice but they left me alone and picked on the w*****s mostly.

borobuddah Posted on 31/3 16:05

re: Middlesbrough Urban Legends

Worked for Uncle ICI in the long hot summer of '76, and again in 1978. Never heard those tales.

When I left British Steel to go to ICI in '76 I got tied up on the last day and me head wrapped round with masking tape while they went for lunch.

F*****g hurt coming off me hair.

Cogeur_le_Conq Posted on 31/3 16:14

re: Middlesbrough Urban Legends

Stories three and four above were told to the new apprentices by the security guards on Induction Day.

ridsdale Posted on 31/3 18:06

re: Middlesbrough Urban Legends

The guy nicking mercury in the bike frame is true. He got jailed.

Another one I remember was when Redcar BSC was being built in the '70s.

A guy working on site constructed a homemade cannon using pipe.

He fired it at a portalav and the projectile went all the way through the bog.

He got jailed as well.

post_edit Posted on 31/3 18:26

re: Middlesbrough Urban Legends

"The guy nicking mercury in the bike frame is true. He got jailed."

Absolutely true... he is/was my brother-in-law's father (remains nameless to save embarrassment).

OPEO Posted on 31/3 18:45

re: Middlesbrough Urban Legends

Swordtrombonefish, the story of the winch is maybe the one about a guy who was on a tug boat when a winch line snapped and decapitated him. True. I sit next to his younger brother in the Riverside.

swordtrombonefish Posted on 31/3 18:49

re: Middlesbrough Urban Legends

OPEO - the way I heard it was that two guys got dragged in but in true Chinese whisper fashion, it was probably a very different story that started out. Either way - a nasty event.

JonSina Posted on 31/3 22:23

re: Middlesbrough Urban Legends

Heard a rumour that some people on this board were once seen running naked around North Ormesby whilst pissed late at night!

That's a hoof!

Eddie_Catflap Posted on 31/3 22:58

re: Middlesbrough Urban Legends

Well I don't know anything about that (cough).

Some great stories on here. The bike one especially.

Recently I went for a few pints at the Pudsey (Leeds) Beer Festival with a bloke from work. He'd arranged to meet a mate there and introduced me to him - seemed like a nice enough bloke, told me some stories about being a copper during the miner's strike. What he didn't tell me and what I only found out today from the lad I work with is that he's married to Mike Neville's cousin*. I've told my work mate that I need to find out the truth about Billy Paul's, and will let you know if I get news from the horse's mouth, so to speak.

* unfortunately according to the lad at work she looks like Mike Neville as well

Cogeur_le_Conq Posted on 31/3 23:07

re: Middlesbrough Urban Legends

Roger Melly on the Telly in Viz comic is based on Mike Neville.

The Canadian version is William Shatner.

tweedle Posted on 31/3 23:16

re: Middlesbrough Urban Legends

Once, and this really is pushing the boundaries of belief, Steve McClaren put out an attack minded team.

Eddie_Catflap Posted on 31/3 23:19

re: Middlesbrough Urban Legends

Have you seen Shatner on that Bran Flakes advert? He's mutated!

Another story. Does anyone remember a bloke that used to wander around Middlesbrough? We used to know him as kids as 'The Phantom Whistler?' He pushed a pram or some sort of cart around collecting rubbish, whistling as he went. He once placed an advert in a shop window that said "Wanted: Wife".

And I suppose Boro's famous tramp Keyo/Keough (?) is worth a mention seeing as he once told me on a bus that Joan Collins was waiting for him in a room in the Dragonara.

tonybiriyani Posted on 31/3 23:25

re: Middlesbrough Urban Legends

I was going to mention Keo. The story was that one time he was in a top job, intelligent bloke etc, then he got sent down for manslaughter, came out of prison and hit the bottle and was living on the streets.

Anyone heard this one?

PNGfulham Posted on 1/4 4:47

re: Middlesbrough Urban Legends

What about the looney fella who wanted to be a jet fighter pilot and failed the test 'cos he was blind?

Then years later he got his mates around for a BBQ and he tied 44 red helium weather balloons to his garden chair, strapped himself in and armed himself with an air rifle to pop them to aid descent - and a six pack of Budweiser, of course.

His mates untied the ropes which were tethering him down and off he went, not the thirty feet above his back yard which he figured on... but to 10,000 feet into the LAX airport corridor airspace...

Anyway he made it down after a while and got arrested... and failed to make it into the Darwinian awards 'cos he didn't die...

But then I think he hanged himself another ten years later so he made it in for trying hard.

Big_Shot Posted on 1/4 9:51

re: Middlesbrough Urban Legends

I once heard that before Keogh hit the bottle he was in the forces.

Bonus point for anyone knowing Keogh's first name.

borobadge Posted on 1/4 18:38

re: Middlesbrough Urban Legends

Hang on... how can we have a thread like this and no one's mentions the... Gazette sellers! Surely a more alternative group of characters have never ever existed on the soil of Zetland...

'The Fly Swatter'... white shirt with the sleeves rolled up and a tank top... spent hours with a rolled up Gazette swatting flies and midgies - a cross between Norman Collier and Norman Wisdom - had his pitch on the window sill of the bank on Linny Road opposite Triads...

'Humpty Dumpty' was pitched out in the Gothic archway of the Town Hall crypt... large bloke of the 25st variety, squeezed his frame into the doorway and never flinched a muscle for hours, possibly days.

'The Assassin'... mirrored lenses over the eyes, two days stubble and a variety of camouflage to keep a whole nest of chameleons in disguise for the whole of the four seasons. Bullet belts, adjustable spanners and night torches were accessories... sold the daily rag from outside the Great American Panthouse shop opposite Billy Paul's...

'Inky Midget' worked the old bus station... short bloke, thick glasses, loved the Boro and could be seen on away days late '70s, covered from head to toe in grey clothes and ink smudges... shouted as he sold the rag, like a foghorn exploding in the Holgate during a fifth round cup run, 'EVENIN' GAAZERT'. Dockers, welders and tug boat crews cowered at the volume from the 'Inky Midget'...

There were more than those four crazy, crazy, crazy cats...

TOPIC

MESSAGE

POST

REGISTER

Grrreds Posted on 1/4 18:46

re: Middlesbrough Urban Legends

Keogh's first name is Ronnie.

He has more stories than any other Middlesbrough character, including Bam Bam.

He used to regularly impress the magistrates with his tales of why he was drunk and disorderly and would usually be fined 1p less than the amount of money he had in his pocket.

Magistrate, "Mr Keogh, we find you guilty."
Ronnie, "Right."
Magistrate, "How much money have you got?"
Ronnie, "29p."
Magistrate, "Fined 28p."

He would like to tell the court to hurry up because he was on the first tee with the Chief Constable at 2.30pm (in his poshest voice) and he even turned up at court once in red silk ladies' hot pants.

A Boro legend.

Anyone remember Tommy McLeneghan? - home address Ladbrokes doorway, Borough Road, Middlesbrough.

Shaun71 Posted on 1/4 18:50

re: Middlesbrough Urban Legends

Didn't Keogh pass away not so long back?

tonybiriyani Posted on 1/4 18:54

re: Middlesbrough Urban Legends

I think Keo must have died about 10 times.

littleboro Posted on 1/4 20:17

re: Middlesbrough Urban Legends

Well remembered, borobadge. Certainly had forgotten about them.

They always used to bring a smile to my face. When life has been a b*****d, watching them made life seem not too bad. Naturally no conversation with them.

The Fly Swatter's pitch was where the TS1 bar is now on Linny Road.

You are certainly correct about his mannerisms, but he had a few more strings to his bow, mannerism wise.

The heat used to get to him during the summer months. He seemed to be forever mopping his brow with the largest hankie ever seen. In fact its size would put to shame some of the recent Boro banners.

When not mopping his brow, the brow would be leaning on his arms that in turn would be leaning on the window sill of the bank for hours. People would pick up the Gazette, leave the money and go. Nobody ever used to nick the cash. When not doing any of the above, he simply wouldn't be there. AWOL I think they call it. Again people pick up the Gazette, leave the money and it was never nicked.

'Inky Midget' was another strange creature.
I was once behind him in a queue for Leeds away tickets that went on sale after a home match. He was wearing a white beanie hat with penned Boro slogans on it. 'Boro rule OK', 'Come on Boro' etc. However there was one slogan that drew my attention in particular.

'Bernie is Slaven'. Wished I'd asked him what it meant.

Does anybody know which Gazette seller used to shout "Gazette, Gazette, get it"?

Does anybody know what happened to 'Fly Swatter' and 'Inky'?

mattrich Posted on 1/4 20:35

re: Middlesbrough Urban Legends

Surprised the old bloke who used to sell hot dogs outside what is now Dixons hasn't had a mention yet. Is he dead or is that just the people who ate his food?

tonybiriyani Posted on 1/4 20:41

re: Middlesbrough Urban Legends

You mean the snot-dogs and bogeyburgers from outside the Madhouse?

mattrich Posted on 1/4 20:42

re: Middlesbrough Urban Legends

That's the same guy. He used to put some hours in!

Grrreds Posted on 1/4 20:43

re: Middlesbrough Urban Legends

'Salmonella Sam' in his white coat and greasy hair. Push bike with a box on the front.

We've all eaten them when hungry at 2.30 in the morning.

tonybiriyani Posted on 1/4 20:46

re: Middlesbrough Urban Legends

Yeah, the good old days!! After leaving a nightclub you had a choice between him or the Boro Fish Bar.

littleboro Posted on 1/4 20:51

re: Middlesbrough Urban Legends

'Salmonella Sam of Madison' - yep, he had the hot-dog/burger cycle, er, booth, er, van thing. It was definitely on a bike, unless I was always that pissed and always missed the van and thought it was a bike. Is possible.

If my memory is correct he was a bit bad tempered and who wouldn't be at 2am serving pissed people giving verbals about food poisoning. "Onions?"

Always had white jacket on. Part and parcel of hygiene regulations. Hair well greased.

mattrich Posted on 1/4 20:53

re: Middlesbrough Urban Legends

He had a right attitude problem. Did you ever eat in the Madison's upmarket diner? Think it was called Madison Garden? As you walked in you turned right, or the downstairs part where they used to play Elvis, Four Tops etc etc?

littleboro Posted on 1/4 20:59

re: Middlesbrough Urban Legends

Oh yes, oh yes. The Boro Fish Bar.

Pictures on the wall of a Boro match at home in the big game against Portsmouth. Score unknown.

Picture of Alan Foggon, hair combed before match, going up for rare header.

Remembered 'A Night with Brian Clough'. Somebody asked Cloughie if he had ever been interested in signing Foggon. He said he had been very interested but after a few discreet inquires found out that he was strictly a 'beer and chips man'.

Foggon must be one of the few players to be signed by Man Utd and then sold a week later.

Makes Foggon's legend even better.

Where is he now?

littleboro Posted on 1/4 21:06

re: Middlesbrough Urban Legends

Can remember a pizza place they had as you turned left on the entrance just before the steps that went to the downstairs bit. Pizza tops there were not, probably straight from Kwik Save's freezer cabinets a few hours earlier.

If I remember, the stairs to the downstairs bit were a bit dodgy as you had to take a sharp right half way down. Any drunken slip and it would be down the next flight of steps, ending up with head lodged against fire doors until the cleaners arrived in the morning.

Somebody must have done that.

jk1311 Posted on 1/4 21:14

re: Middlesbrough Urban Legends

Maddo's upmarket diner was 'The Square Garden'.

The burger on a bike fella can be seen selling cheap tack toys and Christmas wrap in Linny Road pedestrian area near Debenhams.

littleboro Posted on 1/4 21:17

re: Middlesbrough Urban Legends

Didn't he try and sell his burger bike on eBay recently?

mattrich Posted on 1/4 21:29

re: Middlesbrough Urban Legends

Can't believe the burger bloke can use a computer!!

littleboro Posted on 1/4 21:31

re: Middlesbrough Urban Legends

Sunday league referees.

Small, thin, bald-headed referee that looked in his 50s during the early '90s. Apparently worked on the railways.

The manager: "Oh God, no. He plays to the crowd."
The players: "?"
The manager "You'll see."

Anyway half way though the 1st half there is a foul.
The referee comes running up to the defender.

"Do you like pop music?"
"What?"
"Take that!" as he flashes the yellow card.

carlosthebiscuit Posted on 1/4 21:43

re: Middlesbrough Urban Legends

Can't see no "Cancer Castle."

I have seen the block just to the right of the road as you come in from the Grangetown gate just after the cyclohexane tanks and before you get to the power station.

TOPIC

MESSAGE

POST

REGISTER

The cancer castle is indeed very true. As I speak, I'm working not that far from it and have to drive past it every day to go home.

Eddie_Catflap Posted on 1/4 21:56

re: Middlesbrough Urban Legends

I thought the hot-dog bloke was called Salmonella Bob, although it's easy to see how he would have several names.

As for his bike, a mate of mine bought a shop/house off Princes Road near old Psyche and told me he discovered said bike complete with cooking facility in the garage at the back. This is the mid-nineties.

He told me he'd given it to a friend (I don't know who - Faulkner again?) who was going to hang it in one of the pub windows in town. I guess it vanished.

A mystery indeed. Where is it today? It's almost like the car that Franz Ferdinand got shot in or something.

littleboro Posted on 1/4 22:06

re: Middlesbrough Urban Legends

The location of Princes Road as his living abode I can sort of confirm.

One day, mid afternoon, he nearly knocked me over as I crossed Princes Road at the junction of Linthorpe Road, opposite where the TS1 bar is now and the bank was. He was riding the previously mentioned cooker bike but, alas, no white jacket.

So I presumed that he lived in that area of town.

I must have been concentrating on looking at the antics of Flyswatter, the Gazette seller, by the bank across the road and forgot my Green Cross Code.

Shaun71 Posted on 1/4 22:08

re: Middlesbrough Urban Legends

The cancer castle is indeed very true. As I speak, I'm working not that far from it and have to drive past it every day to go home.

If you're not on the Wilton site you won't see it!

ThePrisoner Posted on 1/4 22:13

re: Middlesbrough Urban Legends

So where and what is this cancer castle? Never heard of it.

Eddie_Catflap Posted on 1/4 22:13

re: Middlesbrough Urban Legends

As for Geeeeezzzzeeet sellers, there was a particularly ill looking one used to pitch outside McDonald's. Anyone claim to know/be him on here? He was often talking to another couple of Boro Legends, Andy X and Rockin' Robin, both of whom I'll cover in a bit.

Also down Princes Road was a blues bar. Is that still on the go?

Grrreds Posted on 1/4 22:17

re: Middlesbrough Urban Legends

I remember the blues' on Kensington Road, but not Princes Road!

littleboro Posted on 1/4 22:21

re: Middlesbrough Urban Legends

Princes Road - I was informed that there was indeed a blues bar in the road in the early '90s.

ThePrisoner Posted on 1/4 22:23

re: Middlesbrough Urban Legends

Most of those ICI ones sound like bollox but there is enough Cyclohexane, Naphtha, Ethylene etc, etc to put most of Teesside on the moon.

What about the bloke who allegedly got a splash of cyanide solution on his boots at Cassel works but didn't realise? Then he went and sat in a warm mess-room and hydrogen cyanide gas was given off and he died where he sat.

Cogeur_le_Conq Posted on 1/4 22:23

re: Middlesbrough Urban Legends

Ramsey's Blues used to move about more than something that moves about a lot.

Kenny Road, Princes Road, Woodlands Road, The Jamaican Cafe at the Longlands and Duffy's resting place at the Afro-Carribean Centre on Marton Road.

Sensi and curry... mmmmm.

10pintsB4Parmo Posted on 1/4 22:24

re: Middlesbrough Urban Legends

Roger took a good shoeing from the lads more than once as he took the walk to that gantry at Ayresome. "Come On Roger - Walk The Walk, You Mackem b******d". Ha ha ha. "Shoot". Ha ha ha!! If any plod are reading I heard the above in a transit van going to Hull! Eddie, put me down for a "I'm sure this is true says our kid".

Shaun71 Posted on 1/4 22:25

re: Middlesbrough Urban Legends

The Prisoner - The cancer castle and the mercury bike are totally true.

Eddie_Catflap Posted on 1/4 23:32

re: Middlesbrough Urban Legends

10Pints, you have made my day. I know it's wrong, and I've never been in a fight at the match ever, but there's something about the thought of that happening and some Neanderthal wag deciding to sing "der-de-de de-der-der der-der-der" at the same time that brings a smile to my face. No wonder we never got any Tyne-Tees coverage despite being the first north-east team in the Premiership.

mad_frankie Posted on 1/4 23:49

re: Middlesbrough Urban Legends

A workmate of mine claims to have seen a punk band (I think it was The Damned) at the old Rock Garden, now The Arena. He claims that during the gig the bass player took a crap on the stage and announced to the audience that anyone who could outdo him for the level of filth would get his guitar and amp as a prize. At which point somebody climbed out of the audience, onto the stage and ate the aforementioned turd. Claimed his prize as well. Can anybody else confirm this story?

bill_ingham Posted on 1/4 23:57

re: Middlesbrough Urban Legends

Andy X - True legend - Come on get the X-Man's stories on here.

I used to play gigs with him occasionally in Stockton and Boro, used to sing "Gordon the Goldfish".

I've lived in London for 8 years now but he spotted me at a gig a few years ago and made a beeline for me... some of his gags... What a guy.

I think he used to valet cars when he wasn't penning classic acoustic songs.

Eddie_Catflap Posted on 2/4 0:00

re: Middlesbrough Urban Legends

Is this true? Andy X is also known as 'the Linthorpe Road man', and was given a name check by Spit the Pips on their 'Never Crib a Boggy' EP - I think that's what it was called anyway. Got record of the week in Melody Maker.

Cogeur_le_Conq Posted on 2/4 0:03

re: Middlesbrough Urban Legends

Another Rock Garden story gone wild.

I seem to remember either Rat Scabies or the Captain puking into a plastic pint glass and Dave Vanian getting the crowd to get him to neck it by saying into the the mike "He drinks it, you know."

This caused the audience to encourage him to neck it in one.

Which he did, to everyone's disgust.

I've since heard the story that it was a pint of gob but it's the first time I've heard the eating turd version.

Don't forget to mention Mensi from the Angelic Upstarts chopping up a pig's head on stage at the Rocky with an axe but I always felt that that stage prop was there more for his own protection.

Eddie_Catflap Posted on 2/4 0:05

re: Middlesbrough Urban Legends

Rockin' Robin; one of the band box kings of Boro. Odd looking lad but never afraid to belt out a rock and roll classic. I was once at the Broadway at Palladium shops when Robin was on and he did a beaut version of Blue Suede Shoes complete with dance moves etc. He was wearing these massive clod hopping boots. At the end of the song the compere comes on the mike - "Call for Robin in the bar, Frankenstein's here and wants his shoes back!"

You had to be there, I guess.

Eddie_Catflap Posted on 2/4 0:07

re: Middlesbrough Urban Legends

I'm amazed reading this Rock Garden stuff that no-one has ever come out with a book about it - it's got a very famous moment after all (the Pistols gig) as well as many others. Cog, you could be the man. Some of the stuff you've posted is class!

Gillandi Posted on 2/4 0:15

re: Middlesbrough Urban Legends

Told the story a few times on here now but I saw Ronnie Keogh sat on a bench in Albert Park once with his feet placed neatly on a square foot of carpet he'd found somewhere. He was smoking and drinking and looking pleased with himself as usual and I asked him how he was. He said "I'll be a lot better when my furniture arrives."

Cogeur_le_Conq Posted on 2/4 0:16

re: Middlesbrough Urban Legends

Me and borobadge have been talking for years about building a webshite dedicated to the Rock Garden but the yagbo gets in the way.

I've got the webspace and the badge has all the contacts.

One day it may happen.

Smog_Monster Posted on 2/4 5:13

re: Middlesbrough Urban Legends

I worked all over ICI, in fact most of Teesside, Seal Sands, Hartlepool etc as a contractor in the late '80s and '90s. Heard the one about the cancer castle loads of times and never really believed it. I also heard one (which stinks of myth) about a guy who drank some of the shit from the cancer castle to kill himself. Allegedly, when he was found his insides had completely melted.

Shaun71 Posted on 2/4 5:20

re: Middlesbrough Urban Legends

Smog_Monster - The castle is true. I'm sat in Wilton site now having passed the block hundreds of times over the past 17 years. My old fella was working on the site (aniline plant) when the 'cancer castle' was hastily filled with concrete.

It still stands there gathering moss, as they say.

Smog_Monster Posted on 2/4 5:29

re: Middlesbrough Urban Legends

Shaun, I don't doubt it now. But at the time I just dismissed it, like most of the stories you hear working in them places. I have seen the block myself.

I'm struggling with the one about Ronnie Keogh being a relative of Jonka's. I used to know him pretty well when he was a scaff and I cannot see the family resemblance. I wouldn't ask him either.

RedJohnnie Posted on 2/4 5:55

re: Middlesbrough Urban Legends

The Wilton cancer one is right. Heard about that when doing my apprenticeship.

It was Scabies drinking the vomit and the Captain naked and slashing on the crowd. Got some photos somewhere from that night.

OPEO Posted on 2/4 6:12

re: Middlesbrough Urban Legends

Sean Arkless of Easterside (lot of characters emanate from there) died of food poisoning after allegedly dining out at the aforementioned wheelbarrow outside Maddogs. His elder sister is married to the REAL Joe Laidlaw. Frankie Bam Bam lives across the road.

darmok Posted on 2/4 7:45

re: Middlesbrough Urban Legends

Cog - the puke drinking incident at the Garden was during a concert by The Doomed. It was Henry Badowski who actually did the deed. Almost a full pint of the stuff as well (ugh).

TOPIC

MESSAGE

POST

REGISTER

It was Scabies drinking the vomit and the Captain naked and slashing on the crowd. Got some photos somewhere from that night.

littleboro Posted on 2/4 8:00

re: Middlesbrough Urban Legends

Mad Frankie - about The Damned at the Rock Garden. The following incident did definitely happen.

The eating of crap etc was actually Frank Zappa or possibly an urban myth from another era and another country, the US of A.

Apparently, Zappa once said on stage that he was the most revolting man alive and challenged the audience to disprove him. Somebody from the crowd got up on stage and shat on the stage.

Impressive, you would have thought.

Not to Zappa, who called for a spoon and ate the shat, thus proving that indeed he was the most revolting man alive.

Back to The Damned at The Rocky, they had been banned by most local councils especially in the north-east and I presume the Boro Council allowed them to play the Boro Rocky.

During a rest bite, Captain Sensible started thanking the Council.

"I would like to f*****g thank the f*****g Middlesbrough f*****g Council for letting us f*****g play. Them f*****g b*******s in f*****g Newcastle are a*******s..."

Being pissed, he repeated this about three times before walking off stage. Upon his return about 20 seconds later he was wearing his er, birthday suit only and proceeded to start pi.ssing on the audience.

There was a massive surge of the audience away from the stage. This in itself was a massive achievement since the Rock Garden was packed liked the Holgate when full. We were like sardines.

As the Sensible one was finishing his toiletry duties, Rat Scabies, The Damned drummer posed the question, "You may be wondering why we have been banned from most towns?"

Anyway the event continued with Sensible playing a la fresco, so to speak, for the remainder.

To finish on a sexist note, there was a lass sat on the stage with large tits. Today, Jordan wouldn't get a look in.

The Dammed used to do a cover of "Ballroom Blitz" by The Sweet. Dave Vanian, the singer, changed the lyrics of the chorus, while pointing at her, from "it's, it's a ballroom blitz, it's, it's a ballroom blitz" to...

"She's the girl with the f*****g big tits."

I hope this may have cleared up some misunderstanding about The Damned and Frank Zappa not using HP Brown Sauce. Truly a revolting man.

Cogeur_le_Conq Posted on 2/4 10:32

re: Middlesbrough Urban Legends

Darmo - The Doomed - yeah, you're right. The Damned actually split up in 1978 and reformed as the Doomed cos Brian James nicked the Damned name.

guyb Posted on 2/4 10:42

re: Middlesbrough Urban Legends

This thread is mint.

Has anybody got any stories about Stockton or Stockton characters?

The only ones I can impart are the Keymaster (who was a dead ringer for the bloke in Ghostbusters) who used to hang around outside the Castle Centre in the same grey jacket, always holding a pasty.

And the original 'Old Man' who was about 90 in the late '80s/early '90s and was always out on the lash on a Saturday night in the High Street and wore a Sherlock Holmes coat. We saw him kicked out of the Royal Exchange one night with a roll yer own paper stuck to his bottom lip.

gibson Posted on 2/4 12:03

re: Middlesbrough Urban Legends

How about Sinbad's Tattoo Parlour? Truly rubbish tattoos, I seem to remember.

However, a story I heard was that a lad went in to get his name tattooed inside his bottom lip and on his way home, took out the 'packing' and sucked out all the ink.

He went back to Sinbad who re-did the tattoo and told him,"Under NO circumstances remove the packing until the next day."

On looking in the mirror the following day, his tattoo read 'T**T'... as in T**ty vagitus... a la Avid Merrion... Urban myth?

mattrich Posted on 2/4 12:06

re: Middlesbrough Urban Legends

OPEO: Once again consulted the family elders (from Easterside) who reckon Sean Arkless died after eating food from the burger bloke bike. He was ill for a long time and then died. He knew my uncle and his sister's marriage to Joe Laidlaw didn't last long, although one of the elders disputes this.

KEN_M Posted on 2/4 12:15

re: Middlesbrough Urban Legends

With the exception of the Rock Garden, I can confirm most of the stories on here, especially the ICI ones.

There is a plant buried in concrete. It was knocked down and inwards into the plant space. The bulldozer, truck, forklift and all of the plant equipment were left inside. It was then shuttered and concrete poured in day and night. The shuttering was raised 2.0 metres at a time. The plant was called Alpha Nap and for those who remember Wilton it was located as you drive past the main power station between the station and the Aniline Plant, set back between the two. I was working in one of the maintenance workshops close by at the time. I remember it well.

The bike story is true.

The tank story is also (partially) true. The army display was outside the Medical Centre and a lad took the tank for a spin (for a bet) on the back night shift. He drove it down past the power station and then towards the Dormanstown Gate and panicked and ran it into a pipe trench.

Another true story is about the guy who wanted a piece of metal mesh to cover a window at home that kept getting broken. He found a piece, got a "scrap chit" and went and paid ten pence for it. It was later found out that it was a piece of platinum mesh, worth about £2,500 (in the seventies). ICI wanted it back but he reckoned that he owned it legit. They compromised, ICI built him a double garage, he returned the mesh.

Cogeur_le_Conq Posted on 2/4 12:46

re: Middlesbrough Urban Legends

A few more Boro characters:

1. Ginger George. I've mentioned him on here before. He was a 6 foot odd beanpole and looked about 40 but had a gang of kids knocking about with him in their early teens.

He used to work on Crow's Fair and went to the matches. He was bald on top of his napper but had a shock of ginger clown's hair like her out of Mary, Mungo and Midge and a ginger zapata tash.

He kicked his heel like he was giving a ball a backheel every fifth pace when he was walking.

2. Golden Goal Gadge. Just inside the turnstiles at the Bootboy Alley entrance of the Holgate End.

His bottom jaw protruded a couple of inches more than his upper jaw and must have been the person that the phrase 'looked like a bulldog licking piss off a thistle' was based on.

Goldennnnnn Goallllllll! Tennnnnnnnn Pennnnnnnce!

3. Polpetti Man. Took over the chippy on Clarrie Road and started serving curries in there for the first time. The place was manky but was open between dinner time and tea time when all the other chippies were shut. Every single time you went in he tried to sell you polpettis.

"You want polpetti?"
"No thanks."
"You tried polpetti?"
"Yeah I have."
"You sure? You try my polpetti."
"No thanks, just a bag of chips and scraps."
"I'll put a polpetti in there for you. They're only 15p."
"No I don't want a f*****g polpetti."
"I'll put one in for you to try....."

4. Mr WHADDOYAWAAAANNNNNNNNNNNNNNNNNNNNNNT? The Gazette shop on Clarrie Road just near Polpetti's chippy. He used to scream at you in a foul mood always...

"Whaddddaaaaaayou wannnnnnnnnnnnt?"

It put the shits up you as an 11 year old.

Smog_Monster Posted on 2/4 13:34

re: Middlesbrough Urban Legends

Polpetti man, I wonder if he's still there? He even scrawled 'Delicious Polpetti' on his door in felt tip.

He gave me a free one once, but I can't remember what it was like as I was pissed, but my mate reckoned they were alright.

WTF is a polpetti anyway?

Big_Shot Posted on 2/4 13:36

re: Middlesbrough Urban Legends

Cog, we knew Ginger George as Chicken George.

tonybiriyani Posted on 2/4 13:45

re: Middlesbrough Urban Legends

What about the Angelic Upstarts gig that was called off at Gaskin's at the time of the riots? The rumour going round was that there was a coach load of NF skins coming down from Geordieland and the locals were going to ambush them on arrival using this to start confrontation with the coppers. Apparently the police got word of it and cancelled the gig.

Fischer Posted on 2/4 13:49

re: Middlesbrough Urban Legends

"Roger Melly on the Telly in Viz comic is based on Mike Neville."

Not true, Cog - I've just read Rude Kids, the autobiography of Viz's main man Chris Donald. Roger was based on '70s Tyne Tees presenter Rod Griffiths, who the Viz boys overheard swearing in the studio canteen after one of their early TV appearances. There's even a picture of Rod in the book, posing with a huge Roger Mellie cardboard cut-out.

This thread is gold dust, by the way. One day I'll rip you all off wholesale and turn this into a best-selling book.

Editor's Note: Beat you to it, Bob!

Cogeur_le_Conq Posted on 2/4 13:57

re: Middlesbrough Urban Legends

tonybiriyani - That was when there was loads of copycat riots after Brixton like Toxteth.

There were loads of different gangs of kids playing cat and mouse with the coppers all night. The coppers successfully managed to keep them all from forming one large unruly riot mob.

There were always rumours of Upstarts fans supposedly coming to cause trouble but it never happened. The rumours were started by that manager of theirs who hated my brother's band, No Way, and saw them as rivals.

Smog_Monster Posted on 2/4 14:03

re: Middlesbrough Urban Legends

I remember vaguely another old pisshead who used to wear a weird leather rock climbing/cycling helmet thing. He used to go into the Empire, most likely the only place he could get served. One time he had his face spray-painted blue by someone but never seemed too bothered by it.

Ronnie Keogh used to come in now and then, probably when he had a bit of cash. I remember him carrying a leather doctor's bag with 'Keogh for PM' written on it. I also saw him one time with a dressing gown and hospital band on his wrist. He used to sit with a couple of like-minded people who were known as The Brown Bottle, Cider Woman and The Green Midget.

jam_the_parmo Posted on 2/4 14:09

re: Middlesbrough Urban Legends

I'm a Teesside legend!

darmok Posted on 2/4 14:27

re: Middlesbrough Urban Legends

Cog, The Doomed were The Damned in all but name.

Dave Vanian - Vocals
Captain Sensible - Guitar
Henry Badowski - Bass
Rat Scabies - Drums

Another Damned/Rocky story. Can't remember if it was before or after the vomit drinking incident, as by 1979 they were The Damned again.

Rat Scabies sprayed 'The Damned' in silver paint on the wooden panels in front of the stage and got caught by one of the bouncers who proceeded to throw him out, despite protests that the gig wouldn't be too good without a drummer. Ian Lister finally rescued him just near the bar.

This was about the time that a Boro lad (Paddy) toured with them and the Captain once said of him in an interview "He's like a toilet; you only miss him when he's not there".

Captain Sensible also nicked Sav's fluffy jumper.

TOPIC

MESSAGE

POST

REGISTER

Ronnie Keogh used to come in now and then, probably when he had a bit of cash. I remember him carrying a leather doctor's bag with 'Keogh for PM' written on it.

Cogeur_le_Conq Posted on 2/4 14:32

re: Middlesbrough Urban Legends

Another Teesside Urban Legend, Paddy Durnan, getting done by the RSPCA for bleaching and dyeing his dog fluorescent lime green.

It was Benny Fuscia's fluffy jumper that the Captain nicked.

OPEO Posted on 2/4 15:22

re: Middlesbrough Urban Legends

Mattrich! You can't leave it like that! I lived at Easterside from the age of 3 'til 21. We got the first 4-bedroom house opposite the club which was built on the site of my old man's allotment. Question is, who are the elders?

MontagueWithnail Posted on 2/4 15:30

re: Middlesbrough Urban Legends

For years there was a tramp-type character on Stockton High Street. He was black and had dreadlocks, always had a biro and a piece of paper and would hold the pen up at you as if he were an artist and then pretend to write some notes down. Rumour was he used to be a lawyer! I think he must have been put away as I haven't seen him for ages.

OPEO Posted on 2/4 15:35

re: Middlesbrough Urban Legends

Also there was a big lad with a bushy beard who just went to the dogs after his mother died and he found comfort visiting the nuns at the convent in Normanby. Always dressed very scruffily with his toes sticking out of his boots. And there was Nature Boy who I think lived in Normanby but walked everywhere with his shirt wide open and resplendent gold pendant hanging round his neck. Face was always full of sun.

Eddie_Catflap Posted on 2/4 16:28

re: Middlesbrough Urban Legends

Whilst listening to the game I've been trawling the dark world of Eastenders fan-sites (shudder), trying to track down the official Shane Ritchie website (which is www.shaneritchie.biz). Thought I'd ask the man himself about him being pursued around the mean streets of Coulby. He's got a forum on there - the members look a fearsome lot so I posted the following which I thought was suitably crawling and therefore might not get deleted by their admins. I also dropped a couple of Steve Mc'isms in there as well. Didn't mention fmttm. We might have been invaded.

"Hi everyone, I wonder if anyone can help? Is anyone aware of the Shane Ritchie urban legend from his Daz Doorstep Challenge days? The story goes that the wrong estate was picked to do the challenge on and Shane and his crew were chased by an angry mob of residents (or more likely a crowd of admirers!).

"Is there any truth in this rumour? I've heard it several times - I'm from Middlesbrough and it was supposed to have happened here. I've also heard the same story with different towns/cities involved. Can anyone tell me if this is true?

"Magnificent site, by the way, and I think it's tremendous that the man himself takes time to drop in. Regards, EddieCatflap."

mad_frankie Posted on 2/4 18:09

re: Middlesbrough Urban Legends

Cheers for that, littleboro, that's mint to have it confirmed. Didn't believe it myself until reading your thread. Fantastic stuff!!

j_orourke Posted on 2/4 18:48

re: Middlesbrough Urban Legends

Chicken George is alive and well collecting glasses in the Garden City Club. He looks the same as he did thirty years ago.

sasboro Posted on 2/4 19:06

re: Middlesbrough Urban Legends

Once Keogh told me he was throwing the javelin, with a toilet seat round his neck at the time.

Anyone remember the old bloke in the old Empire pub who used to come in on his own? Used to see him all the time walking down Linthorpe Road.

I always remember the dodgy geezers stood near the door or back room.

RedJohnnie Posted on 2/4 20:19

re: Middlesbrough Urban Legends

Used to be an old gadge kicking about the town and in the pubs who would whip out a plastic comb and bit of paper and start humming songs on it. Remember him also being in the Westminster before games on a Saturday (remember them?)

Had a mate at the time we named Wavey Davey, and took the P out of him, saying it was his dad as they were very similar (except Davey could not play the paper and comb!!)

Cogeur_le_Conq Posted on 2/4 22:04

re: Middlesbrough Urban Legends

"Anyone remember the old bloke in the old Empire pub that used to come in on his own? Used to see him all the time walking down Linthorpe Road."

That describes me, my dad, my grandad, my best mate, my best mate's dad, his grandad etc.

Cogeur_le_Conq Posted on 2/4 22:06

re: Middlesbrough Urban Legends

"I always remember the dodgy geezers stood near the door or back room."

That was defo my dad.

The first crack dealer in the Boro.

Leedsclive Posted on 2/4 22:10

re: Middlesbrough Urban Legends

Surprised no-one's mentioned the guy in Grangetown who was arrested for shagging his dog. Silly bugger forgot to close the curtains one night. But that one's true, not an urban legend.

banbridge_boro Posted on 2/4 22:19

re: Middlesbrough Urban Legends

What about the old Boro song?

"Harry Roberts is my friend, is my friend, he kills coppers."

Who the f**k was Harry Roberts?

Cogeur_le_Conq Posted on 2/4 22:22

re: Middlesbrough Urban Legends

Harry Roberts had nowt to do with the Boro.

red_rebel Posted on 2/4 22:27

re: Middlesbrough Urban Legends

I'll throw another name in here: Anth Sowerby, the Wolfman. Mental, goofy, death-obsessed cartoonist and ginger spikey-haired punk with a distinctive bouncy walk. He looked like the Sid Vicious cartoon character on Rock And Roll Swindle.

He drew weird alien/sci-fi/porn comic strips while under the influence of substances and was always waffling about morbid things. He went to Borneo to collect shrunken heads.

I think he opened a second hand shop behind the police station that was more like a freak show and I believe he got involved in some bizarre legal battle with a foreign government over the rightful ownership of a human skeleton in his possession.

Cogeur_le_Conq Posted on 2/4 22:34

re: Middlesbrough Urban Legends

Anth reminded me of Whispering Bob Harris' estranged son to a '60s mama.

He was harmless and hardly qualifies as an urban legend.

heine Posted on 2/4 22:35

re: Middlesbrough Urban Legends

Tom Robinson from Boro? Nah.

User inserted link which included this quote;

"Born June 1st 1950 in Cambridge, Tom Robinson was a choirboy until his voice broke, and everything else broke along with it."

Source; http://www.tomrobinson.com/pages/biog.htm

Eddie_Catflap Posted on 3/4 0:01

re: Middlesbrough Urban Legends

Was the bloke with the comb called Speedy or something like that? I'm talking mid nineties. Used to go in the Empire/Hog's Head. He allegedly played for the Boro too. He'd walk into the take-aways down Linthorpe Road at kicking out time and burst into song. I was in Gigi's once when he did some stirring rendition of 'My Way' or something and Abdul (who's Libyan) shouted "Dad! I've told you before about doing this!"

ridsdale Posted on 3/4 0:14

re: Middlesbrough Urban Legends

Not a person, but a place - who remembers Paddy's Cafe?

littleboro Posted on 3/4 0:21

re: Middlesbrough Urban Legends

bainbridge, Harry Roberts was a 'villain' who was involved in shooting three coppers outside Wormwood Shrubs in the '60s.

Just in from Palace match, hurrah, so will try and fill in more details tomorrow.

coq is right, nothing to do with the Boro, but still a story to tell.

ridsdale Posted on 3/4 0:24

re: Middlesbrough Urban Legends

Another one from the early '70s. The bloke who sold his council house to a Pakistani bus driver and got four years in jail. Not PC, I know, but very funny.

Another thing you do not see these days are the hawkers. Better off ones had a horse and cart. Many just pushed a hand cart.

And all the old alkies. Used to have a little bit of ground on Victoria Road.

Also the proper prossies under the bridge. Nothing like the young smackheads of today. Drove a hard bargain, these ladies.

What about the Jimi Hendrix lookalike that done the rounds of the pubs in the '70s? He was quite good.

Where is Franni Michna? Brother Joe is a councillor.

And all the bent coppers? Oh, they are still with us.

Smog_Monster Posted on 3/4 0:47

re: Middlesbrough Urban Legends

Anth's skeleton was nicked from Kirby College. He found out the guy was coming to check it out with a UV lamp, so he took it to his mate's house and put it on a sunbed to find the ID marks and then filed them off.

Didn't realise he was a Boro legend. I've still got a few things I got from Anth. I remember one time he tried to make a THC patch, a bit like a Nicotine patch. He boiled up some ganj and soaked an Elastoplast in the foul green froth, then cut his arm and stuck it on. When I enquired what it was like he said, "It's alright, but it's giving me palpatations." I expect he's still doing the same kind of thing now.

Smog_Monster Posted on 3/4 0:55

re: Middlesbrough Urban Legends

Remember the guy from the Linthorpe - Miff? Used to look like Lemmy. He wore nothing but a pair of denim hot pants from spring until autumn. He killed himself a few years ago. Also, Christ on a bike with his bag of second hand records. And the guy who used to draw pictures and claim they were by poor African students. He was an alcoholic and used to draw them himself (my mate's mother was his parole officer).

ridsdale Posted on 3/4 1:03

re: Middlesbrough Urban Legends

"And the guy who used to draw pictures and claim they were by poor African students. He was an alcoholic and used to draw them himself (my mate's mother was his parole officer)".

He was a bit of a mate of mine. From South Africa. Rumour was he came from quite a well off family.

I still have (somewhere) one of his pictures. Nice enough guy. As far as I know he went back home. His son and wife are still over here. His piccies were a bit cartoonish and all looked the same.

Joe Michna was a mate of his as well. And Paul Barker. All Empire drinkers at one time or another.

Smog_Monster Posted on 3/4 2:02

re: Middlesbrough Urban Legends

I liked his pictures, but they were all quite small. A big one would have been excellent. I bought one once, but I don't think it made it home.

TOPIC

MESSAGE

POST

REGISTER

Remember the guy from the Linthorpe - Miff? Used to look like Lemmy. He wore nothing but a pair of denim hot pants from spring until autumn.

Beerwulf Posted on 3/4 2:06

re: Middlesbrough Urban Legends

Re 'Christ on a bike with his bag of second hand records' - that is Tony Day, who, as far as I know, is still peddlin' his wares to this day. He was the feature of a thread on this site not long ago.

Grrreds Posted on 3/4 8:41

re: Middlesbrough Urban Legends

OPEO, you are talking about Nipper Harris. He spent his nights asleep on the field near the reservoir up behind Eston Equestrian Centre and his days wandering around Eston Square and Normanby Top.

borobadge Posted on 3/4 9:32

re: Middlesbrough Urban Legends

To keep the thread running, the mention of Mr Michna... you have to run a thread/stories on 'The Barbarians'...

Enter the Cog!

Cogeur_le_Conq Posted on 3/4 10:18

re: Middlesbrough Urban Legends

Haverton Hill,
Haverton Hill,
The Transporter's knackered,
I'm in Haverton Hill.

gadgemasterfunk Posted on 3/4 10:20

re: Middlesbrough Urban Legends

Anyone got any urban myth stories about Duffy?

Eddie_Catflap Posted on 3/4 10:26

re: Middlesbrough Urban Legends

Is Paul Barker the same Paul Barker who was a whiz with electronics and a sometime drummer? Had a TV repair shop off Parly Road? Mate of a mate of a mate. Small town, if it is him!

Cogeur_le_Conq Posted on 3/4 10:30

re: Middlesbrough Urban Legends

Yeah, that's Paul Barker. I was there when he almost got killed off some kid in the back room of the Empire because Paul had accused him of being a paedo or something. Colin Connors saved Paul's life by dragging the lad off him.

How many people on this thread went to Colin Connors' 40th at the Hollywood. That was one helluva hash party?

borobadge Posted on 3/4 10:33

re: Middlesbrough Urban Legends

Cogeur, do some more lyrics from The Barbarians' songs...

Binns' corner,
Binns' corner...

Cogeur_le_Conq Posted on 3/4 10:45

re: Middlesbrough Urban Legends

I don't know any more lyrics, just some song titles/choruses.

What Ever Happened To The Clean Air Bus?

Binns' Corner was a beaut.

'With a pocket full of action...
I won't go Ohhhhohhhhh
To Binns' Corner Ohhhhnnnohhhhh.'

Mebbees Rob Nichols has some Barbarian info/lyrics/tapes etc. cos I know he was once in cahoots with Dave Barbarian organising music nights upstairs at the Empire before Dave's untimely departure.

Dave Robbo from borobadge's and my band must qualify as a Boro legend. He used to please the crowds with his one man punk takeover of gigs.

He would start pogo-ing at an Abba concert would Robbo, and his party piece was sticking a dirty big nappy pin through his cheek.

littleboro Posted on 3/4 11:47

re: Middlesbrough Urban Legends

Dave Robbo used to work at British Steel in the Eighties for a brief spell - the Sinter Plant at Redcar. He'd got taken on as a relief worker.

While he was there, he told me that they were going to finish him as they no longer required a load of people services. The union told the management that they couldn't lay him off as he'd worked there for more than a year and therefore was part of the workforce. The rest got laid off.

About a year later, he told me he'd put in for his redundo as he wanted to do an electronics course. He got the redundo and this paid for his electronics course at Teesside Uni. He used to mend TVs or something so was really interested in electronics. Good luck to him.

Strange that if the union hadn't been there he would have lost the opportunity. Good bloke and dead friendly.

Cogeur_le_Conq Posted on 3/4 12:03

re: Middlesbrough Urban Legends

But the shytes at electronics.

He studied HND IT at Uni years later but electronics used to be his hobby in the late '70s.

I'd actually studied electronics as part of my TEC at Longlands College so I could see through all his bullshyte about mosfets and diodes etc and always corrected him when he was boring the arse off everyone in the Linny or somewhere.
He wired up a load of LEDs along the neck of his bass guitar so that he could see which fret he was playing in the dark and the solder joints were always cracking loose and he never understood the concept of the electronic noise being picked up by the guitar's pickups and amplified along with the signal.

He'd spend most of the gig f*****g about with the bass instead of playing it.

Smashing lad like.

littleboro Posted on 3/4 12:10

re: Middlesbrough Urban Legends

The Harry Roberts song was always sung at Boro matches and appeared to make a brief comeback in Valencia.

I watched, from a safe distance, about 20 young Boro fans (?) singing it to the Spanish police at about 2am on the day of the match. I presume it was the same lads who'd been swimming in the fountain some 4 hours earlier when we wandered past.

Harry Roberts was stopped outside Wormwood Scrubs by the police on a routine stop. He was wanted at the time for questioning about an armed robbery. He then proceeded to shoot the three coppers dead, some of whom were begging him not to shoot. Hence the song's lyrics.

You have to remember that this happened in the '60s and the death penalty had just been outlawed. In today's media there would certainly be an outcry if a policeman was murdered on duty, but three?

Another problem was that you would get an automatic life sentence for armed robbery, but would also get a life sentence for killing somebody and especially the police. Presume he thought he had nothing to lose.

Anyway he got caught and served 30 years before his release a couple of years back.

So the only connection with the Boro was that the Holgate used to sing the song.

There is a book loosely based on these events called 'He Kills Coppers' by Jake Arnott. Very good book, as it describes the dress codes and music styles of the day - reggae, ska, hippy music etc.

Big_Shot Posted on 3/4 12:18

re: Middlesbrough Urban Legends

Harry Roberts is still in prison.

littleboro Posted on 3/4 12:29

re: Middlesbrough Urban Legends

Big_Shot, oops, you're right. It must have been the press coverage a couple of years ago and I thought he had been released.

Have just found a site with full info on him.

User inserted link which included this quote;

"Harry Maurice Roberts (born Kennington 1936) is one of the UK's most notorious murderers and longest-serving prison inmates. He was the instigator of the Massacre of Braybrook Street, a triple-murder of policemen in 1966."

Source; http://www.answers.com/topic/harry-roberts-murderer

borobadge Posted on 3/4 13:56

re: Middlesbrough Urban Legends

When the coppers used to stand in front of the Holgate, being a complete nuisance, the Holgate would start to sing it.

"Harry Roberts is our friend..." This made the coppers go mad so they used to come into the Holgate to get the ringleaders who started the song off. This in turn started a lot of pushing and pulling, then a fight between Boro fans on the Holgate and the local cops. It usually finished with a few coppers' hats flying in the air and a few arrests.

Then one season some wag started it and just as it was about to finish, without the cops coming in, someone else started a new 2nd verse.

There was absolute f*****g hell on. It was crazy. Must have been around 1977.

Cogeur_le_Conq Posted on 3/4 14:08

re: Middlesbrough Urban Legends

"Who's that copper with the big red knob?"

borobadge Posted on 3/4 14:10

re: Middlesbrough Urban Legends

No, that was a different song...

The 2nd verse started, "Let him out to kill some more..."

Cogeur_le_Conq Posted on 3/4 14:13

re: Middlesbrough Urban Legends

That must have been the 3rd verse cos the 2nd verse was... "Shoots the b******s with a gun..."

littleboro Posted on 3/4 14:15

re: Middlesbrough Urban Legends

There were other songs that were sung from the Holgate every match that always brought laughter.

At about 10 past 4, two lasses would always walk past the front of the Holgate carrying two bags of money to spontaneous choruses of "Get yer tits out for the lads..."

Why they didn't just walk around the back of the Holgate only God knows. Maybe the lasses liked it, which is probably nearer the truth.

20 minutes later, at about 4.30, the coppers would form a line and march off in front of the Holgate before stopping and facing the Holgate to a spontaneous chorus of The Laurel and Hardy theme tune, and Mackay from Porridge, neck wrenching from the boys in blue, no doubt thinking, "What purpose does this have every home match? Oh sod it, we get paid for it."

Oh what clever wags we were.

borobadge Posted on 3/4 14:16

re: Middlesbrough Urban Legends

As usual, you're not wrong... ...new 3rd verse then... What I was getting at was it was NEW to us on The Holgate.

Can we mention Ernie Ragbo on this thread? He was a Middlesbrough legend. I remember when he threw your lad in the Albert Park pond.

Cogeur_le_Conq Posted on 3/4 16:16

re: Middlesbrough Urban Legends

There's a picture of Ernie Ragbo behind the bar in the side room of The Cleveland in The Village.

borobadge Posted on 3/4 16:24

re: Middlesbrough Urban Legends

That wasn't his local bar, so why?

Grrreds Posted on 3/4 16:27

re: Middlesbrough Urban Legends

I take it you lads will know Tommo (Cut Price Wallpaper variety) well, if you use/used The Acklam?

borobadge Posted on 3/4 16:27

re: Middlesbrough Urban Legends

In response to a reply earlier about Tom Robinson, I don't care what his official website says, Tom told me he was from Stokesley.

Or was he just trying to become an urban legend?

Miss Brahms... she's from the Boro... honest.

The_Gatekeeper Posted on 3/4 16:50

re: Middlesbrough Urban Legends

I've always thought Tom Robinson was from Stokesley too. On his website that was linked earlier on this thread, although it says he was born in Cambridge, there is a pic of him receiving an honorary degree at Teesside Uni which suggests a connection to this area. My guess is he was actually born in Stokesley and moved down south as a child.

darmok Posted on 3/4 16:53

re: Middlesbrough Urban Legends

I've told dozens of people over the years that Tom Robinson was from Stokesley.

Cogeur_le_Conq Posted on 3/4 17:16

re: Middlesbrough Urban Legends

He came on the stage at the Town Hall with a Boro scarf when he played there.

guyb Posted on 3/4 18:19

re: Middlesbrough Urban Legends

What has Ernie Ragbo done? I've heard his name before but don't know why.

OPEO Posted on 3/4 18:22

re: Middlesbrough Urban Legends

Ernie Robinson, to be precise. First met him when my year younger brother twatted him in the playground at Bertram Ramsey.

roswell Posted on 3/4 18:24

re: Middlesbrough Urban Legends

Talking of Holgate coppers, remember the one who looked like Mickey Quinn?

borobadge Posted on 3/4 18:28

re: Middlesbrough Urban Legends

OPEO, Eric Robinson - 'Ernie Ragbo' became his nickname following the release of A Clockwork Orange...

Cogeur_le_Conq Posted on 3/4 18:37

re: Middlesbrough Urban Legends

They were all dressed as Clockwork Orange skins when they shot our kid in Albert Park lake.

Were you there, badge? Was Jonah (Peter) there?

littleboro Posted on 3/4 19:49

re: Middlesbrough Urban Legends

Shop keepers - ah yes, the all singing Boro fans that were Robinson's on Borough Road, next to the old ABC on the corner. They sold fruit and veg and would always have a chalked up sign willing the Boro on, on matchdays.

It was always worth going in as they always seemed to be singing Boro songs. Obviously not Harry Roberts etc songs. They've gone now, sadly.

Dean, of the record shop that used to be in the Cleveland Centre, was always a top gadge. Saw him in the Princess Alice about a year ago having a couple of pints and listening to a live band. The strange thing was that he looked exactly the same as he looked about 30 years ago. Either that or the Guinness was having a fuller effect than I expected.

There must be stories about Hamilton's, Fearnley's and Austin's.

Mind you, Austin was so keen on music that he'd get other records out that were sort of linked and play them for you. You had to go in when you'd got plenty of time on your hands.

Gingerpig1 Posted on 3/4 20:46

re: Middlesbrough Urban Legends

Who was the bloke who brought the Gazettes around the Holgate?

"GEEEEEEZET... ALL THE HALF TIME SCOWERS!"

Bloke used to give people tinitus.

The dreadlocked bloke in Stockton years ago was known as 'Eddie Grant' to most. He was always decent and harmless enough but on and off the rails constantly. But when he got himself tidy, he scrubbed up well... only to fall off again!!

bill_ingham Posted on 3/4 23:11

re: Middlesbrough Urban Legends

Just thought of another one... the old fella without a tooth in his head who sold the Sports Gazette after the match. He always wore a muffler. Surely dead by now but it'd be nice if he wasn't.

red_rebel Posted on 3/4 23:37

re: Middlesbrough Urban Legends

The Record Shop (prop. Dean Wycherley). My mam says Dean had been big on the club circuit all over the North and a dashing singer of some renoun before his stroke. "He could have been as big as Tommy Steele", she says.

The posh South African gadge was called Charles (Mazebulu?). He briefly crashed at my house in the town in the early eighties after a dispute with his landlord.

He was a refugee. Or a political exile as they were known in those days before they were demonised. His dad had been high up in the ANC and was a top communist lawyer before the family had been forced to leg it to London.

He was at Teesside Poly doing something technical, avionics or something. Nice bloke but mad as a hatter. He drew a massive ANC Spear of the Nation mural on our living room wall. Class.

Cogeur_le_Conq Posted on 4/4 0:04

re: Middlesbrough Urban Legends

That posh South African guy, Charles, can't have been much of an alkie. He only ever stayed around for half a pint even if you offered to buy him a pint.

red_rebel Posted on 4/4 0:12

re: Middlesbrough Urban Legends

No Cog, but he liked a smoke.

Cogeur_le_Conq Posted on 4/4 0:17

re: Middlesbrough Urban Legends

That's why he stopped around for a half.

forza_boro Posted on 4/4 0:52

re: Middlesbrough Urban Legends

As a fireman's son, I grew up with some of these legends and I can tell you about things that officially didn't happen that I know did.

One was the tanker leak in Stockton town centre about 10 years ago. I know that the fire brigade didn't have a clue what was leaked or how to handle it despite what the press said. That was a very nasty leak.

The same plant that killed thousands in Bhopal has a sister plant on Seal Sands (Union Carbide).

There is a hydrogen plant on Seal Sands that, if it ever went up, would take half of Teesside with it (and it almost blew in the 1980s).

There was a plant that blew up in the US that took half a town with it that is also based on Seal Sands.

I asked my dad and he has never heard of 'cancer castle' (though he was based more in Stockton and Billingham).

mad_frankie Posted on 4/4 0:58

re: Middlesbrough Urban Legends

True about the h2 plant. I used to work there.

KEN_M Posted on 4/4 2:01

re: Middlesbrough Urban Legends

Another plant on Wilton was built to the highest possible standards. Quality assurance/control standards were still a fairly new concept but they were used to the full. It was near the transport maintenance depot, close to Nylon.

A mate was part of the site fire brigade (long dead now). He was on duty when they decided to give it a trial on a Sunday morning. They used a talcum powder derivative as a trial compound because it was the closest in particle size to the real stuff.

Result – 10 minutes after start up, Trunk Road covered for miles in white powder. Looked like it had been snowing in the middle of summer. They reckoned that it spread over a 15-20 mile radius.

Plant was never commissioned, later scrapped totally.

Mate later told me that the chemical intended for production was lethal, the same as a plant that had been given 24 hours to be closed down in the USA. The US owners tried to rebuild in other locations but governments in South America, Pakistan and India had all refused. Teesside Council gave the go-ahead. He reckoned that if the Sunday morning trial had been the real stuff it would have been the biggest peace-time problem the UK had ever faced.

mad_frankie Posted on 4/4 2:20

re: Middlesbrough Urban Legends

Plant that blew up in the States was an ethylene oxide plant and there was (is?) one on Wilton. There also used to be an ethylene oxide derivative plant at Billingham, which was the first one I was ever on.

Before my first day at work (a 7-2), I put the late night news on to see footage of the ethylene plant exploding in a fireball approx 2 hours before I was due to start work on the Billingham one. Very scary!

mad_frankie Posted on 4/4 2:23

re: Middlesbrough Urban Legends

'In response to a reply earlier about Tom Robinson... I don't care what his official website says... Tom told me he was from Stokesley.'

True, borobadge, he is. I know one of the other band members from Cafe Society who told me about how he used to go to Tom's house in Stokesley for jamming sessions.

KEN_M Posted on 4/4 4:39

re: Middlesbrough Urban Legends

mad_frankie, the one in the States that I referred to did not blow up. It was given 24 hours to close down by US OHS.

mad_frankie Posted on 4/4 6:15

re: Middlesbrough Urban Legends

There was one that went up big style in the States, apart from the one you mentioned. I watched it go up on the news the day before I was due to start work on the Billingham ethylene oxide derivative plant - scared the shat out of me!

PNGfulham Posted on 4/4 6:20

re: Middlesbrough Urban Legends

Keogh doesn't have a brother named Trevor, does he?

boros_moggy Posted on 4/4 9:32

re: Middlesbrough Urban Legends

Forza - the leaking road tanker in Stockton was carrying Cresol (creysilic acid). The emergency services blew it out of all proportion. The leak was very minor and we had to offload the tanker after it was escorted back to our site at Seal Sands.

The main problem was that it was Christmas Eve and the police evacuated all of Stockton town centre leaving traders and pub owners rather miffed. The product is not that dangerous compared to some of the dodgy chemicals we store at work.

Was 20 yards away when a 60 foot storage tank blew up a few years back. That wasn't a good shift!

green_beret20 Posted on 4/4 9:40

re: Middlesbrough Urban Legends

Not so much Middlesbrough (although you would have seen a very large fireball on the northern horizon) but about two months ago half of Peterlee nearly ceased to exist...

mattrich Posted on 4/4 10:31

re: Middlesbrough Urban Legends

Sorry OPEO. Been away from the computer for a few days. Mother's family are called Mohan and moved to Easterside when it was built from Cannon Street.

borobadge Posted on 4/4 14:33

re: Middlesbrough Urban Legends

Cogeur, I wasn't there and as far as I know neither was Jonah.

Smiffy the Dustman was there, as was Leggy Collins, Bluesey, Northern Soul Dave, Barney Brannigan, Squinter Sam, Baby Bob and Stuttering Trev, amongst others...

Cogeur_le_Conq Posted on 4/4 14:57

re: Middlesbrough Urban Legends

Kinnel. It sounds like the Bash Street Kids.

Yeah Grreds, I knew Tommo. Used to be a wrong 'un but turned out alright. Didn't he used to knock about with Fatty Clarkson?

A few names that used to fly about the back room of the Empire:

John the Windowcleaner (alias Scare The Kids)
Dave the Baker
Eric the Red
Steve the Taxi

And everyone must know Tex at the Linny.

TOPIC

MESSAGE

POST

REGISTER

Official word from the Shane Ritchie site admin is that the story about him being legged round Coulby is false.

Eddie_Catflap Posted on 4/4 17:41

re: Middlesbrough Urban Legends

Bloody hell, I've got some reading to do here to catch up with this thread.

Official word from the Shane Ritchie site admin is that the story about him being legged round Coulby is false. They offered me some story about him catching a woman cheating on her husband instead but I haven't followed it up.

borobadge Posted on 4/4 17:47

re: Middlesbrough Urban Legends

Flat-top Tex?

Cogeur_le_Conq Posted on 4/4 17:53

re: Middlesbrough Urban Legends

No. Mucky ginger/blonde, long haired sound engineer from the Little Theatre.

wilfym Posted on 4/4 18:29

re: Middlesbrough Urban Legends

With regard to ethylene oxide, the little place near the Riverside used to process that and had an atomic bomb style map in the offices... everything in a 3 mile radius levelled if a tank of this stuff exploded. 3 to 8 miles seriously damaged, 8 to 10 miles lightly toasted!

AtomicLoonybin Posted on 4/4 20:44

re: Middlesbrough Urban Legends

On the Frank Zappa eating poop story... it's false.

User inserted link which included this quote:

"I was in a London club called the Speakeasy in 1967 or '68. A member of a group called the Flock, recording for Columbia at the time, came over to me and said:

"You're fantastic. When I heard about you eating that shit on stage, I thought, 'That guy is way, way out there.'"
I said, "I never ate shit on stage." He looked really depressed — like I had just broken his heart."

Source; http://www.snopes.com/music/artists/grossout.htm

borobadge Posted on 4/4 21:19

re: Middlesbrough Urban Legends

What about the so called curse on Ayresome Park? What's the background and story about that?

ccole Posted on 4/4 21:23

re: Middlesbrough Urban Legends

I think the story is that they scattered some gypsies to build the ground. As they were leaving, an old woman put a curse on the ground.

Was there really a workhouse called the Holgate?

Cogeur_le_Conq Posted on 4/4 21:31

re: Middlesbrough Urban Legends

Old Gate according to old maps.

mattrich Posted on 4/4 21:33

re: Middlesbrough Urban Legends

Thought that was St Mary's?

tonybiriyani Posted on 4/4 21:34

re: Middlesbrough Urban Legends

Yes, according to this...

User inserted link which included this quote;

"From 1837 until 1875, Middlesbrough (frequently misspelt as 'Middlesborough') was part of the Stockton Poor Law Union. Following the development of iron mining in the area, the population increased substantially. As a result, a new Middlesbrough Poor Law Union was set up, taking in parts of the existing Guisborough, Stokesley and Stockton unions."

Source; http://users.ox.ac.uk/%7Epeter/workhouse/Middlesbrough/Middlesbrough.shtml

littleboro Posted on 4/4 21:35

re: Middlesbrough Urban Legends

borobadge - Oh bloody hell. That's a good one. I'm expecting some good theories on this one. All I know, or think I know, is that it's something to do with gypsies? Or was it witches?

I've never believed that it was the ghosts of Gazette sellers past. Mind you, I suppose a collective name for Gazette sellers would be "Gadgiegazetties".

Whatever the reasons for the curse there was no need to give us Mr Burns as chairman. That was beyond the pale. Long live Gibbo.

littleboro Posted on 4/4 21:41

re: Middlesbrough Urban Legends

Just put in the following on Google - 'gipsies curses Middlesbrough'.

Got this...

Medicine "oop North"... First off, the last time Hull played Middlesbrough there was massive crowd trouble... So there you go, our patient was stolen by gypsies - we were ...

www.medschoolguide.co.uk/ forum/archive/index.php/t-105.html

Cogeur_le_Conq Posted on 4/4 21:55

re: Middlesbrough Urban Legends

Here's Uri Geller's slant:

BORO'S GYPSY CURSE

If you've seen my work you'll realise my biggest interest in life is the human condition, and what goes on in the greatest supercomputer of all - the mind.

I believe that much of what we perceive as strange or paranormal comes from within. It fascinates me if a sportsman talks about a 'jinx team' or says their performance suffers because of a 'bad atmosphere'.

That's how I got caught up with the Boro story. On a charity visit to the area I was told that a gypsy curse from Ayresome Park had followed the club to their new ground, I was intrigued by tales of builders consulting charts to determine the positions at which the sun would rise and fall over the stadium. To me that's a belief in other forces, although judging by the panels in the roof that allow extra light as the season wanes, there might be a more down-to-earth reason.

Having spoken to fans who have visited both grounds, I gathered that Middlesbrough has a 'feel' they can't explain. A curse? Well, who knows - but don't rule out the power of collective thought, in both positive and negative ways. How many times has the crowd turned an impossible situation with a goal out of the blue? How many times have teams been two up at home with 10 minutes to go, the crowd has gone quiet and then the visitors have a scoring spree and take three points home with them? It happens, but you just can't put your finger on the reason, can you?

Ask Gerry Francis about the mysterious Black Cat of Loftus Road. Its appearance always seemed to prompt victory, and the fans came to rely on a last-minute feline appearance to salvage problem fixtures. Luck made real? Or a prompt for the faithful to use their collective thoughts to empower the players? I'd love to see if we could use the power of positive thought to fire up a team who are down on their 'luck'. Which brings me back to Boro!

Uri Geller is consultant editor to Uri Geller's Encounters magazine. Visit his website at www.urigeller.com

OPEO Posted on 4/4 22:37

re: Middlesbrough Urban Legends

Mattrich, Mary and Frank ring any bells?

mattrich Posted on 4/4 22:43

re: Middlesbrough Urban Legends

Nana and Grandad were called Mary and Frank.

OPEO Posted on 4/4 22:44

re: Middlesbrough Urban Legends

What about Colin and Alan?

mattrich Posted on 4/4 23:22

re: Middlesbrough Urban Legends

Uncles, guess you know them then?

outoftowner Posted on 4/4 23:46

re: Middlesbrough Urban Legends

How about Elaine Boksic as a legend... rain, hail or shine, head to foot in Boro kit, trainers, bag etc wandering around town. I worked in a hostel a few years ago which dealt mainly with those from out of area... and managed to convince one of the clients she was Frontline. Maybe a little in bad taste, but funny all the same.

mattrich Posted on 4/4 23:54

re: Middlesbrough Urban Legends

Is that the one who is always with her dad who dresses the same? Think they sit in the East Stand. Have seen them in the concourse and around town during the day!

outoftowner Posted on 5/4 0:01

re: Middlesbrough Urban Legends

Couldn't tell you, pal. Not my stand... but worth sitting there to see it! Only the once mind. She's always alone when I've seen her in town. And must be rolling in it too... would be cheaper to shop solely in Triads than buy every item you own from the club shop.

OPEO Posted on 5/4 6:25

re: Middlesbrough Urban Legends

Mattrich, is Sheila yer mam or auntie?

borobadge Posted on 5/4 8:08

re: Middlesbrough Urban Legends

There's a Ghost in My House - R Dean Taylor.

boksic Posted on 5/4 8:14

re: Middlesbrough Urban Legends

Has anyone ever heard of 'Paddy's Wood?' My old fella used to go on about this. Sure it's a myth. A piece of wood stuck in a narrow gap between 2 buildings that could not be retrieved, somewhere near top end of Marton Road/Royal Exchange.

mattrich Posted on 5/4 9:22

re: Middlesbrough Urban Legends

Sheila is my mam.

Muppet_Hi_Fi Posted on 5/4 22:37

re: Middlesbrough Urban Legends

1. I can confirm The Damned at the Rock Garden legend. Henry Badowski did puke into a beer glass and drink it with the Doomed in '78. The Captain did appear for the encore in his birthday suit and relieve himself on the front row with the Damned in '79.
2. Sadly, the story of the BSC apprentices is true. They did take a ride on the conveyor and end up in the lime bunkers.
3. Kevin Mooney out of the Antz was game for a scrap with a few of the Garden faithful. He had his bass off ready to smack a few but things calmed down. Adam Ant also called the Rock Garden "the biggest toilet he'd ever played in."
4. I thought the Angelic Upstarts gig at Gaskins did go ahead with only the support band playing? King Crab they were called and Jimmy 'Big Nose' Nail was supposed to be singing for them?
5. The bloke in the white coat selling those lovely pink Wessler burgers must have used the fat from them to style his hair. It was dripping in it.
6. Who can forget Keogh busking with that guitar with no strings?
7. Nipper, the Eston Square tramp. A lovely sight in the summer basking in the sun with his knackers hanging out.
8. Alice Bun. Nit Noo. Anyone remember them?

Muppet_Hi_Fi Posted on 5/4 22:44

re: Middlesbrough Urban Legends

This one was kicking around years ago. Some lad got off with one of the lovely ladies of the night at the Bongo. On getting down to business some bloke burst out of the wardrobe in a Batman suit and gave the lad a very sore bottom!

mattrich Posted on 7/4 11:26

re: Middlesbrough Urban Legends

Not strictly Middlesbrough but anyone heard the one about the Viking ship buried beneath the hill near Lockwood Beck on the way to Whitby?

RedJohnnie Posted on 7/4 12:17

re: Middlesbrough Urban Legends

Nit Noo and Alice were regulars around Grangetown in the '70s. Wasn't that round hill near Whitby supposed to have been a Roman burial site?

TOPIC

MESSAGE

POST

REGISTER

Adam Ant also called the Rock Garden "the biggest toilet he'd ever played in."

sandancer Posted on 7/4 12:20

re: Middlesbrough Urban Legends

Who was that Jock who used to hang around Linthorpe shops trying to sell cheap perfume? Is Paul Clifford still inside after the Sarfraz Najeeb affair?

mattrich Posted on 7/4 20:47

re: Middlesbrough Urban Legends

No, he will be out by now. Think we are on about the same hill, mate!

Smog_Monster Posted on 8/4 6:32

re: Middlesbrough Urban Legends

Not a Viking ship or burial ground. It was formed during the last Ice Age. A crack in the ice allowed debris to fall through causing the mound below, like an egg timer.

borobadge Posted on 8/4 13:41

re: Middlesbrough Urban Legends

When we were kids for a day out in the summer we'd go to Fairy Dell...

Or try and dodge the farmer and his legendary supply of 'salt pellets' that he'd fire at yer arse as you crossed his field trying to get to The Blue Lagoon...

Or, as we called it as kids in Grove Hill, 'The Blula'...

These were places of intrigue and fun, of dares and scrapes...

Goal_Scrounger Posted on 8/4 15:58

re: Middlesbrough Urban Legends

Those adult-authority figures were scary, weren't they, borobadge?

I remember legging it several times from Parkie and Frenchie in Smith's Dock Park because, as every self-respecting schoolboy knew, if they caught you, they'd lock you in the cricket score hut and you'd be there until the next cricket match. A scary thought if it was November!

Talking of bands, a more recent story is of The Libertines. An article in the NME a couple of years ago mentions the band saying that they would never be able to play Middlesbrough again after an incident following their Cornerhouse appearance. Apparently, one of the band was trying to cop off with a barmaid and the security were none too impressed by this, for some reason. The incident ended with the band helping themselves to as much of the bar's top shelf as they could carry before doing a runner.

Goal_Scrounger Posted on 8/4 16:02

re: Middlesbrough Urban Legends

Anyone know the origins of the 'Spies For Peace' graffiti that was written on the wall of a brick building next to Gillbrook School in 3 feet high white letters in the late '70s/early '80s?

The building was a dark red brick changing room (I think) on the field further down Normanby Road from Gillbrook's sports hall (behind which many schoolboy/girl 'liaisons' took place after school!!)

mattrich Posted on 11/4 20:30

re: Middlesbrough Urban Legends

There was supposed to be a Grey Lady at King's Manor School library. Think it is part of Middlesbrough College now.

borobuddah Posted on 11/4 21:04

re: Middlesbrough Urban Legends

That mound (near Jolly Sailor's) has as much to do with the hobs, which I'm surprised haven't had a mention; too rural rather than urban.

GS - I'm sure 'Yankees go home' or summat similar was on the same wall?

boro74 Posted on 11/4 21:26

re: Middlesbrough Urban Legends

Is it true that The Sex Pistols once did a gig in Boro under the psuedonym of Acne Rabble?

Muppet_Hi_Fi Posted on 11/4 23:33

re: Middlesbrough Urban Legends

Yeah, the Pistols played at the Rock Garden, now The Arena, under the name Acne Rabble on Friday 26th August 1977. They also played the Town Hall Crypt supporting The Doctors of Madness on 21st May 1976.

Cogeur_le_Conq Posted on 11/4 23:45

re: Middlesbrough Urban Legends

What's all this S.P.O.T.S

User inserted link to Sex Pistols flyer for Middlesbrough gig as S.P.O.T.S.

Big_Shot Posted on 12/4 23:17

re: Middlesbrough Urban Legends

I was told the other day about a place called Pansies (sp). Apparently it was somewhere to go drinking on a Sunday afternoon when all the pubs shut. I'm assuming it was '70s/'80s, and possibly over the border. Anybody remember it?

apl1970 Posted on 13/4 0:20

re: Middlesbrough Urban Legends

The BSC apprentice one is true. There were actually 3 lads on the conveyor but one managed to get off.

For anyone who doesn`t know. Lime is a bleeding `orrible substance that burns mucous glands (eye ducts, mouth, sweat pores etc) and has the same consistency as talcum powder. Once they were in that bunker they had no chance.

Death by drowning in Lime. I can think of nothing worse.

On a lighter note - urban legends; can we not put Bam Bam and Keogh down as these?

ridsdale Posted on 13/4 0:31

re: Middlesbrough Urban Legends

Big_Shot, it was Paddies Cafe. And was on the Rivers Estate. Just as you go over the flyover to North Ormesby.

A terraced house that sold cans of beer between pub opening hours. I lived nearby, in Lune Street. I think Paddies was on Clyde Street.

A proper place for plonkies.

apl1970 Posted on 13/4 0:40

re: Middlesbrough Urban Legends

And I`ve thought of another. How about Rea`s cafe between the bus station and Jack Hatfield's, I think, on Newport Road. It was a hang out for our ladies of the night, salt of the earth, call them what you will.

Big_Shot Posted on 13/4 8:33

re: Middlesbrough Urban Legends

That'll be it, Paddies. A mate said he went once and that was enough. He said it was a cafe that sold cans when the pubs shut.

borobadge Posted on 13/4 9:23

re: Middlesbrough Urban Legends

The miniature railway in Albert Park and Bell Hill, the fenced off area behind it... the scene of a girl's murder?

Muppet_Hi_Fi Posted on 13/4 19:27

re: Middlesbrough Urban Legends

Southgate and Parnaby On Tour Secretly. le Conq, where did you dig that flyer up from?

Redbrian Posted on 13/4 20:51

re: Middlesbrough Urban Legends

The story about the two BSC lads getting killed was indeed true. There was actually three of them on the conveyor but one jumped off and the other two went into the lime bunkers in the BOS plant. The one who survived still works there. Everyone on the plant knows him. He was a very lucky lad. He's about 44 now.

mattrich Posted on 13/4 21:30

re: Middlesbrough Urban Legends

Is it true that there used to be a topless fish and chip shop in Redcar?

Muppet_Hi_Fi Posted on 13/4 23:18

re: Middlesbrough Urban Legends

Topless chippy seems to ring a bell. Wasn't it the one behind The Sandpiper, now The Aruba?

Eddie_Catflap Posted on 13/4 23:33

re: Middlesbrough Urban Legends

I'm pretty sure the Albert Park murder story is right, borobadge, although I can't find anything with a quick Google search. I was definitely told it when I was younger anyway.

boros_moggy Posted on 14/4 8:07

re: Middlesbrough Urban Legends

mattrich/muppet - you are both correct, the chip shop was indeed behind Aruba (the Sandpiper in them days) though the lady serving topless was not young and not, shall we say, a real looker.

mattrich Posted on 14/4 21:02

re: Middlesbrough Urban Legends

Ouch, the fat must have burnt!

Muppet_Hi_Fi Posted on 16/4 9:57

re: Middlesbrough Urban Legends

Talking to someone last night who actually went to the topless chippy after a session in The Sandpiper only to be confronted by a topless bloke dishing the chips out. Depends which side you like your bread buttered but they left disappointed.

Goal_Scrounger Posted on 3/9 9:24

re: Middlesbrough Urban Legends

Bloody hell, Cogeur_le_Conq, I can only assume you either a) had it bookmarked or b) have a lot of patience to be able to resurrect this one!!

The_Commisar Posted on 3/9 9:29

re: Middlesbrough Urban Legends

Without doubt the board's finest hour.

The Linny - who was the bloke who wore cut-off jeans as shorts? He looked like Iggy Pop? 'Albert' Frank at the far end of the bar near the snug, used a tankard which was NEVER washed?

The burger bloke off Linny Road once leapt off his bike to thump my mate Kev who complained about the quality!

Why did it ALWAYS rain when the Cleveland Show was on?

Whatever happened to the HMM - Hemlington Mau Mau's - and their arch enemies, the NPT?

The day that we played Celtic, a million Jocks invaded. I was in the off-licence on Linny Road to hear the owner say "No, we haven't got any ***kin' heavy or Irn ***kin' Bru!" to yet another 'sweaty sock'.

Cogeur_le_Conq Posted on 3/9 9:40

re: Middlesbrough Urban Legends

Miff was the bloke who wore cut-off jeans as shorts. He topped himself. The mother of his kid was living with my mate at the time. He's already mentioned above, as is Salmonella Sam the Burger Man.

The NPT is actually the NTP (Netherfields, Thorntree, Pally Park) or Joeys and there is a new hoolie book coming out called 'The Brick' by Paul Debrick which chronicles a lot of their exploits, apparently.

The_Commisar Posted on 3/9 9:51

re: Middlesbrough Urban Legends

Paul Debrick? Bloody hell, there's a name from the past!

Yeah, I heard Miff had topped himself but not sure if that was a myth itself.

You an ex-Linny man?

hells_bells83 Posted on 3/9 9:54

re: Middlesbrough Urban Legends

The first post was on my birthday!

tonybiriyani Posted on 3/9 9:55

re: Middlesbrough Urban Legends

I think nearly everyone from the Boro of a certain age is 'ex-Linny'.

mattrich Posted on 3/9 10:05

re: Middlesbrough Urban Legends

Sadly, The Linny is a shadow of its former self.

tonybiriyani Posted on 3/9 10:06

re: Middlesbrough Urban Legends

Do many get in there now?

Whatever happened to the HMM - Hemlington Mau Mau's - and their arch enemies, the NPT?

Cogeur_le_Conq Posted on 3/9 10:15

re: Middlesbrough Urban Legends

It used to be great in the late '70s/early '80s.

The_Commisar Posted on 3/9 10:38

re: Middlesbrough Urban Legends

I used to frequent the Linny before it was done out for the first time. I had a bike so that was OK! I remember Satan's Slaves holding a wake in there. That was 'interesting'.

Sez_Les_Boro Posted on 3/9 10:42

re: Middlesbrough Urban Legends

Bloody Hell!!

I remember 'Candles' outside the Maddo. Every now and then there'd be a sudden sizzle as a bit more mucous dropped onto his hot plate.

Anyone remember the lad who used to constantly orbit the old Ayresome Park carrying a Brixton Brick and towing along an old mankie dog on a piece of hairy string? I think some on here know him.

The_Commisar Posted on 3/9 10:45

re: Middlesbrough Urban Legends

I know the lad you're on about. He used to orbit Ayresome with his radio. I spotted him outside the Riverside the other week. Bless him, he's a cheery soul who has never offended anyone and just gets on with his life.

Andy X - I used to be at Kirby and the lads from the Student's Union used to pay Andy to do a lunchtime gig. That Goldfish song had them bouncing.

He's now a "JAAAACKPOT" seller at The Riverside. Still has a grin like the Joker's.

Eddie_Catflap Posted on 3/9 12:45

re: Middlesbrough Urban Legends

Cheers Coga - I never thought I'd see this thread again. The Terry Scott picture Fischer dug up still makes me laugh.

jonny_giles Posted on 3/9 13:12

re: Middlesbrough Urban Legends

Is there a ghost town on Eston Hills? Or was there one?

Cogeur_le_Conq Posted on 3/9 13:14

re: Middlesbrough Urban Legends

That'll be SS Castle, as featured in 'A Century of Stone'. An old iron ore mine entrance.

I think they may have built a false town up there during WWII to confuse the German bombers.

comfortable_shoes Posted on 3/9 13:22

re: Middlesbrough Urban Legends

I was told a story about Dorman Long steelworks by my dad years ago. As they all went in to work on the bus one day, one of the old blokes (Jimmy) who worked one of the cranes was found dead.

Now back then it was union rules that if someone died at work, everyone got the rest of the day off. So, they got this dead bloke, walked him into the changing rooms, got his overalls on him, carried him to his crane and then all went to work.

After about five minutes someone shouts out, "Hey, Gaffer, I think there is something wrong with Jimmy in crane 6." The nurse came, then a doctor, then an ambulance and took poor Jimmy away. They all got knocked off and went on the piss all day!!!

Piquet2 Posted on 3/9 13:40

re: Middlesbrough Urban Legends

Charlie Kray was a regular visitor to the Inn off the Park. My dad's best mate is Barry Faulkner's cousin. My dad said you could cut the atmosphere with a knife when he turned up. Definitely Princes Road, lived there long enough, and Keogh once dropped his pants and did one outside our tea room window. Tom Robinson is definitely from Stokesley.

borobadge Posted on 3/9 13:59

re: Middlesbrough Urban Legends

Is that Debrick on the front of his new book, or an actor?

Last time I saw him (in real life) he had a deep, deep suntan and a head of blond quiffed/spikey hair...

As an all too infrequent visitor to the Boro, I see great changes each time I come back. Can't say that they're all for the better. Are there still characters kicking around in town these days, or has the place been completely sanitised?

Grrreds Posted on 3/9 14:16

re: Middlesbrough Urban Legends

"Anyone remember the lad who used to constantly orbit the old Ayresome Park carrying a Brixton Brick and towing along an old mankie dog on a piece of hairy string? I think some on here know him."

Eric is his name.

borobadge Posted on 3/9 14:45

re: Middlesbrough Urban Legends

Marvellous... he named his dog after McMordie ......

AyresomeMark Posted on 3/9 15:15

re: Middlesbrough Urban Legends

OPEO - was the natureboy about 60 with white hair and perma tan?

tonybiriyani Posted on 3/9 15:51

re: Middlesbrough Urban Legends

borobadge - yes, that is him, not an actor.

As for the characters around the town, I don't think there are any these days, but that might be a sign of me turning into an old git!

PhillyMac Posted on 3/9 16:54

re: Middlesbrough Urban Legends

New urban myth:

"Hark now hear
The Boro sing
United ran away
And we will fight for evermore
Because of Boxing Day."

I know this used to be sung by just about every club going in the '80s but what happened on Boxing Day? Which United? Is there any substance behind the lyrics at all?

j_orourke Posted on 3/9 16:56

re: Middlesbrough Urban Legends

Leeds, '79-'80 season, now I have consulted my Boro library!

Jonny_Greenings_sock Posted on 3/9 17:12

re: Middlesbrough Urban Legends

Lived next door to one of the Gazette sellers mentioned above, in Thornaby, the one who looked like Onslow out of 'Keeping Up Appearances' and always wore tank tops.

He only had one record, 'I Am The Music Man,' and every Saturday morning he'd play it twice through at an earth-shattering volume. "What can you plaaaaaay?"

borobadge Posted on 4/9 17:00

re: Middlesbrough Urban Legends

Traditionally, St Stephen's Day - Boxing Day - was the day of lots of local derbies... hence a punch-up. That's in relation to the song, not an explanation for why it's called Boxing Day...

Dirty Leeds or the Jawdees... 'cos whenever we played Man Utd, the Holgate sang "There's only one United and that's a bus."

Anyone recall a lad who was always in Albert Park? He was called "Monkey Alan."

tonybiriyani Posted on 4/9 17:08

re: Middlesbrough Urban Legends

Did he used to hang about in the trees?

borobadge Posted on 5/9 10:34

re: Middlesbrough Urban Legends

You clearly don't know the lad...

He was a big large lump and he used to bite his fisted hands and grunt like a chimp... hence the name 'Monkey Alan'. He was as strong as an ox and had great bursts of power and energy...

I know it all sounds rather odd, but believe me, he was a character, circa 1972/73/74.

mattrich Posted on 5/9 10:37

re: Middlesbrough Urban Legends

Before my time, mate.

gravy173 Posted on 5/9 14:30

re: Middlesbrough Urban Legends

This must be the best thread written on FMTTM. Was laughing in my office reading some of Keogh's witicisms. I remember the auld duffer well. Is he still doddering about?

Grove_Hill_Red Posted on 5/9 15:51

re: Middlesbrough Urban Legends

Cancer Castle - definitely true. I used to work out the back of it.

Anyone remember the old bloke in The Green Tree who used to use boot polish on his head? Talking late '70s here.

Sex Pistols at the Rock Garden had an associated ruck. Mate of mine had his jaw broken (top and bottom, both sides) by a punk with 2 bricks. Was wired up for several months having it set.

Some great nights out down there though, and several drunken sprints to Ayresome Park after pre-match strips.

blotonthelandscape Posted on 27/10 16:10

re: Middlesbrough Urban Legends

My dad was known as the bloke who kicked a nun.

starbecksmoggy2 Posted on 27/10 19:44

re: Middlesbrough Urban Legends

My dad, who is from South Bank (or was, he's dead now) would have loved this and he'd probably have joined in with loads of stuff.

Come_On_Boro_the_1st Posted on 27/10 21:20

re: Middlesbrough Urban Legends

I've just read this whole thread and I'm worn out!

The 'Spies for Peace' sign was allegedly written by my brother-in-law. I can't remember why he said he did it. He was too intellectual for Normanby, that's for certain.

I knew someone who went to school with Nipper Harris. Nipper was your archetypal tramp in his latter years, string round his coat and big beard. They used to drag him in every now and then, give him a wash and a de-louse, but he always went back to the streets. My mate used to chat with him and asked him why he lived like he did. Nipper would just say he liked being out in the open. He often slept on Eston Hills.

Wasn't there a dodgy burger van outside Madison in the 1970s called Duffy's Diner?

Sex Pistols at the Rock Garden had an associated ruck. Mate of mine had his jaw broken (top and bottom, both sides) by a punk with 2 bricks. Was wired up for several months having it set.

littleboro Posted on 27/10 21:33

re: Middlesbrough Urban Legends

There was a character of interest - well, an interest - that was best kept at a listening distance. The era would be 1970s and early 1980s.

He roamed the Linthorpe area pubs - The Linthorpe, the Roses and The Cleveland.

A tall, gangly gadgey who, if mind remembers well, used to wear a suit, minus tie. When he talked he would always chump his lips, almost spitting. Winter wear was the same, except he had a long black overcoat that the Bunneymen would have killed for.

You would listen to him talking to barmaids about his recent sexual conquests. These would always turn out to be prostitutes.

His real talent lay in this brilliant ability to play the ivories. He was regarded by all the locals as being a great pianist and even used to have a Yellow Rose residency for a few Christmases, with his 'double pint glass' on top of the piano, in the then old man's bar.

His name was Basil.

During the early 1980s he seemed to disappear. I did hear that he had been sent to an asylum. Whether or not this is true, I don't know.

Does anybody else remember this legend?

borobadge Posted on 27/10 21:54

re: Middlesbrough Urban Legends

Sir Steve Gibson...

I heard he was a Labour councillor in Park End!!

littleboro Posted on 27/10 22:30

re: Middlesbrough Urban Legends

Amazing what a change of hair style, suit and name change can do?

Mind you, how did he manage to lose the height?

JoeLaidlaw Posted on 27/10 22:33

re: Middlesbrough Urban Legends

Nipper Harris is all cleaned up and lives behind St Andrew's Church on Fabian Road, Eston.

I've mentioned before that I once bumped into Roger Tames outside the South Stand at Ayresome Park many moons ago but there was no singing or dancing going on, just Roger banging on the door screaming for help. He even mentioned why he was sporting a black eye on 'Midweek Sports Special' with my dad saying 'They're nothing but bloody animals.'

That was in my dark days and I have repented since then.

Sorry, Roger.

It might have happened again.

erimus11 Posted on 27/10 23:32

re: Middlesbrough Urban Legends

Littleboro - I remember that gadge, Basil. He was a cracking piano player and would do a spot on the ivories in any pub with a 'Joanna,' e.g. The Trooper.

Eddie_Catflap Posted on 27/10 23:39

re: Middlesbrough Urban Legends

Did you sing the theme tune from 'Shoot' though, Joe? That's the big question

blotonthelandscape, you can't leave that story about the nun hanging like that. Did he really boot a holy sister?

Not really a Boro urban legend but I live out at Sedgefield now (since moving back from Leeds). I live on a new estate just outside of the village. It is the site of the old psychiatric hospital. The other week I was getting a taxi back home and got chatting to the driver - "You used to hear some tales coming out of that hospital," he said."Oh aye?" says I, imagining some kind of Michael Myers-style mass murderer on the loose and ghosts of the victims wandering round my garden shed. "Er, yeah" he said. "Apparently there was a bloke in there with a massive cock, used to f**k all the women".

So there you have it, the legendary King Dong of the Sedgefield looney bin.

The_COAT Posted on 28/10 9:26

re: Middlesbrough Urban Legends

Alright, not Boro, but... my dad told me of a bloke in the '60s who would spend his whole day walking around Stockton with his head bent over looking for the spanner that hit him on the neck when he was working at Dorman Long Steel Works. He would walk across Victoria Bridge and turn around before setting foot in Thornaby and he would then go back. If he wasn't walking, he could be found in the pub near where what was the 'Employment Exchange' was situated, just off the bridge opposite what is now DFS or similar. My dad went on to say that the spanner had actually hit this bloke square on the head, nearly killing him, hence his problem!!

Note - I signed on at said 'Employment Exchange' for one week in the early '70s... I was so ashamed. I was waiting to start a career in the forces but had to wait two months, so took a job labouring on a building site instead.

PumpingGnome Posted on 28/10 10:48

re: Middlesbrough Urban Legends

Bloke I knew was quite well known around Billingham - married a German girl who in her youth looked like Bridgit Bardot but by the time she was 20 she looked like Cushy Butterfield (a big sack o' taties tied round with a string). Parties at their house were always entertaining, often including things like bottle fights, the weapon of choice being the old fashioned Lowcocks' Lemonade bottles.

One true story about this guy - he was in the Catholic Club bragging about his new dog (Great Dane) and one of the locals (related to Corcaigh of this list) told him that the way to stamp your authority on a dog is to do as dogs do and give it a little bite on the ear.

Next time he came in he had bite marks all over his face. He'd gone home pissed, bit his dog on the ear and she'd gone for him big style. Apparently the ear bitey thing only works with pups. The Great Dane was 3.

Another Billingham character I know well decided that the ornamental koi carp pond in the town centre (now gone) could do with a bit of livening up and he put a pike in it. Only one fish left in it by the time they managed to get it out - and it wasn't a carp.

The concrete-encased chemical plant you refer to used to make alpha naphthylamine, one of the most dangerous carcinogens ever made. Very, very dangerous stuff, and I remember somebody telling me that 100% of the people who worked in the final stage at a plant somewhere else in the country had died of bladder cancer.

extratomato Posted on 28/10 12:11

re: Middlesbrough Urban Legends

Red book holders get first choice on home and away cup matches!!

Sorry, couldn't resist.

I'm not bitter honest... I'll get my coat.

Come_On_Boro_the_1st Posted on 28/10 19:24

re: Middlesbrough Urban Legends

Re: the 'Spies for Peace' sign on the wall at Eston Rec [near the sports centre], my brother-in-law has confirmed his involvement with another two lads from Keswick Road, Normanby. They took a dark sheet and held it up between the wall and Normanby Road so that the white paint wouldn't be seen until they'd finished. Part way through they realised there was a mistake so it looked a bit odd.

It's a while since I've been past there. Is it still on the wall or has it been painted over? Or has the wall disappeared?

Glad to hear that Nipper Harris has sorted himself out a bit. He was part of the Eston scene for a long time. I felt proud that we had our own bona-fide tramp. People would buy him food from the shops on Eston Square, but whenever folk gave him dosh he was in pretty smartish for a bottle of cider or whatever.

On the Holgate hooliganism era, I often remember coppers' helmets flying around above the crowd. Who'd have been a policeman in those days?! If they were stood in the Holgate they went home with their coats covered in gob.

jimmyrav Posted on 28/10 19:41

re: Middlesbrough Urban Legends

I once saw Natalie Imbruglia in the Star and Garter! You may have been there, Catflap.

Rumours she went home with one of the lads (or all of them) have never been proven!

MontagueLongfellow Posted on 28/10 23:40

re: Middlesbrough Urban Legends

I remember Nipper and reckon he only used to doss about so the nuns at Normanby Convent would take him in for a good scrub

soxy Posted on 29/10 0:22

re: Middlesbrough Urban Legends

Great to read stories that bring back memories. As a Teesville scally from the '80s, the stories of the 'Sportsie' and Nipper Harris bring back great childhood memories. Thanks FMTTM peeps for a great thread.

NorthDownSouth Posted on 29/10 10:42

re: Middlesbrough Urban Legends

One story I heard about Lee Duffy was that someone poured petrol all over him but couldn't get his lighter to work, which was bad news for him as Duffy promptly broke his back. Can anyone confirm this?

j_orourke Posted on 29/10 11:00

re: Middlesbrough Urban Legends

It was 2 brothers in the Commercial Pub in South Bank and it was a jaw, not a back!

Cogeur_le_Conq Posted on 29/10 12:52

re: Middlesbrough Urban Legends

Duffy went up to Newcastle looking for the gangster Viv Graham, who was boss of all the jawdee bouncers.

He was dropped off on his own at one end of the Bigg Market and went from one pub to the next, knocking all the doormen out.

According to the book 'Viv Graham and Lee Duffy's Parallel Lives' he said 'Go and tell your boss I'm here!'

JoeLaidlaw Posted on 30/10 20:18

re: Middlesbrough Urban Legends

The petrol story about Duffy is true and it happened in the Commercial in South Bank. The lad got a good kicking, not his back broken, for his troubles. If he had managed to ignite the lighter then the whole pub would have gone up because everyone was covered in petrol and fumes. Apparently Duffy managed to scramble to the toilets, ripped his clothes off and then went outside and gave the lad a good kicking.

The story goes that the lad who did it had been paid by other local drug dealers in the South Bank area to do it because Duffy was taxing them.

mattrich Posted on 30/10 20:27

re: Middlesbrough Urban Legends

There must be an easier way to 'do' someone than throw petrol over them. What's wrong with a gun?

trev_seniior Posted on 30/10 21:52

re: Middlesbrough Urban Legends

I was told Nipper Harris died earlier this year. Don't know if this is true but he had sorted himself out and was working at one of the hospitals (possibly St Luke's!)

Come_On_Boro_the_1st Posted on 31/10 11:12

re: Middlesbrough Urban Legends

The 'Spies for Peace' sign. A quote from one of the perpetrators:

"It was all over the news back then and people painted the slogan on all kinds of buildings to show support for the 'spies' and to protest at the government's plans to take care of their own in the event of nuclear attack and leave the rest of us unprotected. We chose that building because it had an unbroken flat wall facing the road. Nobody knew what the building was for anyway - we tried to find out but couldn't so I guess that fuelled speculation that it might be sinister. I don't think anyone actually believed it and personally I think it was probably to do with one of the utilities."

What was that building for? A storeroom for the Rec?

green_beret20 Posted on 31/10 11:53

re: Middlesbrough Urban Legends

Yes, jonny_giles, there was once a little village on Eston Hills where everyone got trapped from one really bad winter and was deserted ever since, or so the story goes.

Quite surprised Nipper's gotten such a large mention. I'd have thought he'd have been long dead by now, although I suppose the long beard and all probably made him look thirty years older than he actually was.

BoroE17 Posted on 31/10 12:40

re: Middlesbrough Urban Legends

In the early '70s, Dave Coverdale of Whitesnake and Deep Purple worked in a clothes shop on Coatham Road in Redcar called Gentry and my mam bought our dad a leather waistcoat from him.

MGinKSA Posted on 31/10 15:21

re: Middlesbrough Urban Legends

Speaking of famous graffiti - does anybody remember the old railway bridge in Normanby that as you drove in from the Ormesby direction had the legend "ALEC THE DUMMY" painted on it? People were unsure whether it meant Alec Douglas-Home or Alec the parky from Smith's Dock Park.

In the early '70s, Dave Coverdale of Whitesnake and Deep Purple worked in a clothes shop on Coatham Road in Redcar called Gentry and my mam bought our dad a leather waistcoat from him.

Come_On_Boro_the_1st Posted on 2/11 23:31

re: Middlesbrough Urban Legends

MGinKSA - I'd forgotten all about that sign, but now you've said that I do remember 'Alec the Dummy'. I always assumed it was Alec D Home, but does anyone know who did that one?

This time, my brother-in-law wasn't involved.

Come_On_Boro_the_1st Posted on 27/12 22:56

re: Middlesbrough Urban Legends

I never did get a reply on 'Alec the Dummy' in Normanby.

mattrich Posted on 3/1 20:13

re: Middlesbrough Urban Legends

Well worth another hoof. Welcome to 2006!

Maccarone_Is_Me Posted on 19/3 20:30

re: Middlesbrough Urban Legends

"Eddie Grant" - Stockton Tramp.

Me and our kid used to call him Jimmy Hendrix. He must have been the first black fella in Stockton.

Maccarone_Is_Me Posted on 19/3 20:39

re: Middlesbrough/Stockton Urban Legends

The Smiths got refused entry to Madison's after they played Middlesbrough Town Hall in 1986 - Can anyone confirm this?

Can anyone remember the scruffy guy from Swainby Road in Norton who used to push around fridges and other white goods while wearing high heels - He really used to disturb me!

bertiefrontline Posted on 19/3 21:27

re: Middlesbrough Urban Legends

Coga, I remember you once got arrested twice in one day! Swansea away in the FA Cup 'bout '81...

the_righteous_one Posted on 20/3 2:05

re: Middlesbrough/Stockton Urban Legends

Took me over two hours to read this - brilliant!

Anyone remember a bloke called Marty Farty Rubberlips?

He used to go to Nazereth House, I seem to remember.

borobadge Posted on 20/3 6:40

re: Middlesbrough/Stockton Urban Legends

As mentioned earlier... but worth another mention after the latest news...

B.J. McQuade.

boro_fan_in_China Posted on 20/3 8:36

re: Middlesbrough/Stockton Urban Legends

Like many other users, I've spent a long time reading this great thread. What prompted me to write was the mention of Ernie Ragbo. I used to work in No.9 Mill at Cleveland. Ernie would come in pissed more often than not! I was also present when he almost killed his mate in an accident one night (I can't remember the exact details). Ernie cried his eyes out that night...

bertiefrontline Posted on 20/3 14:02

re: Middlesbrough/Stockton Urban Legends

Some more Boro legends...?

Keogh - the tramp.
Bob the Bucket.
Sweaty Betty.

holgate69 Posted on 20/3 14:28

re: Middlesbrough/Stockton Urban Legends

the_righteous_one, yeah I remember him. I used to live on Abingdon Rd near Nazareth House. The poor old sod used to get tortured by all the kids around there.

holgate69 Posted on 20/3 14:48

re: Middlesbrough/Stockton Urban Legends

Anyone remember "Dennis The Menace?" He used to live/lodge in the street next to Victoria Rd School. I am sure the lad had a learning disability or something. But he was great fun to be around and used to keep all the kids amused by telling daft jokes and dancing around the school.

the_righteous_one Posted on 20/3 15:01

re: Middlesbrough/Stockton Urban Legends

I think he used to go to Nazareth House for his meals, holgate69. I remember the kids used to follow him, shouting "Marty Farty Rubberlips." I lived on Waterloo Rd as a kid, opposite the launderette.

holgate69 Posted on 20/3 18:06

re: Middlesbrough/Stockton Urban Legends

I think we probably know each other then. I lived in Abingdon Rd for about 17 years. Next door but one to what was Wiggins' Wet Fish Shop. There was a big family of us, 8 kids in all, if that's any help. My mam worked at the Odeon.

borobadge Posted on 20/3 19:50

re: Middlesbrough/Stockton Urban Legends

"Ernie Ragbo"... was his Clockwork Orange moniker... droog!

His real name was Eric Robinson...

Maccarone_Is_Me Posted on 21/3 0:55

re: Middlesbrough Urban Legends

Someone told me this one tonight:

Two lads working at Jennings on Yarm Road drank what they thought was a bottle of Lowcocks' Cherryade. It turned out to be anti-freeze. I don't know what their fate was. Doesn't it make you go blind?

borobadge Posted on 21/3 0:58

re: Middlesbrough Urban Legends

No, mate... it's w*****g that makes you do that...

borobadge Posted on 21/3 0:59

re: Middlesbrough Urban Legends

Chris the Goat... legend.

jarazinho Posted on 21/3 2:02

re: Middlesbrough Urban Legends

holgate69 - did you know the Mangans from Abingdon Rd?

freethenorton7 Posted on 21/3 5:53

re: Middlesbrough Urban Legends

Geggy Moon - Stockton, I think he is still alive and now 175 years old.

Kenny Harrison - Stockton/Billingham/Port Clarence legend.

Cogeur_le_Conq Posted on 21/3 7:53

re: Middlesbrough Urban Legends

I knew Keith Mangan until he got kidnapped in Kashmir.

A great lad.

the_righteous_one Posted on 21/3 13:17

re: Middlesbrough Urban Legends

Yep, I know who you are, holgate69. I remember your mam used to work in the Odeon as well. I remember there were about four brothers and your sister used to knock about with my eldest sister when she was young. She worked in Romer Parrish, if that's any help.

rkangel Posted on 21/3 14:28

re: Middlesbrough Urban Legends

Fantastic thread. Wasted a bluddy big portion of my day, mind. But, oh, the romantic memories... Alice Bunn used to terrify me. I used to sit next to Lee Duffy at Beech Grove. My mam helped get Nipper Harris into accommodation and he came to offer his condolences when he heard she'd died. Barnaby Moor was the ghost town on Eston Hills. You could still make out the patterns of the foundations of the houses when it snowed. Mental places to go and see bands, Killing Joke (I think) at The Empire, Alex Harvey at the Coatham Bowl, 9 below Zero at Thornaby Cons Club. It seems so strange now to think that there were so many places with live acts on.

holgate69 Posted on 21/3 20:06

re: Middlesbrough Urban Legends

Jarazinho - yeah, I knew them, mate. Keith, the lad who was kidnapped, was a good mate of one of my brothers.

the_righteous_one - yeah, I think I have sussed who you are as well, mate. How you doing? What you up to these days?

borojam Posted on 29/3 15:55

re: Middlesbrough Urban Legends

borobadge, what years did you hang out round Fairy Dell? Does Blue Tarzee Mountain ring any bells with you?

Archie_StephensElbow Posted on 30/3 9:37

re: Middlesbrough Urban Legends

This thread is one year old today!

Happy birthday.

the_righteous_one Posted on 30/3 11:26

re: Middlesbrough Urban Legends

Doesn't time fly...

South_Stand_Steward Posted on 30/3 12:33

re: Middlesbrough Urban Legends

What a great thread.

Possibly how the Father/Son legend started. At BSC Lackenby in the late '70s. A young apprentice went to turn the boiler on and put tins of food in a small oven (didn't have microwaves in them days) for fellow workers. Anyhow, when everyone went for their breakfast, the young apprentice was nowhere to be found. A large metal door was noticed to be laid on the floor. When they picked it up, they found the young apprentice under it crushed to death by the heavy door. One of the blokes who was lifting the door was the dad of the young apprentice. This is fact as my dad was also there lifting the door.

Ronnie Keogh's grand daughter works at St Luke's.

The Grey Lady at King's Manor lived in the library. There was also supposed be a secret tunnel behind the fireplace in the library. If you pulled one of the niches on the fireplace it opened. However, it had been painted that many times it wouldn't budge (I did try it once, for a dare).

A girl was killed in Albert Park near to the train. I remember riding my bike to my Nanna's one Sunday morning and the middle of the park being blocked off with crime scene tape.

One that I would like confirming is whether the big hill on the way to Whitby (A171 road) is a cholera burial ground and full of bodies. My Grandad told me it but I think he was winding me up.

boroboroboro Posted on 30/3 12:35

re: Middlesbrough Urban Legends

I was told the Transporter story but I was told that it was the actor Ian Carmichael who drove into the river! He has always lived near Whitby apparently.

the_righteous_one Posted on 30/3 12:38

re: Middlesbrough Urban Legends

I remember a story about a teenager hanging himself off the bridge across the beck in Albert Park and the fireman that came and cut him down was his dad. He apparently lived above the DIY shop on Waterloo Rd.

The_DiasBoro Posted on 30/3 14:08

re: Middlesbrough Urban Legends

Boro's sectarian heritage (myth?). Rumour last heard aired in the '70s was that Boro fans had a 'permit' to sing the Celtic song, and that this could actually be found in the boardroom at Ayresome. I guess it expired before anyone learned the words.

wiganbo_ro Posted on 30/3 15:34

re: Middlesbrough Urban Legends

South-Stand, I was always told the big hill (Freeborough Hill?) was a Viking burial ground and that in the middle was a Viking longboat.

Does anyone remember around 10 years ago all of the funny poles appearing on top of the hill in the middle of the night? No one saw anything and I don't think I ever heard of a reasonable story as to why/how they appeared. Could anyone shed any light?

TOPIC

MESSAGE

POST

REGISTER

The Grey Lady at King's Manor lived in the library. There was also supposed be a secret tunnel behind the fireplace in the library. If you pulled one of the niches on the fireplace it opened.

AwesomeSwells Posted on 31/3 20:15

re: Middlesbrough Urban Legends

A Hoof, plus:

After a Sunday morning footy game, we had a pint in a Thornaby club. Just outside the door was that Kenny Harrison guy, always on the cadge.

He was slumped on the deck with his hoppo shouting: "Pound to see the dying man, pound to see the dying man!"

That was the Seventies. As far as I know he's still kicking around Stockton.

By the way - where are the Norton 7?

boredreceptionist Posted on 5/4 15:11

re: Middlesbrough Urban Legends

Bob the Bucket! First name on this I actually recognized. Shares his birthday with my grandma and would always bring her a bunch of flowers on the day. She would always take them off him and tell him she was on her way out despite going back in the house with all of us inside. She knew him from the Longlands Club.

Also does anyone know of the Helium brothers? Bit slow, they used to sit in North Terrace at Ayresome, always shouting for the opposition as a joke? They sound like the Vic and Bob characters who do 'This is Your Life'. The last time I saw them was queuing for the subway, trying to start conversations with people as a hush fell over the crowd, everyone avoiding eye contact.

Chutney Posted on 5/4 16:12

re: Middlesbrough Urban Legends

Gotta be worth a nudge down towards third man to bring up the quadruple ton...

Butters1406 Posted on 5/4 16:18

re: Middlesbrough Urban Legends

Bored, the Helium brothers sit in the West Lower now, they must be the same ones you're on about.

blotonthelandscape Posted on 5/4 16:47

re: Middlesbrough Urban Legends

Someone mentioned Nipper of South Bank above, but who was the woman with the wig, always walking, always in the pub? I haven't seen her for at least 15 years.

guyb Posted on 5/4 16:58

re: Middlesbrough Urban Legends

The Helium brothers are called Stotty and Kingy. I know this because I was behind them after the Hednesford match and a Hednesford fan was trying to wind them up about how close they had run us, not realising who or what they were.

One of them turns round and says "Do Ya Wanna Punch?" in his trademark voice. The other says: "Yeah, hit him, Stotty! He'll give ya a punch" in the same voice.

Everyone cracked up and the Hednesford fan had that look on his face when you think you're being wound up but aren't sure enough to retaliate.

I've just clicked - Stotty = David and Donald Stott. Mortimer must know them.

Come_On_Boro_the_1st Posted on 5/4 17:14

re: Middlesbrough Urban Legends

Strike a light - Alice Bunn. She was scary - cheeks redder than a ripe tomato. Was she really a 'Lady of the Night?' I can't imagine anyone wanting to get within five feet of her, never mind... well... let's move on shall we?

I'm still awaiting a reply on 'Alec the Dummy' on the old bridge at Normanby - someone must know who painted that.

blotonthelandscape Posted on 5/4 17:18

re: Middlesbrough Urban Legends

That's the lady(?). I should have read all the responses, the good lady has been mentioned already.

Anyone mentioned Mattie Innis, the barber/club comedian? He did a turn at our wedding night, great bloke.

bertiefrontline Posted on 5/4 17:20

re: Middlesbrough Urban Legends

How about Willie Whigham on and off the pitch (a bit of a sad story really)? Or does he qualify? (With them lips I'm sure he was related to Marty Farty...!)

Come_On_Boro_the_1st Posted on 5/4 22:16

re: Middlesbrough Urban Legends

Yeah, top bloke, Matty [actually Innes]. I worked with one of his sons.

I must ask my brother about Alice Bunn - he'll know more.

ReidyDog Posted on 20/4 3:16

re: Middlesbrough Urban Legends

Anyone remember Wendy Woo, the mad flasher lady from Hemlington? Got some good un's about her.

BoroInNC Posted on 20/4 4:55

re: Middlesbrough Urban Legends

Hoof to this magic thread and oh yes, she ended up out the back of where I lived (and where my parents still live) in Coulby Newham. Lots of "Wendy Woo will get you" stories at school.

Cogeur_le_Conq Posted on 20/4 9:03

re: Middlesbrough Urban Legends

I'm not sure how many people will remember Cowboy Joe from Mexico. He was the nightwatchman on the site of the Doggy flyover when they were building it. He used to wear a Stetson or Ten Gallon Hat with cowboy boots. We used to have his life with Dead Shot gatties and he'd never sussed out our den in the cavern under the flyover which was only accessible via the beck tunnel.

Does anyone remember that dozy dog that sat on the bend of Ingram Road near Bradhope waiting for buses?

Every time one passed it would belt round in circles trying to catch its tail.

ReidyDog Posted on 20/4 10:40

re: Middlesbrough Urban Legends

BoroInNC... when were you at Coulby? I was there '82-'87.

BoroInNC Posted on 21/4 7:22

re: Middlesbrough Urban Legends

Moved to Coulby from sunny Thorntree in '79 (when it was three estates and a lot of shiny plans) and didn't leave till college in '92. Here now, in fact, staying with the parents while back from the States to catch up and take in the matches. No sightings of Wendy Woo, though.

ReidyDog Posted on 21/4 9:40

re: Middlesbrough Urban Legends

Moved to Coulby Newham (Tollesby Bridge) in 1980. Joined the Army from school in '87. Back to same house in '97 until I moved in 2003.

sambaDTR Posted on 21/4 13:10

re: Middlesbrough Urban Legends

Just thought I'd add a few (from local clubland)...

1) Harry Morgan from South Bank St Peter's. Used to play snooker for the club. Always used to play with his coat on. Even when he was on 'Invitation Snooker' (ITV).

2) Alfie Cooke from Redcar. Always played in a flat cap. Remember him making a 100 billiards break in the Redcar League when he was in his 80s against Micky Fiddes.

3) The Masseys from South Bank Albion (Wilf, Billy, Tony etc). Could have had a table team of their own.

4) The 'Paid Lads from Horden'. Used to get paid 'Travel Expenses'. Bernie Jones, Bobby Honour, Arthur Price, Kevin Sumpton. The best player was Billy Clarkson who "could have made it but was a ladies' man". When there was a money match after the games he always used to win for himself and his backers.

5) Remember the 'Clarence Club' (now Dickens Inn)? One of the lads went into the lounge. There was a sack in the corner. He looked in and it was full of gas meters!

Row_7 Posted on 21/4 13:52

re: Middlesbrough Urban Legends

After the small loss of the Tuxedo yesterday, does anyone remember Teesside's first floating nightclub?

Think it was called the Bonaventure and was a ramshackle affair moored to the riverside near where the Princess Di Bridge is now. Used to attract the cream of Stockton's 'café' society and was notorious for illicit goings-on in dark corners.

I remember it being closed down on public health grounds sometime in the mid-'80s but what happened after that - did it sink or was it scrapped?

TOPIC

MESSAGE

POST

REGISTER

The Phantom Whistler! Whatever happened to him? The last time I saw him he was walking over the white bridge with a budgie in a cage!

johnhicktonsrunup Posted on 21/4 14:40

re: Middlesbrough Urban Legends

Bob the Bucket...
The Longlands' Club car park...
1984...

About 20 odd years ago, my mate let Bob clean his brand new two litre Ford, insisting that a thorough job be done or Bob would miss out on the agreed sum of £2.

It was a scorching day and my mate had left the driver's window open and Bob, with pound signs in his eyes, somewhat predictably emptied the contents of his bucket straight thru' the aforementioned open window. The scene ended with Bob legging it towards Albert Park but still gallantly keeping a firm grip on his beloved bucket.

Also, we would sometimes suggest to Bob (usually in Blaises) that "that girl over there fancies you, Bob, it's obvious" whereupon he would either rugby tackle or dive-bomb the startled/terrified lass.

Lastly, Keogh. Simply THE Boro legend.

spiderbaby Posted on 21/4 14:54

re: Middlesbrough Urban Legends

Fanstastic thread, just spent an hour reading it...

I've got a picture of Jack Hatfield!

The Uri Geller bit below about the Curse of Ayresome Park seems quite pertinent at the moment. Just think of the Basel Game:

"Having spoken to fans who have visited both grounds I gathered that Middlesbrough has a 'feel' they can't explain. A curse? Well, who knows - but don't rule out the power of collective thought, in both positive and negative ways. How many times has the crowd turned an impossible situation with a goal out of the blue? How many times have teams been two up at home with ten minutes to go, the crowd has gone quiet and then the visitors have a scoring spree and take three points home with them. It happens, but you just can't put your finger on the reason, can you?'

Keep the positive 'curse' going for another week, I say, and of course this thread, although some of the things in it are a bit scary, like the ICI stories...

ospreyheights Posted on 21/4 15:10

re: Middlesbrough Urban Legends

red rebel, you posted a bit about Anthony Sowerby (mad cartoonist, went to Borneo etc). I can tell you that it's all true. I know his brother Jack, also an artist, and he verified all these stories as true. By the way, the family are from Easterside.

boro74 Posted on 21/4 22:43

re: Middlesbrough Urban Legends

Reading about the sack full of gas meters reminds me of a story from '97. This gadgie I knew couldn't pay his gas bill coz he'd spent all his money following the Boro (three finals, four semis and so on). Anyway, he had to get a pay-as-you-use meter installed or they were gonna cut his gas off. The bloke that came round to do it told him he'd been run off his feet. He'd never had so much work. He was on overtime trying to fit all these meters. It seemed like half of Middlesbrough hadn't paid their gas bill. They were all skint from following the Boro! I think it was at Hillsborough where the fans started chanting "stand up if you're f*****g skint"

mendymagic Posted on 22/4 0:25

re: Middlesbrough Urban Legends

I also left Thorntree in '79 (remember the Binger Picker) and moved to Coulby where I was introduced to Wendy Woo, who always lurked outside our school. Scary.

gibson Posted on 22/4 0:32

re: Middlesbrough Urban Legends

Row-7, I used to frequent the Bonaventure in Stockton. One memory was a very drunk Norwegian sailor who kept dropping his keks on the dance floor. DJ said "Anyone want a Viking to take home? Anyone?" after he passed out on the dance floor and all the punters just continued dancing around him.

bertiefrontline Posted on 22/4 10:45

re: Middlesbrough Urban Legends

How about the legendary if not unsurpassable Rendezvous restaurant on Linny Road, where for my money the best parmos of all time were served. Had my first one there in 1980 on recommendation (actually not really knowing what to order) but in my opinion far better than the Europa. The Rendezvous is now sadly closed but I had some fond, delicious and gut-bursting times there.

guyr Posted on 22/4 14:00

re: Middlesbrough Urban Legends

The mechanics at a local car dealer drank the anti-freeze as it was in a spirit bottle. I think they thought it was cherry brandy or similar. Either two or three died, one seriously ill in hospital.

Great thread.

freethenorton7 Posted on 22/4 14:04

re: Middlesbrough Urban Legends

Tug Boat Annies, she/he was a strange one. The original boat in Stockton, best place for punk/ska music in the town, but you had to take a broken bottle or a baseball bat to get in.

Come_On_Boro_the_1st Posted on 25/4 22:07

re: Middlesbrough Urban Legends

No luck with my elder brother and sister in getting details on Alice Bunn. They both remember her and her lipstick, but neither knew her background or what became of her.

Posted on 30/4 20:45

re: Middlesbrough Urban Legends

I'm new on here but the Phantom Whistler! Whatever happened to him? The last time I saw him he was walking over the white bridge with a budgie in a cage! And the hot-dog man, we used to call him Salmonella Bob, always had loads of hair coming out of his ears and nostrils. Davey bought his old shop on Princes Road and that bike was in the garage, I saw it. The kitchen was manky but it did have a 'no smoking' sign on the wall, next to the ashtray! Davey gave it to Faulkners Bar and Paul Zuk rode it down there on a Friday night!

the_righteous_one Posted on 30/4 21:02

re: Middlesbrough Urban Legends

The Rendezvous on Linthorpe Road certainly did a very good parmo. I remember the owner was a big Greek bloke called Steve. Got all his veg from a shop on Waterloo Rd.

Cogeur_le_Conq Posted on 1/5 15:11

re: Middlesbrough Urban Legends

Does anybody have any evidence or direct quotes from Viv Anderson when he came back from Kiev after being sent to check out on Shevchenko by Robson?

It was reported that Anderson said that he's no better than what we already have at the club.

Apparently we could have had him for a million. Spurs got the other fella.

I have a shed load of newspaper articles from that period filling two sports bags. It'll take me ages to sort through them but it'll be worth it cos they are from when Robbo first took over and the papers were getting excited about us buying Bolivians etc.

OPEO Posted on 1/5 15:39

re: Middlesbrough Urban Legends

Hearing about that lad who died in a crash under the bridge at Ormesby after the West Ham semi reminds me that someone I went to school with also died in a crash under the same bridge a few years ago. Apparently his head was severed from his body. I can't remember his name but he was from Berwick Hills. Gary?

jono_feds Posted on 1/5 19:40

re: Middlesbrough Urban Legends

Did a bus get trapped under Albert Bridge?

flabby66 Posted on 1/5 21:23

re: Middlesbrough Urban Legends

Can this thread be turned into a book so it can be read at leisure?!

delgrapos Posted on 2/5 0:36

re: Middlesbrough Urban Legends

Bibi's apparently did a mean parmo, and the Asteria used to be good. The problem now is finding a good pork one. Most of the takeaways are owned by Muslims so they only do chicken, which for me isn't a proper parmo. The first one I had was veal. I've heard they were invented by a chef in what used to be Fatso's.

delgrapos Posted on 2/5 0:41

re: Middlesbrough Urban Legends

The old guy who used to come in the Empire, whip his comb out and sing "New York, New York" was known as Speedy because of the way he used to whizz around the pub. His real name was Billy, haven't seen him for years. I'm sure he never recognised me one night from the next but when I said "now then, Billy" he ALWAYS replied "BY, YOU GET ABOUT!"

delgrapos Posted on 2/5 0:51

re: Middlesbrough Urban Legends

For Eddie Catflap,
About the witches' coven. About sixteen years ago some lads I used to knock about with told me about the table in the woods and we went. It was between Hutton Rudby and Seamer. We went to a derelict farm, through the woods and there was a table there with some drinking vessels. Whether they were put there by someone to wind people up, I don't know but they were there.

Also four of my mates swore they saw a UFO up Clay Bank. Whether that was something to do with mush or not I don't know either but they all swore they saw it...

delgrapos Posted on 2/5 1:01

re: Middlesbrough Urban Legends

Cogeur le conk, I remember that dog, used to chase its tail whenever a bus passed. It was like a border collie, if I remember rightly.

neiltrodden Posted on 2/5 1:09

re: Middlesbrough Urban Legends

I remember Speedy Eddie! Used to croon the night away, if I remember.

Does anyone remember Damage? (I think it was Mr Damage Control).

Bit of a goth-type, used to bomb around on a skateboard and, later, in-line skates?

neiltrodden Posted on 2/5 1:12

re: Middlesbrough Urban Legends

PS: I do save this thread regularly and I agree it needs putting into a book! Or maybe on-line somewhere else if Rivals delete it. A bit like the Snopes Urban Legends page.

delgrapos Posted on 2/5 12:27

re: Middlesbrough Urban Legends

Yeah, I know that Damage who you mean! He's still about, often seen shouting at invisible people. Proper strange lad him. Not the type you'd invite round for a bit of cake and some tea!

delgrapos Posted on 2/5 12:33

re: Middlesbrough Urban Legends

I once met Chris Quinten (Brian Tilsley) in the Empire and I told him it was an honour to meet him cos I was half pissed but he seemed a nice enough chap. I said I reckon he'd easy knock Martin Platt out.

Smog_Monster Posted on 2/5 12:56

re: Middlesbrough Urban Legends

I used to know Damage, not really a bad lad, just all image. He used to sit outside his flat playing his guitar for the local kids, the door of his flat propped open with a chainsaw. I haven't seen him for about ten years but I wouldn't be surprised to hear that he had gone down the 'shouting at invisible people' route.

Cogeur_le_Conq Posted on 2/5 13:29

re: Middlesbrough Urban Legends

The bus getting stuck under the Ferodo Bridge on Albert Road is part of Boro folklore.

Apparently they had a team of engineers scratching their heads wondering how best to get it from under the bridge and some schoolkid asked them if they'd thought about letting the tyres down.

It became a Boro p**s-take in the way the monkey hanging was for the Poolies.

A p**s-take of Sunlan was when they supposedly hung nets offa the Monkwearmouth Bridge to stop the plague coming up the river.

Another p**s-take of the Boro was the new fire station for Boro's first ever fire engine.

They built the station before they took delivery of the engine and when it turned up they couldn't fit the b*****d in. They'd built it too small.

CliveRdCorner Posted on 2/5 14:56

re: Middlesbrough Urban Legends

Mid-'70s - local nutter who ended up a drug addict had the idea of sending three Newcastle Brown Ale bottles with a molotov cocktail inside them into the away end from the Clive Road outside the ground ten minutes into the match against the Geordies. He ended up setting fire to himself and what could have been a major disaster was averted.

Penny Leechman used to travel around the estates on a Monday morning selling leeches to treat black eyes - there would be a queue of women waiting patiently after every payday.

Nunthorpe School riots around '78? The Nunthorpe w*****r who used to flash in the early '70s until gangs of lads used to roam around singing ''Oh when the lights are flashing we're going w*****r hunting.''

The gamekeeper at Pool Lake that was found with his eyes scratched out in the early '60s. Also the Hell's Angels that used to hang out there in the '70s.

Roger Tames getting robbed in the late Seventies outside the main entrance.

Robbo and Viv on the lash from the night before when Nick Barmby comes down to breakfast...

borobadge Posted on 3/5 19:59

re: Middlesbrough Urban Legends

Anyone recall Frankie Dee's supermarket on Linny Road, near the Empire?

Who the f***k was Frankie Dee?

During the early '70s there were three great teenage discos/youth clubs in town. One was on Woodlands Road, opposite the original Ayresome Angels club, that was the first teenage club where I ever heard David Bowie. The second was the Sacred Heart club on Linny Road and the third was St. Oswald's in the centre of Grove Hill...

There must have been others out on the estates but if you lived central they were the places for early doors grooving, party sevens and teenage gropes...

mr_r_soles Posted on 3/5 20:23

re: Middlesbrough Urban Legends

This time last year I had been shopping on my birthday in York. Waiting at the train station for the train home I met Gareth Southgate. He was a really sound bloke and gave me his autograph and I got my photo taken with him.

borobadge Posted on 3/5 20:35

re: Middlesbrough Urban Legends

Mr arse ole... I think that was Gareth Gates...

kirky35 Posted on 3/5 20:36

re: Middlesbrough Urban Legends

"Every single time you went in he tried to sell you polpettis."

That would be Tony... the little bloke with the 'tache... he moved the shop to Princes Rd a good few years ago.

kirky35 Posted on 3/5 20:42

re: Middlesbrough Urban Legends

Pavs do a nice pork parmo, Hartington Rd, I believe...

PS Is that you, Mr Walton... boot hill boy ;) soon to be married.

Jastie Posted on 3/5 20:49

re: Middlesbrough Urban Legends

As a young man I worked for a while at Redcar Ore Terminal and had to share an office with the ladies of the night, notably 'Redcar Lil' (I'm sure a few of you will remember her). One day I heard on the car radio that her taxi had parked too close to the dock and a load of pellets had landed on top of it with her and the driver in it. There was a rumour that they would have been killed if she hadn't had her legs open.

longpig Posted on 3/5 21:01

re: Middlesbrough Urban Legends

I used to know Damage quite well but haven't seen him for a few years. Always stood like a statue on his skateboard, no expression whatsoever. God knows how he got round corners.

Real name was Gareth if I remember rightly, once smashed up a ZX81 computer so he could glue the keyboard to the sleeve of his leather jacket. I ended up in his flat after a night out once. Very dungeonesque, he was dead keen to show off his sword-swallowing skills but he only got it halfway down before everyone started to baulk on his behalf.

Anyone still see the other one, Morbid, knocking about? Local poet/p**shead?

borobadge Posted on 3/5 21:12

re: Middlesbrough Urban Legends

Damage! Morbid! Makes me laugh.

Anyway I have an idea that a reference to one of my earlier posts about Monkey Alan is also the same guy quoted here as Marty Farty Rubberlips...

mattrich Posted on 4/5 0:33

re: Middlesbrough Urban Legends

Frankie Dee's is now Linthorpe Beds. I've got a feeling it might have closed due to fire damage from Gaskins night club above when it burnt down.

delgrapos Posted on 4/5 20:23

re: Middlesbrough Urban Legends

Yes, it's me, Mr Walton, who dat?

By the way, Tony Trumfio who had the polpetti paradise on Princes Road, I used to work with his son Joe (Giuseppe) and he told me his dad used to charge him for the use of the iron!

delgrapos Posted on 4/5 20:28

re: Middlesbrough Urban Legends

I also once had a Polpetti. There was a sign on the wall saying "POLPETTI ARE IS DELISCOUS" and someone had written in marker pen underneath "BIG KING KONG BALLS." I actually thought they tasted alright.

jonny_giles Posted on 18/5 11:10

re: Middlesbrough Urban Legends

I was sat outside Tony's the barbers this morning and I thought to myself "Why is the Trunk Road called the Trunk Road?" Any answers?

borosown Posted on 18/5 12:15

re: Middlesbrough Urban Legends

What a coincidence. I was driving down the Trunk Road yesterday on the way back from Redcar and my stepdaughter asked me the same thing. Can't help with the answer though, but I think there are plenty of trunk roads across the country.

deganya Posted on 18/5 12:43

re: Middlesbrough Urban Legends

Two characters from Billingham/Stockton - one has already been mentioned. Kenny Harrison and Snibsey. You won't see much of Snibsey these days as he is always in prison but Kenny is still about. Both of them were always on the cadge and were amateur thieves (crap ones). Ask Snibsey for a new TV and he would put on a brown overall coat so he looked like a warehouse man and just walk into a major store and walk out with it.

The pair of them were always willing to do anything for money and once Snibsey walked into the Smiths Arms, Billingham, with just his shirt and tie on, with his tackle hanging out. He talked to the landlord who was unaware of his attire while the rest of the pub wet themselves laughing.

Once saw the both of them in a doctor's waiting room, which as usual was very quiet so they both got up and did a couple of Deep Purple numbers, complete with air guitar to the waiting patients.

deganya Posted on 8/6 12:12

re: Middlesbrough Urban Legends

Brilliant thread - someone should write a book on our legends. Come on, you budding writers, make a name for yourselves. All this material should be made available in written form for our children to know which characters made Teesside what it is.

borobadge Posted on 8/6 12:23

re: Middlesbrough Urban Legends

A very unusual one for this thread.

A goofy southerner, not a cockney, mind, or a mockney but a Surrey boy. Not been around that long, but apparently he is.

Goes by the name of... Southgate: Gareth

stimo Posted on 8/6 12:30

re: Middlesbrough Urban Legends

A large amount of copper piping kept disappearing from ICI many years ago. The Wilton security raided an employee's garage and found several hundredweight ready for the scrap yard. It was all bent into small square lumps. They then were told that it had all been sneaked out inside a lunchbox one bit at a time.

TOPIC

MESSAGE

POST

REGISTER

Another was of a bloke who made some 'adjustments' to his bike and managed to cycle home each night out of ICI with a load of mercury in the bike frame.

deganya Posted on 11/6 8:44

re: Middlesbrough Urban Legends

I heard a story of some blokes nicking a train and driving it into ICI Billingham, filling it up with scrap and driving it out again. Now who would think of stopping a train, eh?

There is also a story of some guys who went into ICI on a bank holiday when there was a shut down on. They nicked the platinum plates out of some tower but I think they got caught.

Another was of a bloke who made some 'adjustments' to his bike and managed to cycle home each night out of ICI with a load of mercury in the bike frame.

Big_Shot Posted on 11/6 12:00

re: Middlesbrough Urban Legends

First time I've looked at this thread for a while and find Morbid has been mentioned. I used to know him quite well. Always looked odd with the way he dressed and cutting his own arms and stuff but he's actually a decent bloke. Used to be always in the Empire/Hogshead, whatever it's called now. Not seen him for a few years now but I don't drink down there very much any more so he might well still drink in there.

Cogeur_le_Conq Posted on 11/6 12:21

re: Middlesbrough Urban Legends

The first Catholic to play for Glasgow Rangers wasn't Mo Johnston, as many believe.

It was a Boro gadgie called Tom Murray who went to St Patrick's School on Cannon Street.

He became the first Englishman to play for Rangers when they signed him from Aberdeen back in 1907.

Smog_Monster Posted on 11/6 12:40

re: Middlesbrough Urban Legends

The little bikie - Satan's Slaves guy - with the bulging cross/Marty Feldman eyes and spider tatt on the side of his head. I heard he was pretty normal until he went out pinching copper from ICI and put his hack saw into a 11KV cable. Needs a pace-maker and shakes a bit now.

smogbynumbers Posted on 11/6 12:52

re: Middlesbrough Urban Legends

deganya, the mercury story (and others) are covered at the top of the thread.

I wonder if anyone has a picture of the big mural (of a man with a guitar) that used to be on Linny Road, near where Riley's pool hall is now. Not really urban legend but I'd sure like to see that again.

si_cun Posted on 11/6 12:52

re: Middlesbrough Urban Legends

Remember the Grey Lady at Acklam College (formerly King's Manor School) who used to scare the crap out of all of us? Apparently it is/was the ghost of Charlotte Hustler, the lady of Acklam Hall, as it was then. Her grave is at the back of St Mary's Church near what we used to call Ivy Wall and the Secret Garden (err... basically a walled off area with a pond in the middle!)

towz Posted on 11/6 13:45

re: Middlesbrough Urban Legends

Phil Stamp threatened to knock my mate out at Redcar amusements coz he was laughing at Stampy playing on the 2p slot machines.

boro_daley Posted on 11/6 16:58

re: Middlesbrough Urban Legends

Someone mentioned The Blue Lagoon. Wondered if that's the one near Roseberry Topping?

borobadge Posted on 11/6 17:30

re: Middlesbrough Urban Legends

I was a regular at the Bluela in the mid '70s, but I had and still have no idea where it's near... but I was told that the reason it's so blue is because of the cobalt in the ground... it made the water go blue...

There was one of the lagoons that you had to go underwater and swim for about 25 metres and it brought you up in a different 'lagoon' that you couldn't reach from earth. In fact you couldn't even see it...

Thing is, how did someone find and work that out?

bored_at_work Posted on 11/6 17:47

re: Middlesbrough Urban Legends

This thread is fantastic. First time reading has made my day at work enjoyable. I agree with many others that this should be turned into a book.

I've got a few to add to this evergrowing list.

From Norton: Hairy Mary, the old woman who lives in Albany, wandering the streets all day long scaring the kids with her amazing facial hair. Commonly linked to Penny Pick Nick, the old bloke who walks around Albany shops at dinner time picking up pennies off the floor.

Also does anyone drink in The Central after the game and has seen the bloke who I think is called Dougie who sings "Win, Lose or Draw" at the top of his voice? He also has a habit of getting on the karaoke.

Cogeur_le_Conq Posted on 11/6 18:39

re: Middlesbrough Urban Legends

The Blue Lagoon was near the caravan park just before you get to Great Ayton.

The best ones were Big Fern Deep and Little Fern Deep up Gribdale between Rosebery Topping and Captain Cook's Monument.

There's supposed to be a horse and cart at the bottom of one and they're interconnected by Whinstone mines.

boro_daley Posted on 11/6 22:07

re: Middlesbrough Urban Legends

Yes, I've been there a few times. Would have been good on a day like today.

Steaknife Posted on 11/6 22:25

re: Middlesbrough Urban Legends

The Blues on Princes Road? Is that the one Duffy managed to avoid getting shot outside by some blokes from Handsworth?

James Dorothy I believe was the name of the guy who drew the same picture over and over again. Was always saving up to get back to South Africa yet never got past the Star and Garter.

The ghost of Charlotte Hustler was supposed to haunt the library and staircase at Acklam Hall (King's Manor). Usual story, spurned lover/tragic suicide. As she's buried in St Mary's cemetery next door, aged 72, it's unlikely to be her.

Last time I saw Damage he was spraying anarchy signs on bins on Corporation Rd. He used to go to stick fighting and insist on wearing a black karate suit. Got uppity if anyone called him Gareth. Morbid used to slash his arms a bit (I remember seeing him after in Kwik Save with them all bandaged), but he did give the world Dwolma 19 and the delightfully named Killydogbox.

I remember a Carless Chemicals tanker making the national news after threatening to explode. It would have been about 1983 and the fire brigade were training hoses.

The Frank(ie) Dee Shop was below Gaskins. I first shoplifted in there (a boiled sweet). Gaskins burned down in 1983 taking the Dee with it. Gaskins was rebuilt but lay empty and was accidentally torched again in 1989.

It was great fun watching Keogh molesting unsuspecting students; not so good when he caught you for 50p. I remember seeing him near The Trooper. He had a small tree over his shoulder and was explaining that he was the new man in the Duchess of York's life. He was sometimes in The Empire/Hogs with an unusually shaped woman in a green leotard.

Regarding the bus under the bridge there was also the Low Grange bus that hit a piling drill on the Portrack Roundabout in about 1974 and killed a few people. Some more died when a Bee-Line overturned on the roundabout a few years later. Me old man used to tell me about four or five apprentices who got killed at Oxygen Corner at Haverton Hill after the trench they were digging got filled with oxygen during a leak and someone lit a fag. On a happier note, does anyone remember the disabled bloke with the impossibly large ghetto blaster who used to wander up and down Linthorpe Road?

Big_Shot Posted on 11/6 23:29

re: Middlesbrough Urban Legends

Dwomla 19, that was his band, wasn't it? Branny was in it too. It took me a few minutes to work that out there, the name instantly rang a bell. Never saw them play and have no idea what it meant, although it was explained to me a few times and I just can't remember.

mattrich Posted on 12/6 10:16

re: Middlesbrough Urban Legends

Remember hearing a story at school that one of Jack Hatfield's sons drowned at The Blue Lagoon?

glippy Posted on 12/6 10:46

re: Middlesbrough Urban Legends

Does anyone remember Uncle Bernie who used to be the manager at the Odeon in Stockton in the '60s? He used to march up and down terrorising the kids when we were queuing up for Saturday morning pictures. He regularly used to stop the films and get up on the stage hurling abuse if we were making too much noise, dropping things on other kids from the balcony etc.

Bazooka_that_Viduka Posted on 12/6 10:53

re: Middlesbrough Urban Legends

I left Acklam Grange school in 1989. Towards the end of the '80s a group of us would camp out during summer holidays. The favoured location was near to Fox's Wood where the two becks meet.

This sounds a bit Blair Witch but honestly it's absolutely true.

One night (it must have been around 2am) we all are awoken by children's voices outside. Now bearing in mind there are about ten of us in three tents we all hear the same thing. Laughter and then talking as though the kids are speaking to an adult.

A few of us stick our heads out to have a look but cannot see anything. The sound appears only to be metres away.

We all are absolutely scared stiff. After about ten minutes the noise stops. Nobody leaves the tent until next morning when it's light.

One of us nips off to have a pee. He walks back holding a kid's teddy bear. Not one of the modern type but a really old, fur-rubbed-off type but it had no dirt on it. By now we are thinking ghosts. Not knowing what to do we started up the camp fire again and burnt the teddy.

Looking back, it still sends a shiver down my back.

wishin_well Posted on 12/6 21:38

re: Middlesbrough Urban Legends

No mention yet of 'Mucky Maureen' or the two twins (I think they were called Wilson) who used to sneak in the pubs in the town supping everyone's dregs, forever getting chased out of the back door of the Shakey!

Class acts.

longpig Posted on 12/6 22:22

re: Middlesbrough Urban Legends

Morbid's band Dwolma 19; saw them play on the Teesside Princess up and down to Yarm. Damage joined them on stage for a bit and possibly played violin. Branny, who should've been playing bass, just sat watching them saying they were shyte and drinking Pils. I think everyone on the boat had had a good dose of mushrooms. I remember getting barred out of Blaises afterwards that night for not stealing a bottle of Jack Daniels off the bar (it was skinny Pete).

Also remember a time Dwolma or Killydogbox played in Dr Brown's, Morbid screamed this song at some poor old fella just sat having a quiet pint, smashed his bottle of brown, and cut his arms open, had to go to the General to get stitched up.

wishin_well Posted on 15/6 0:55

re: Middlesbrough Urban Legends

Gilkes St Baths. That attendant, I think he was Scottish, sheep's head, "RED BAND OUT! You could hear him underwater. "STOP RUNNIN". "Wash yer feet".

delgrapos Posted on 15/6 10:06

re: Middlesbrough Urban Legends

I know a couple of lads who used to be right rogues and they broke into King's Manor about sixteen years ago about three in the morning with the intention of thieving. They're in the library when one noticed a phone and said to the other "Here, why don't you ring your mam?" As he said that the phone started ringing! They were out of there like a shot and ended up getting caught! They swore this was true!

delgrapos Posted on 15/6 22:21

re: Middlesbrough Urban Legends

I heard a few times off people that the old Borough Hotel (now Dr Brown's) was haunted and it's supposed to be the reason why it ended up called Dr Brown's. A mate of mine used to work there and an old geezer came in one day who reckoned his dad knew the landlord, Herbert or Horatio Brown, I think. He was a surgeon and in the First World War, there was an air raid one night and the cellar was used as a makeshift morgue. Dr Brown is said to have ignored everyone's screams to get to the shelter because he'd left his woodbines in the cellar where he was wrapping corpses and slipped down the cellar hatch, breaking his neck. Allegedly, he was found slumped over a naked corpse with his trousers round his ankles but some people reckoned there was a conspiracy theory as he had previously been arrested on suspicion of being a necrophiliac.

The same lad resigned only days later as he swore when he was down there rolling barrels through he heard someone whisper: "Have you got any faaags."

He won't even go in there now.

delgrapos Posted on 15/6 22:30

re: Middlesbrough Urban Legends

...and Andy X is definitely the king of Linthorpe Road and I have had the pleasure of his company for Christmas dinner the last two years and hopefully every year. He still rocks. He used to have a wicked cowboy shirt for gigs and his chest was that hairy it used to stick out the top even with his top button done!

DrBuck Posted on 7/7 0:21

re: Middlesbrough Urban Legends

Apparently there used to be a ghost that wandered the seventh floor of Billingham House (ex-ICI) offices.

There are also supposed to be mines that run under Billingham and out to the North Sea in which there are still old lorries because the cost of bringing them out was too high back in the old days.

There used to be a ghost called the White Lady haunting Kia Ora Hall in Roseworth too.

neiltrodden Posted on 7/7 0:30

re: Middlesbrough Urban Legends

Was Morbid the one who had a crow nailed to the wall of his bedroom?

the_righteous_one Posted on 7/7 0:33

re: Middlesbrough Urban Legends

Was it still alive?

Rondo_1 Posted on 7/7 0:58

re: Middlesbrough Urban Legends

That'll be the old salt mines which they wanted to fill with nuclear waste.

Speed Walker in Billingham is a legend, she could walk faster than a car can drive.

We also have the old bloke who walks about with a rucksack and talks to everyone.

jax_1 Posted on 7/7 1:20

re: Middlesbrough Urban Legends

Did anyone else have Colin the window cleaner come to their houses? He used to do Grandma's regularly (every fortnight I think it was) and he would bring his guitar on his rounds with him. So after he'd done the windows, he'd be given a cup of tea and he'd play a few choons. Anyway, he must have done that for a couple of years, when all of a sudden he stopped appearing. No explanations or anything. Ages later I saw him cycling along Linny Road all done up like a woman, from make-up to mini skirt. I thought at first that maybe he had been going to a fancy dress party or something but I saw him a few times after that and he was always dressed in women's clothes.

Rondo_1 Posted on 7/7 1:22

re: Middlesbrough Urban Legends

Might have been to a few fancy dress parties...

OPEO Posted on 7/7 7:18

re: Middlesbrough Urban Legends

Rag 'n' bone! Our mam lost some of her Sunday best in exchange for a bow and arrow in the days when Easterside had a mere ten houses complete.

longpig Posted on 13/7 20:20

re: Middlesbrough Urban Legends

neiltrodden - that rings a bell about the dead bird. He definitely had a bit of string across his window with a row of used tampons dangling from it. He and a few mates shared a house on Clifton Street for a while and it was the most disgusting place I have ever seen. Always good for a party though.

Big_Shot Posted on 13/7 23:54

re: Middlesbrough Urban Legends

The dead birds were supposed to be at Morbid's. I never saw them myself but only ever went round a couple of times but I definitely have heard of both the birds and the tampons. That was the house on Clifton Street.

wishin_well Posted on 14/7 4:59

re: Middlesbrough Urban Legends

The Central, Friday afternoon Bandbox:

Dennis Cordell and the 'Dream Team' give The Flaming Flames a run for their money any day. The drummer looked like a pissed Les Battersby.

The Danimac Girls fighting to get up and sing on payday.

The bloke who looked like, and thought he was, Dean Martin. Beats Karaoke any day. No sound check. Real 'live' Instruments too…

borobadge Posted on 14/7 11:28

re: Middlesbrough Urban Legends

The Danimac Girls… now they were legendary.

TOPIC

MESSAGE

POST

REGISTER

Anyway, whatever happened to Speedwalker from Billingham? Remember the thin (probably anorexic) woman who sped everywhere on foot?

erimus11 Posted on 14/7 12:42

re: Middlesbrough Urban Legends

I married a Danimac girl. Told me she was a stiffener - bloody liar!

Cogeur_le_Conq Posted on 19/7 12:21

re: Middlesbrough Urban Legends

Did you know there's two ICI tunnels running under the River Tees?

I've worked down there.

The gadgie that used to sign you in and out had a little hut at the top of the south entrance to one of them.

His name was Wilf Mannion and he was the greatest player to play for the Boro.

clag01 Posted on 19/7 17:19

re: Middlesbrough Urban Legends

I know Morbid. He used to have a rabbit called Alan when he lived in Clifton St. It used to have the run of the house. It was also mad. It hated me and attacked me on several occasions. The house was truly bad. He lives on Parli Rd now and has cleaned up his act.

AtomicLoonybin Posted on 26/7 9:49

re: Middlesbrough Urban Legends

Billog now has its very own tramp. We call him 'Bag Man' because he has an enormous rucksack on his back that seems to be entirely full of plastic bags - so many that they are overflowing. He seems a creature of habit.

The story is that he was a high ranking gadgie in ICI, his wife died suddenly, and since then he's been a gentleman of the road. He lives somewhere near the Horse and Jockey and every day walks up to Castle Eden/Thorpe Thewles, then along the Wynyard Hall Road, past Northfields School and into Billingham, where he hangs round the town, occasionally going into shops, stinking the place out, while looking intently at the goods on offer. Then presumably, he walks home the same route. He does this on Sundays as well, when there's nothing open. Seems awfully sad.

Rondo_1 Posted on 26/7 10:29

re: Middlesbrough Urban Legends

ALB, he walks up Whitehouse Road most days. He seems quite a nice chap, always says "good morning" or "hello". We even spoke to him outside the Wynyard pub when we were drinking.

Anyway, whatever happened to Speedwalker from Billingham? Remember the thin (probably anorexic) woman who sped everywhere on foot?

borobadge Posted on 11/8 20:27

re: Middlesbrough Urban Legends

I heard a story about a woman in Billingham in the '70s who was reported for having sex in front of her neighbours. They could see through the curtains and with lights on, silhouettes.

The police were called but they didn't stop it, they just set up a roster and a shift system so they could watch. Every Tuesday and Thursday evenings it was.

The cause of such intermittent interest? Her alsatian dog!

But I'm more than sure it was just an Urban Myth that we told each other in Middlesbrough about our neighbours from the north...

Unless of course someone on here knows differently!!

acklam_lad Posted on 11/8 21:27

re: Middlesbrough Urban Legends

Just using my mate's login at work but as I am originally from Grangetown, I thought I'd add a bit about a few things:

(1) The bloke caught shagging his dog is TRUE. They called him Pissy George. The RSPCA were called as neighbours heard the carry on from the dog. They turned up to find the dog with its back legs tied together and Pissy George givin' it one.

(2) As the story goes, Nipper the Eston Tramp had a breakdown after lending his old dear 50p for the gas meter, going out to return to his Mum with her head in the oven... she had gassed herself.

Last but not least anyone remember the old bird from Grangetown, Nit Noo... all the kids used to torture her and she'd shout "If I get ya I'll nit noo" (she was obviously short tongued!).

Corcaigh_the_Cat Posted on 11/8 21:53

re: Middlesbrough Urban Legends

I pass the Billingham tramp most nights on the Wynyard Road. He did live in the woods just off Castle Eden Walkway, not sure where now but can't be far away. My father in law followed his tracks through the snow one day and found his camp.

Anybody know this fella from the Boro, don't know whether he's had a mention before or not on here?

User links to image of Spiral Island, a floating artificial island in a lagoon near Puerto Aventuras, on the Caribbean coast of Mexico, south of Cancún. It was built by eco-pioneer Richart (or "Rishi") Sowa who is from Boro.

Eddie_Catflap Posted on 11/8 22:51

re: Middlesbrough Urban Legends

I pass that Billingham tramp too, all the time. Must be fit as a fiddle doing that trek every day. Think I'll buy him a bottle of whisky for Xmas.

the_woolyback Posted on 12/8 7:52

re: Middlesbrough Urban Legends

Wonder if it's the same Richie Sowa that went to St Thomas' in the Sixties? Had a sister called Katherine, I think.

delgrapos Posted on 18/8 0:50

re: Middlesbrough Urban Legends

Does anyone remember Catwoman from Doggy?

Bessie Posted on 19/8 1:53

re: Middlesbrough Urban Legends

A brilliant thread and bringing back some memories. I've just spent two hours reading it. I remember Nipper very well and the fact he used to sleep rough up the hills and get cleaned up by the nuns now and again.

Also, I remember Alice Bunn who roamed the streets of South Bank. I vaguely recall her actually buying me a glass of milk one day. My dad used to own a 'niknak' shop in South Bank and I think there must have been a cafe close by. This must have been in the early to mid '70s.

The story about the ICI man with his bike of mercury is true. My ex worked at ICI for over twenty years and told me that one. Not heard about the cancer castle but it wouldn't surprise me. Judging by the amount of cancer in the area, I wonder if they dug it deep enough?

Someone mentioned the Satan Slaves. The man with the spidery tattoo on his head is still around and drinks in the Station in Redcar every now and then. Quite a few of the 'old' Satan Slaves go in there.

norfolkred1 Posted on 5/9 11:30

re: Middlesbrough Urban Legends

Did we get to the bottom of the two lads getting killed at the BOS plant? I can confirm one was called Dave Metcalf from Dormanstown. He was on my JPT course at Cargo Fleet Lane. I also went to his cremation at Acklam Road Crem.

zappa909 Posted on 5/9 12:47

re: Middlesbrough Urban Legends

norfolkred, I remember this well as my brother was good mates with both lads, Dave Metcalf and the other lad was called Eric but his nickname was Eza, also from Dormo. It was tragic at the time, like. They both lived near the Kingfisher, I believe. I was about eight at the time... it also made the front page of the Gazette, I'm sure.

PumpingGnome Posted on 5/9 12:55

re: Middlesbrough Urban Legends

I used to know Richard Sowa - his cousin was my best mate. He had two sisters and a brother if memory serves me right. He's built himself an island of 100,000 plastic bottles off Yucatan in Mexico, where he lives. He went through a lot of phases - was a Jehovah's Witness for a time.

I also knew one of the lads who drank the anti-freeze, the one that survived. The anti-freeze was in a cherry brandy bottle. He said it was nice and they just thought they were pist. He woke up in intensive care with liver damage, kidney damage, all sorts. Haven't seen him for a lot of years.

norfolkred1 Posted on 5/9 13:24

re: Middlesbrough Urban Legends

Zappa909, I used to keep a diary and looked it up when this was brought up recently. I still have the date in some dark cupboard. Rumour was that one had gone over the top and the other tried to grab him. Obviously there was nobody else there to confirm it. Thing was, all were under 18 at the time and working all hours including nights to keep the unemployment figures down. My son now can't find a job at 16 because of insurance. How times have changed...

zappa909 Posted on 5/9 13:38

re: Middlesbrough Urban Legends

Now then norfolkred1, the story I heard, and remember this must be about 25-26 years ago, was that they were on a conveyor belt and one did try to save the other. I mentioned the incident to our kidda when I read about it on this post and apparently there was another lad there or in the proximity and he still works for BSC, ahem, sorry Corus, and is now in his 40s. I dare say health and safety in them days wasn't the beast it is today. Not a bad thing when we look back on stuff like this, mate.

norfolkred1 Posted on 5/9 13:48

re: Middlesbrough Urban Legends

Zappa, it was before the 16 week strike in 1980, about 1978/9. I will dig the dates out a bit later but I think it was Dec '78. There were loads of near deaths at BSC when I was there but the unions ran the place and were OUT, OUT, OUT at the drop of a hat. I now have a hatred for them. Where did your kid work? I hung out in the Rod Mill...

zappa909 Posted on 5/9 13:58

re: Middlesbrough Urban Legends

Now then norfolk. Nah mate, our kidda knocked around with them socially round Dormo and Redcar, like.

Sadza Posted on 5/9 15:52

re: Middlesbrough Urban Legends

A bouncer at the Redcar Jazz Club once stopped a bloke walking to the front of the queue. "Don't you know who I am?" the bloke asked. "I'm Long John Baldry" he said. "I don't care if you're Long John F'kin Silver, get to the back of the queue!" was the response - happy days!

norfolkred1 Posted on 5/9 19:13

re: Middlesbrough Urban Legends

Just to finish this rumour off, it was 13 Dec '78 when the two trainees died at the BSC BOS plant.

smalltime Posted on 5/9 20:15

re: Middlesbrough Urban Legends

Can't remember Catwoman from Doggy?

Along the lines of tramp threads, I remember 'Blind' Bob and his wife Pattie from Doggy who spent their days getting blitzed and knocking f***k out of each other. Very early '80s.

zappa909 Posted on 5/9 21:06

re: Middlesbrough Urban Legends

Leedsclive... about that gadgie caught shagging his dog in Grangetown, yeh it's true alreet, but that's not how it happened.

The feller, let's just call him Ronnie, cos that's his name, had been a naughty boy earlier in the day and when the police went to his house to arrest him, their lass said he's in the shed with the dogs (two German Shepherds, I believe). Police open shed door, embarrassment all round, oh dear.

When questioned about the doggy gang bang, police said: "Ronnie, how low can you get?"

Ronnie replied: "Oh, I dunno, maybe a Chihuahua." OK I made that last bit up but the rest is true, X my heart.

delgrapos Posted on 10/10 23:01

re: Middlesbrough Urban Legends

Does anyone recall King Prawn Collitte? The seafood queen of South Bank? Old Man Wilky or any of the Venises from South Bank?

madlad Posted on 16/10 15:15

re: Middlesbrough Urban Legends

I cannot believe nobody has mentioned the ubiquitous supply teacher who seemed to just turn up randomly at your school throughout the late '70s/'80s. Chain smoked, always smelling of booze, clueless but by f**k he was funny.

Of the time when the Rec had Stapylton, Sarah Metcalfe and Gillbrook (I was Gilly).

Now that, my friends, is a true legend!

B_Hills Posted on 16/10 16:26

re: Middlesbrough Urban Legends

And... just exactly who was Joe Walton? I was a member when it was in the road where the Boro Police station is now. Non-stop five-a-sides in Belle Vue playground every night for members of JWs.

drinkingbob Posted on 18/10 19:17

re: Middlesbrough Urban Legends

What about Tonibell ice cream vans?

BarryBlagger Posted on 30/10 21:50

re: Middlesbrough Urban Legends

I remember Blind Bob and mad mad Pattie of Doggy. Heard of the Catwoman but never seen her!

JillyJ Posted on 17/12 13:24

re: Middlesbrough Urban Legends

Just found this site, me and the hubby have never laffed so much in ages. Thanks, guys/gals.

Yeah, Snotty Johnny we called him. I remember him selling toffee apples and toffee dabs outside the ABC flicks on a Sat morning, that was back in the late '60s. He also rode that bike round the estates selling his toffee dabs. One kid would kick the back of his bike and when he chased him, the other kids would nick everything. Hubby just told me, when he was out with his mates thumbing a lift to Stockton, Snotty Johnny just happened to ride past. So they all chased after him, he jumped off his bike and did a runner. The lads were riding his bike round Newport roundabout. They never quite made it to Stockton as the bobbies were soon in hot pursuit and sent them home LMAO. EEEE them were the good old days.

I loved the '70s. We used to go out with £1.50, 20 fags, beer all night, fish 'n' chips, bus fare home and still had change in your pocket. 16p a pint, 26p for 20 fags, can't remember how much the fish 'n' chips were, like. I wish we could turn back the clock just for one last Christmas, back room in the Shakey, everyone singing. It didn't matter if yer had no dosh like, anyone would buy you a drink back then.

Anyway that's all for now. Hubby said I could talk a glass eye to sleep. Merry Christmas All.

Cogeur_le_Conq Posted on 8/2 12:01

re: Middlesbrough Urban Legends

Does that gadgie still go from pub to pub with his white coat selling seafood from a tray?

I bet he got fed up of the same jokes every night such as: "Got any crabs on ya? Cock!"

My favourite was:

Pisshead: "Have you got any muscles, mate?"

Crabstickman: "Yes."

Pisshead: "Well, give us a hand with this piano."

BOOM TISH.

smoggyramone Posted on 8/2 18:55

re: Middlesbrough Urban Legends

Surprised no-one has mentioned Eric, who could always be seen either outside Ayresome, at the Speedway, or walking down Linthorpe Road with his dog, and listening to his radio. I know he lived with his nanna and when she died, Eric went somewhere else. Anyone seen him lately?

Anyone from Whinney Banks remember seeing "PC FAIRY GODMOTHER BARKER" being written on the fence outside Grimes coalyard?

Another Whinney Banks legend was Tommy Wellies, aka Tommy the Hammer. Always wore a red and white benny hat, a donkey jacket with an orange yoke, national health specs and wellies 3 sizes too big. He lived in someone's wash-house on Bruce Avenue and they charged him rent!! Is he still about?

Also 'The Swinger'. Wierd looking, specky, trenchcoat wearing freak who used to frequent Foxes' Wood. We used to go looking for him after school for a dare.

JimmyMFC1 Posted on 8/2 19:19

re: Middlesbrough Urban Legends

Eric has been mentioned further up somewhere, although not by name, I don't think. He lived with my great grandma and his dog was called Skipper.

signal Posted on 9/2 19:34

re: Middlesbrough Urban Legends

The Helium Brothers used to sit near me when I was in the West - long since moved now, like. I saw one of them a few years ago during SMac's first season after a match. I asked him where his brother was and he said that he doesn't go anymore - he was chucked out for fighting... Is this true or was he winding me up? I could never tell with them.

onthemap Posted on 9/2 19:42

re: Middlesbrough Urban Legends

Anyone ever go tatie-picking with Harkers, getting picked up from Doggy about 4 in the morning? Getting on the wagons was like them Yanks trying to get on the choppers to get out of Hanoi before it all kicked off.

norfolkred1 Posted on 9/2 19:47

re: Middlesbrough Urban Legends

Did anyone mention the gadgie outside the Bob End shouting "Golden goal, ten pence"? Face like a balloon.

Eric the Wireless is a pure legend. You want up-to-date scores, he will tell you there and then, Boro scores, speedway, the lot.

wool_skull Posted on 9/2 22:49

re: Middlesbrough Urban Legends

Anyone remember Mrs Wells who had the cobblers' shop in Doggie? She used to scare the living bejabers out of us kids cos she had this scary ass speech impediment that made her scream out like Fred Ippytittymus halfway thro' soling and heeling your best winklepickers.

I also played footy for Wilton Juniors with Wilf's son, also unfortunately called Wilf Mannion. He was a useful left winger but had far too much to live up to. Canny lad, like... Anyone know if he's still around?

wishin_well Posted on 10/2 2:37

re: Middlesbrough Urban Legends

Eric the Wireless is a pure legend. You want up-to-date scores, he will tell you there and then, Boro scores, speedway, the lot. This guy was before Sky Sports and mobile phones and he's the man. Always on a shitty little transistor, Roberts should look him up...

The digital age, eh...

Dennis Cordell and the Flaming Flames are the best Central bandbox live band ever, period.

smoggyramone Posted on 10/2 11:17

re: Middlesbrough Urban Legends

I was always a fan of "Welcome to the sound of Las Vegas, ladies and gentlemen," Mr Alan 'Bubbles' Robson!!

goughla Posted on 10/2 12:20

re: Middlesbrough Urban Legends

"...also 'The Swinger.' Wierd looking, specky, trenchcoat wearing freak who used to frequent Foxes' Wood. We used to go looking for him after school for a dare."

Is he still about? He fits the bill of someone I pass down Mandale Road when I'm driving to work.

smoggyramone Posted on 10/2 14:00

re: Middlesbrough Urban Legends

Bulbous, bald head, straggly hair, 'tache, glasses, trenchcoat. Used to have a satchel across his body.

zappa909 Posted on 10/2 14:12

re: Middlesbrough Urban Legends

I remember as a kid on our many trips between Grangetown and Redcar, me and the brothers thumbing a lift on the Trunk Road and it was guaranteed that every time he went past a gadgie in a small red van who only had one arm and one of them special knobs (phnarr) on the steering wheel, he would always pick us up. Nice fella, never said a lot. Does anyone remember "The One Armed Bandit?"

I'd go ballistic if I knew my kids were doing the same thing now.

XboroX Posted on 10/2 16:54

re: Middlesbrough Urban Legends

"Another Whinney Banks legend was Tommy Wellies, aka Tommy the Hammer. Always wore a red and white benny hat, a donkey jacket with an orange yoke, national health specs and wellies three sizes too big. He lived in someone's wash-house on Bruce Avenue and they charged him rent!! Is he still about?""

I remember Tommy the Hammer still hanging around Bruce Avenue and Springfield Road when our dad lived there. I still live round that way and haven't seen him or heard any of the younger kids mention him. Maybe he is dead?

As far as Eric the Wireless goes, he is still alive and well. He has a season ticket in the West Lower. I saw him a few weeks ago in Billingham. He still looks exactly the same as he always has.

smoggyramone Posted on 10/2 17:13

re: Middlesbrough Urban Legends

More from Whinney Banks:

Talky - running messages and collecting glasses for free beer in the Roseberry.

Den Grayson telling everyone he'd been nutted by the Yorkshire Ripper outside the paper shop on Burlam Road.

Someone flicking dogshit in the fryer in Nellie Bell's fish shop and then having "shit shop" written on the door.

When the houses started to get modernised in the '80s, everybody all of a sudden had brick fireplaces!

Happy days...

Eddie_Catflap Posted on 11/2 1:28

re: Middlesbrough Urban Legends

I do remember Mrs Wells, although I really was just a bairn. I was told she had shell shock. No idea if this was true or not.

B_Hills Posted on 12/2 12:06

re: Middlesbrough Urban Legends

Mrs Wells did suffer from shell shock, and she did scare the life out of you. Has Harry Bindorf the Doggy club foot barber had a mention on here?

squiffypants Posted on 12/2 13:41

re: Middlesbrough Urban Legends

When I was a kid I went to school on the Acklam Road school complex - Boynton, Hustler, King's Manor and St George's, as it was back then.

Back in the mid to late '70s I remember a lad/bloke who everyone was pretty much in fear of called Billy Conners (I think).

He was a few years older than the rest of us and I think knocked about with the Hemlington crowd. Or maybe Whinney Banks. You would see him hanging around the trees between the schools all the time.

Anyone remember him? He's probably mid to late 40s now. God, I'm getting so old :(

collo1875 Posted on 12/2 15:19

re: Middlesbrough Urban Legends

I've just spent two and a half hours reading this and although I don't know a lot of the mentioned urban legends, it's still a great read.

Eston and Normanby - Anyone remember Scotch Ernie? Used to drink in the Royal and the Miners (think he was born in Leicester) but always started speaking like a Jock the more he had to drink. By the end of the night he was that broad you could hardly understand him. He also went up to everyone (trying to get a free drink) with the same crap, "Jesus, how ya doin'? I used to work with your dad and he was one of the best blokes I ever met."

And Jimmy Tierny, always pulled his own cider when a fight broke out.

Row_7 Posted on 13/2 11:07

re: Middlesbrough Urban Legends

I remember Billy Connors, nice lad (if you knew him). He was built like a barn door even when he was 17 or 18.

Think he was a year or two older than me so he'll be about 43 or 44 now. He's still in the area - saw him in the Chinese in Doggy a couple of months ago.

Got a couple of kids too I think. Last I heard he was working as a scaffy.

smoggyramone Posted on 13/2 18:17

re: Middlesbrough Urban Legends

Yes, Billy Connors. Think he belonged off Levick Crescent.

wool_skull Posted on 20/3 21:32

re: Middlesbrough Urban Legends

Harry Bindoff... I'd forgotten him. Hungarian, club-footed barber who had a shop near the Market Tavern on Doggie market. Ran off with his brother's wife, if I remember right.

fatknackerlardarse Posted on 20/3 21:39

re: Middlesbrough Urban Legends

It's where the haircut came from,

'The Bindoff Alloff'.

Pope_Gregory_IX Posted on 20/3 21:39

re: Middlesbrough Urban Legends

I'm sure I saw Tommy Wellies last year dressed in camouflage and wearing a beret.

smoggyramone Posted on 28/3 15:10

re: Middlesbrough Urban Legends

Charlie Ezzard the Acklam Rd barber. Only knew how to do one haircut, 'the threepenny all-off'.

VodkaByName Posted on 28/3 15:23

re: Middlesbrough Urban Legends

Not sure if this has previously been mentioned but anybody remember that woman who used to wander around the town and then appear in the Raglan, Shakey or the like and dance with the blokes whilst nicking fags and booze etc off the tables?!

She was a bit slow and always seemed to be pregnant...

neilteesside Posted on 28/3 15:27

re: Middlesbrough Urban Legends

The Raglan! Shakey! Remember the Masham?! You're taking me back to the days when I sold Boro programmes on the corner of Parly Road!

She was a bit dippy... She used to try the Trooper, but everyone knew her in there!! Good old days!!!

SmogontheThames Posted on 28/3 15:44

re: Middlesbrough Urban Legends

Roy - ex landlord of the Linny. Might not be a legend as such but he taught me the value of "respect thy landlord and thou shall have a stoppy back."

Yeah, I remember Billy Connors, used to climb on the Whinney Banks school roof with him as a nipper.

neilteesside Posted on 28/3 15:48

re: Middlesbrough Urban Legends

In those days the Brambles Farm Hotel would have a Saturday boxing match... the more the merrier... the last one out had a pint on the house!

smoggyramone Posted on 28/3 15:49

re: Middlesbrough Urban Legends

Anyone know Toya Barnes? Or Fatty Clarkson?

SmogontheThames Posted on 28/3 16:06

re: Middlesbrough Urban Legends

Yeah, I know Toya and Fatty. Was in the same class with Toya at Franny's and then the same year at Mick's. Fatty was not a bad lad when you knew him but he could be a bit wild.

borobadge Posted on 29/3 0:17

re: Middlesbrough Urban Legends

Johnny "Hutch" Hutchinson...

Archie_StephensElbow Posted on 30/3 16:26

re: Middlesbrough Urban Legends

Two years old today.

delier1908 Posted on 30/3 17:19

re: Middlesbrough Urban Legends

What a thread! First time I've seen it.

Aaaah, The Masham. My sister Maria used to always say she knew I was in The Masham when she passed as 'Say It Ain't So Joe' by Murray Head would be playing. Nearly all the time then!

Anyone remember it? Allegedly about Joe DiMaggio.

User reproduces lyrics from "Say It Ain't So Joe" by Murray Head.

wool_skull Posted on 31/3 0:58

re: Middlesbrough Urban Legends

Not true urban legends but I used to book Dave Coverdale's band Denver Mule before he sent in his tape to Deep Purple. The rest is history. A lad called Mick Martin played lead for 'em and ended up in a band called Juicy Lucy (I think he did some gigs with Thin Lizzy as well).

MartinManor Posted on 3/4 11:58

re: Middlesbrough Urban Legends

That hill on the Whitby road near Lockwood Beck is called Freeborough Hill.

Happy days.

User posted link to article called 'Geographical and Historical information from the year 1890', all about Skelton and East Cleveland.

TOPIC

MESSAGE

POST

REGISTER

The Raglan! Shakey! Remember the Masham?! You're taking me back to the days when I sold Boro programmes on the corner of Parly Road!

molten1 Posted on 3/4 13:57

re: Middlesbrough Urban Legends

The swinger you are on about was also known as "Daft Dave" or "Dave the Swinger." He used to live round the corner from me. He used to hang bags of piss in a tree outside his dad's house.

Billy Connors - big lad indeed.

I also remember Damage and Morbid from the Linny and the Empire.

Brings back memories this does.

OurLassesMerkin Posted on 3/4 16:46

re: Middlesbrough Urban Legends

I remember me and my mates always used to walk up Ormesby Bank and along towards Great Ayton, through the caravan park on its outskirts and off swimming in The Blue Lagoon. It got filled in about 15 years ago I think. It was an old mineshaft/quarry and legend has it that a dead horse attached to a cart drowned in it but never got to touch the bottom as it was well deep.

Piquet2 Posted on 3/4 16:54

re: Middlesbrough Urban Legends

We get "Now and Then" delivered through our letterbox... now and then. Used to go fishing in the Blue Lagoon, it was filled in when Whinstone View started to become popular, with more children using the campsite.

OurLassesMerkin Posted on 3/4 17:15

re: Middlesbrough Urban Legends

Yeah, that's the place and the name of the caravan park. Nice one!

emadgin Posted on 6/4 17:54

re: Middlesbrough Urban Legends

Fatty Clarkson, he got done for police assult, a police dog bit him so he bit back. This happened at Manchester, he got three months in Strangeways, that must be 25 plus years ago. I always got on with the lad, I haven't seen him for years.

emadgin Posted on 6/4 18:02

re: Middlesbrough Urban Legends

Eric Nicolson and Dave Metcalfe, the two lads who were killed in BSC. These lads were two good friends of mine. I didn't know the other lad who was there. Both were only kids at the time, it hit the families hard. I remember them well.

smoggyramone Posted on 6/4 18:03

re: Middlesbrough Urban Legends

I saw Fatty last year in the Cambridge having Sunday dinner with their lass and the kids.

norfolkred1 Posted on 6/4 20:09

re: Middlesbrough Urban Legends

emadgin: I was on Dave's course at Cargo Fleet before we were let loose in the adult world of BSC. Their deaths caused a bit of hassle due to their being under 18 and working nights, like we all were. He had another mate, think he was called Dave as well, on the same course, also from Dormanstown. Any ideas?

emadgin Posted on 6/4 20:35

re: Middlesbrough Urban Legends

Red, don't recall anyone else called Dave. I knocked about with them in the late '70s. We all knocked about together in a gang in Dormanstown so I knew both families as well.

ayresomeangel365 Posted on 8/4 9:15

re: Middlesbrough Urban Legends

I can remember going to see the bus station opened by Corra's one and only Elsie Tanner who did a tour of the town on an open top bus.

ayresomeangel365 Posted on 8/4 9:20

re: Middlesbrough Urban Legends

Giggy Moon... brother of Doris and Raymond... Portrack Lane legends.

Teesside Urban Legends

emadgin Posted on 8/4 17:13

re: Middlesbrough Urban Legends

zappa, I remember the "One Arm Bandit" and Ronnie the dog lover, lol. Howz it hanging?

emadgin Posted on 8/4 17:16

re: Middlesbrough Urban Legends

Here's one for ya, Boc Beck Benny. I think his real name was Freddy Taylor. He had a shack over the works for years, always drinking meths. I think he was from South Bank.

AtomicLoonybin Posted on 19/4 10:12

re: Middlesbrough Urban Legends

Eric the Wireless walks past me every home game as I'm selling FMTTM. His mate goes into the Good Food Joint and Eric waits for him outside. He hasn't changed a bit since the Ayresome days.

Non-Boro but "Say It Ain't So Joe" is about "Shoeless" Joe Jackson, not Joe di Maggio. He was a baseball player who helped his team (The Chicago White Sox) throw a world series back in 1919 for a bookie. When he was being tried, some kid stopped him on the court steps and cried "Say it ain't so Joe" - i.e. that he hadn't done it. Got banned for life.

smoggyramone Posted on 5/5 11:17

re: Middlesbrough Urban Legends

Surely Sinbad the tattooist deserves a mention. 30 odd years of professionally done 'tasteful' tattoos, all done in his hygenic, spotless salon situated in the arcade off Grange Rd.

OPEO Posted on 14/5 7:22

re: Middlesbrough Urban Legends

John Rodgers. Has he had a mention? "Gazeeeeeeeeeeeeettttte!" He sold the Sports from being a young nipper 'til... is he still around? Sold them all over the place. In fact he was probably cloned by some mad scientist at Gazette Towers cos he seemed to be everywhere.

Stepper_T Posted on 16/5 23:13

re: Middlesbrough Urban Legends

Best thread ever. Would love it to be put into print.

AyresomeMark Posted on 17/5 10:04

re: Middlesbrough Urban Legends

Can anyone remember Jimmy Saville driving through the town in a convertible car, must be around 1980ish? It was part of a tour of Britain I think.

delgrapos Posted on 23/5 22:19

re: Middlesbrough Urban Legends

I once knew a woman who had 'Jean' tattooed on her arm. I asked her if it was her mam's name or her sisters and she said "No, I got it at Sinbad's, it was supposed to be Gene Pitney."

She had Arther or Aurthur on the other and there was a big Indian Ink blue block underneath which had scrubbed the original one out and he'd spelt it wrong again. She still didn't realise 'til somebody spelt it out! But she was a good lass, Mucky Maureen.

delgrapos Posted on 23/5 22:29

re: Middlesbrough Urban Legends

Also another Sinbad special was "MILD" and "BITTER" on a pair of jugs I happened to come across once! Or should I say happened to come by. Sorry that's even worse...

I remember a story about Jimmy Saville cutting through Ashfield Avenue in Grove Hill in a soft top Cadillac or something and some lad up the road was cattying his Datsun and said "Can you f*****g fix this, Jim?"

acklam_lad Posted on 24/5 0:16

re: Middlesbrough Urban Legends

Ahhh Tommy the Hammer of Whinney Banks.

When we were playing footy on the bit of green at the end of East Crescent and he walked past, we used to shout "Tommy the Hammer!" and he used to chase us every time. Heehee.

Cogeur_le_Conq Posted on 24/5 0:54

re: Middlesbrough Urban Legends

Sinbad started tattooing MC under my mate's Boro lion, which is astonishing considering he must have done the same tattoo over a thousand times. He had to convert the C to an F and the letters are all the wrong size.

Doesn't Danny Boone have 'Dan' tattoed on his neck written the wrong way round cos the dozy get did it himself in a mirror?

burydweller Posted on 21/6 21:12

re: Middlesbrough Urban Legends

Sinbad butchered me in 1982 - several awful tatts that would look good on Popeye. His 'Made In England' around my belly button nearly required a blood transfusion. I then got a couple on from a bloke with a shop oppo the old Odeon. Also had my first tatts put on by a smelly drunk in Hartlepool who had a 'shop' in his upstairs bedroom. I hate tattoos, me.

burydweller Posted on 21/6 21:23

re: Middlesbrough Urban Legends

For me personally, Boro was legendary for having a brilliant youth club culture during the '70s and early '80s. I loved the northern soul dancing at the Sacred Heart in the late '70s, Saint Barns, Grove Hill youth club, Thorntree youth, and the best, Beechwood youth club, great venue, great music.

Does anyone remember little Norman who was a great dancer and went to Wigan casino? Would love to know what happened to his record collection. He lived off Cumberland Road and was a great dancer during the mid to late '70s upstairs in the Sacred Heart.

wool_skull Posted on 21/6 22:47

re: Middlesbrough Urban Legends

Didn't Chris Quentin (real name Bell) do a northern soul dance routine with Georgie Kamara (brother of the local celeb, Chris?) round all the clubs and pubs?

Vague memories of my childhood.

norfolkred1 Posted on 21/6 22:55

re: Middlesbrough Urban Legends

Youth club discos, anyone remember Brian DeBear? He used to run Boro Mobile Disco. He did a weekly at Whinney Banks youth club.

Cogeur_le_Conq Posted on 21/6 23:16

re: Middlesbrough Urban Legends

burydweller

The tatooist near the Odeon was called Dinky. The gadge in Hartlepool was called Duke Webb.

I used to go to the Northern Soul youth clubs like Grove Hill and Beechwood, and even Kader (somewhere in the posh suburbs?).

Me mam let me go to my first all nighter at Doggie YM (sponsored dance marathon) when I was about 13, about '75 ish.

collo1875 Posted on 21/6 23:51

re: Middlesbrough Urban Legends

I'm almost certain Brian DeBear did the Royal in Eston on a Sunday night and used to go through three Chinese meals a night.

burydweller Posted on 22/6 7:24

re: Middlesbrough Urban Legends

Cheers for that. Well then, I was Dinky's first victim in Middlesbrough. He put a tattoo on me the day before he opened his shop, it is the worst tattoo in the world. A friend of his set it up. It's true, Chris and Kamara guy did NS at Beechwood in the mid 1970s.

Who could forget Whinney Banks youth club as well? I think done by Wally Black and his mobile disco.

burydweller Posted on 22/6 7:26

re: Middlesbrough Urban Legends

Le Cog, Kader was in Acklam, I think.

smoggyramone Posted on 22/6 7:38

re: Middlesbrough Urban Legends

Acklam Lad - Tommy the Hammer's name comes from the '60s song 'Lily The Pink' by Scouse band Scaffold.

"Johnny Hammer had a terrible s-stammer."

Discos - the name escapes me of the mobile disco that seemed to be everywhere in the '80s. Every 18th/21st/engagement/wedding seemed to have the same one... was it Tramps?

Re Eric the Wireless. I was reunited with Eric at the Speedway a couple of weeks ago when I came over for a week's holiday. Someone's put blond streaks (none of this highlights poncy shite, they're called streaks!) in his hair. He looked genuinely pleased to see me which was nice, seeing as I haven't seen him for about ten years.

Boro was legendary for having a brilliant youth club culture during the '70s and early '80s. I loved the northern soul dancing at the Sacred Heart in the late '70s, Saint Barns, Grove Hill youth club, Thorntree youth, and the best, Beechwood youth club, great venue, great music.

MarlonD Posted on 22/6 9:10

re: Middlesbrough Urban Legends

Best thread that has ever been on here.

Billy Connors; wasn't he supposedly the first Boro fan on the pitch at 'The Battle of Stamford Bridge'? I also used to live next door to Little Billy, his cousin.

I have had many a happy pint listening to stories from Big Billy from Pally Park.

XboroX Posted on 22/6 9:27

re: Middlesbrough Urban Legends

When I worked in Forbidden Planet, I remember someone telling me that a regular customer had convictions for rogering seals down at Seal Sands...

XboroX Posted on 22/6 9:32

re: Middlesbrough Urban Legends

Jesus, I have millions of Brian DeBear stories, our mam and dad used to do the discos with him in the '70s. He is a good friend of our family. My all time favourite though involves him and our grandad.

My grandad used to work down the docks at British Steel and as a result they always used to go on board the ships to speak to the crew etc.

Brian DeBear, who went with my grandad on board a Philipino boat, dressed up in a gorilla costume as a joke to scare the chef. The chef chased him off the boat and round the dock for a good 30 minutes with a massive knife before he realised it was a guy in a suit.

He now runs Boro Bikes on Borough Road. Dunno if he still does the discos.

borobadge Posted on 18/7 23:01

re: Middlesbrough Urban Legends

Dinky had his first tattoo shop down near the Transporter Bridge (Gosforth Road).

He tattooed Middlesbrough F.C. on my arm in 1977...

norfolkred1 Posted on 18/7 23:13

re: Middlesbrough Urban Legends

Brian run for 30 minutes? This was not your average-sized bear. He only took me and his nephew to help out with Boro Mobile Disco to keep the blue van on all fours.

Borobarmy Posted on 19/7 8:19

re: Middlesbrough Urban Legends

Can't remember whether I've asked this before on here but does anyone remember Jonah the Whale appearing on Clairville Common in the '70s?

Also does anyone remember the parky in Albert Park with a speech impediment who used to scream at the kids back in the '70s?

I also remember the northern soul nights in YMCA, Beechwood and Church of Ascension in Berwick Hills where we all used to get chased back over the Longlands by the NTP.

borolad259 Posted on 19/7 8:41

re: Middlesbrough Urban Legends

I seem to recall the whale too. There were all sorts of things turned up at Clairville... I remember a spitroast ox... spitroast meant something different then.

Reading this thread took me back a bit... St Barnabas' youth club Northern Soul nights... good Lord!!!

kazzaxxx Posted on 19/7 8:45

re: Middlesbrough Urban Legends

coguer_le_conq, I was talking to Paddy Durnin not so long ago. He said he didn't dye his dog lime green.

borobadge Posted on 20/7 15:27

re: Middlesbrough Urban Legends

Yep, I can confirm the whale... it came on the back of a large flat bed lorry.

The roasted ox was part of the Queen's Silver Jubilee in 1977.

And on another occasion, I had to wheelbarrow elephant dung from Clairville to our back garden, so the old fella could use it as manure on his plants! Real genuine elephant shyte, not everyone can have use of such exotic gardening assists.

hicktonspenaltyrunup Posted on 20/7 15:59

re: Middlesbrough Urban Legends

I remember the parky from Albert Park well. He banned me "for life" when I was 12 for soaking everyone who was waiting for a rowing boat. I was quite upset (he was a bit weird). My old man pissed his pants laughing.

Does anyone remember Dirty Dick, a horrendous looking bloke who used to walk around all the back alleys around Lovaine St, Union St, Wentworth St in the late '60s? Frightened us kids to death.

HolgateWall Posted on 20/7 20:39

re: Middlesbrough Urban Legends

Catwoman from North Ormesby lived in Fredrick Street, I think.

borolad259 Posted on 20/7 20:50

re: Middlesbrough Urban Legends

Badgie, re elephant dung... I can remember the odd circus coming to Clairville. Sort of seems bizarre really thinking of tigers in cages just sitting there on the common to drum up business. Now, tiger dung, that would keep the local moggies out the yard.

JuininhoForever Posted on 21/7 13:23

re: Middlesbrough Urban Legends

Anyone got any memories from 'over the border'?

littleboro Posted on 21/7 13:46

re: Middlesbrough Urban Legends

Still makes me smile about this one. I remember walking through Albert Park in the late '70s during a sun blessed summer. As we got to the gates by Linthorpe Road, we heard the parky using his megaphone from the skating rink.

"Stop that now, son. Yes - you in the red top."

borolad259 Posted on 23/7 8:14

re: Middlesbrough Urban Legends

I can remember in Albert Park one day, and I only saw them once, a gang of young blokes all dressed as Droogs laid on the grass by the skating rink. Also, with no relevance to anything at all, wasn't there a curling track out the back of the skating rink? What the heck was that all about?

slaven Posted on 26/8 11:47

re: Middlesbrough Urban Legends

Gram - I remember him. What was in the Gazette about him?

zappa909 Posted on 26/8 12:21

re: Middlesbrough Urban Legends

Gram, is it the same lad, was he a pisshead, big fair hair, few tats? I met him a few times when I was working down Wilson St way, always friendly but quite intimidating due to his size and the fact he was pissed.

Couldn't believe it when I was watching TV a few years later and there he was clean as a whistle, sensible specs preaching about his new found love of all things Christian!

It just goes to show all the religion knockers out there that it does have a positive effect on some, nay many.

Good luck to the lad, I say, cos he was a mess.

Jastie Posted on 13/9 9:34

re: Middlesbrough Urban Legends

Does anyone know what happened to a lad called Mushy Pease who I worked with at BSC Lackenby in the '70s?, I think his first name was Ken. He'd be in his mid-fifties now, I suppose. He was one of the first hang-gliders in the country. He got into the British team after some trials at Saltburn when he lost control and was the first man ever to do a triple loop.

delgrapos Posted on 14/9 16:13

re: Middlesbrough Urban Legends

Whatever happened to that massive boat that bloke built in his back garden in Grove Hill behind the library? I heard he got it finished but not what happened after that?

TMG501 Posted on 14/9 17:44

re: Middlesbrough Urban Legends

delgrapos - he did get it finished eventually and it actually saw water, as far as I'm aware. How many years was it in his garden? Seemed like it was there forever. I used to go past it on me Chopper on the way to Devil's Bridge at Saltersgill. Great summers, they were.

Eddie_Catflap Posted on 14/9 17:54

re: Middlesbrough Urban Legends

The Devil's Bridge, why was it called that? Remember going, like.

gravy173 Posted on 14/9 19:53

re: Middlesbrough Urban Legends

It had a hoof print in one of the bricks underneath supposedly. I had a look when i was 10 and there were a few holes there but nothing really looked like a hoof.

Ima_urnt Posted on 14/9 21:19

re: Middlesbrough Urban Legends

I lived on Ashfield Avenue all the way through the '80s. I don't remember Jimmy Saville driving down there.

The boat that was built in the back of that garden on Sycamore Road was eventually finished and was put in the Tees at Stockton. Not sure if it's still there though.

neilteesside Posted on 15/9 11:20

re: Middlesbrough Urban Legends

I once had a pee in the Holgate. Am I a leg end?

swedish_meatball Posted on 15/9 13:16

re: Middlesbrough Urban Legends

Top thread!

I remember Tommy the Hammer who lived in a wash house.

Also Tongue Dog who lived in Whinney Banks. He was a dog whose tongue was disabled and was always flapping about.

delgrapos Posted on 17/9 16:10

re: Middlesbrough Urban Legends

There is a 'footprint' on Devil's Bridge but it is actually something to do with Ordnance Survey maps or something. I think it indicates the height above seawater, or beckwater in this case. Someone is supposed to have sold his soul to the devil there for a bottle of White Lightning or somat. There was "888" carved on there as well, long before Boro's sponsorship by the same.

nathan007 Posted on 19/9 18:00

re: Middlesbrough Urban Legends

Where did the old church from Eston cemetery go to?

borobadge Posted on 10/10 19:47

re: Middlesbrough Urban Legends

Shoorly the Yak is a leg-end... £11.25m!!!

collo1875 Posted on 10/10 23:05

re: Middlesbrough Urban Legends

neilteesside - you b*****d! I had a wet leg end that day.

Church from Eston was taken down brick by brick and rebuilt at Beamish. Why it went there, I've no idea.

TOPIC

MESSAGE

POST

REGISTER

Whatever happened to that massive boat that bloke built in his back garden in Grove Hill behind the library?

SteveGoldby Posted on 14/10 21:42

re: Middlesbrough Urban Legends

Remember Ray who used to have The Empire in its red and chrome days? He's a donkey farmer in Hartlepool now, no kidding.

Cogeur_le_Conq Posted on 14/10 22:43

re: Middlesbrough Urban Legends

I had plenty of stoppy-backs with Gay Ray (he wasn't gay).

He had his work cut out stopping us smoking 'wackie backie' in the back room and I witnessed him getting twatted on many an occasion.

He'll be better off with the donkeys.

SteveGoldby Posted on 14/10 23:02

re: Middlesbrough Urban Legends

Was it 'World In Action' who parked in a flat over the road and filmed the dealing going on?

d_robinson1970 Posted on 16/10 1:11

re: Middlesbrough Urban Legends

There's apparently still a load of mining vehicles down the Billingham mines.

boro365 Posted on 16/10 9:53

re: Middlesbrough Urban Legends

Was stood at the bus stop outside The Empire years ago when the Wilson twins (mentioned earlier) started going through the bin. It looked like they really enjoyed scranning someone's leftover Kentucky... Dirty b******s.

LTS_3 Posted on 16/10 16:20

re: Middlesbrough Urban Legends

Haven't touched this thread in a good few months, just read it from start to finish (whilst trying to avoid my boss seeing me). Been absolutely pissing myself at some of the stories/characters.

Being from Eston, I remember Pissy George and a couple of the other things on here.

We used to go to Eston Baths with the school in the late 1980s and I'm sure I heard once that there used to be diving boards in there but a lad broke his back/neck on the bottom of the pool so they got taken out.

One graffiti I always remembered was at the top of Jubilee Bank on a fence that belonged to nobody near the allotments that said "ENRON KILLS".

hicktonspenaltyrunup Posted on 16/10 18:53

re: Middlesbrough Urban Legends

Remember the boards at Eston Baths well. A top board that seemed about 300ft high when I was a nipper, and two lower springboards (I think). The lower one was definitely sprung. Great for somersaults and almost splitting your back open.

Most of the local baths had high boards when I was a lad, apart from Middlesbrough old and new baths.

Dolan_ov_Marton Posted on 16/10 21:22

re: Middlesbrough Urban Legends

We used to go to Berwick Hills Baths. They had 3 boards there and I remember the top one being really high (not as high as Stockton Baths though). I also remember going into the kids' pool to look through the windows at all the birds swimming. Happy Days.

ElvisRamone Posted on 23/10 13:21

re: Middlesbrough Urban Legends

I went on the top board at Stockton Baths years ago. I was like Mr Bean.

The_lawmaker Posted on 26/10 19:51

re: Middlesbrough Urban Legends

Anyone else remember when Ayresome Gardens was a cemetery? I remember them moving all the gravestones up against the walls.

ElvisRamone Posted on 26/10 20:28

re: Middlesbrough Urban Legends

Anyone remember the lad from Hemo/Coulby who thought he was a reincarnation of a German pilot? Apparently he used to come out in fluent German all the time. His story was in the Gazette.

nathan007 Posted on 26/10 20:53

re: Middlesbrough Urban Legends

Can anyone remember the cooling tower at ICI Wilton being demolished? What year was it and has anyone got a link to the film? I've looked everywhere but can't find one. I think it was about 1978 or 1979.

delgrapos Posted on 9/11 16:21

re: Middlesbrough Urban Legends

Heard a few people say that Boro's Emerson has a few kids around the area. Anyone know if there's any truth in that?

borodazzlers Posted on 9/11 16:32

re: Middlesbrough Urban Legends

I wouldn't be surprised. He used to love Redcar (for his sins) and spent a lot of time in Sharkey's.

Chapter Two
What Happened to Pogi's Head?

Teesside Urban Legends

TOPIC

MESSAGE

POST

REGISTER

Emanuel Pogatetz has counted to infinity. Twice.

TOPIC - What happened to Pogi's head?

Previous | Next | New Topic | Top Of Board

Designer_Boro Posted on 22/4 11:24

What happened to Pogi's head?

Anyone know?

Turner_86 Posted on 22/4 11:25

What happened to Pogi's head?

He got angry after the Villa game and just started punching himself in the face.

sean_boro Posted on 22/4 11:30

What happened to Pogi's head?

Emanuel Pogatetz's tears cure cancer. Too bad he has never cried. Ever.

JimmytheHill Posted on 22/4 11:31

What happened to Pogi's head?

Thought that was Chuck Norris!!!

JimmytheHill Posted on 22/4 11:34

What happened to Pogi's head?

Maybe Chuck punched him after finding out Pogi's tears were better than his!

sean_boro Posted on 22/4 11:34

What happened to Pogi's head?

When Emanuel Pogatetz has sex with a man, it is not because he is gay, but because he has run out of women.

sean_boro Posted on 22/4 11:37

What happened to Pogi's head?

Rather than being birthed like a normal child, Emanuel Pogatetz instead decided to punch his way out of his mother's womb. Shortly thereafter he grew a beard.

towz Posted on 22/4 11:44

What happened to Pogi's head?

I think he was head-butting a brick wall before kick off to psyche himself up.

sean_boro Posted on 22/4 11:47

What happened to Pogi's head?

Emanuel Pogatetz lost his virginity before his dad did.

the_broken_fridge Posted on 22/4 12:02

What happened to Pogi's head?

Pray that Pogatetz never decides to look directly at the sun. It's a stare down contest and the sun will lose, casting a perpetual night upon us all.

sean_boro Posted on 22/4 12:06

What happened to Pogi's head?

Emanuel Pogatetz uses ribbed condoms inside out, so he gets the pleasure.

JimmytheHill Posted on 22/4 12:09

What happened to Pogi's head?

This is the funniest thread in a while... keep 'em coming!!

Max_Headroom Posted on 22/4 12:09

What happened to Pogi's head?

Emanuel Pogatetz doesn't read books, he stares at them until he gets the answers he wants.

sean_boro Posted on 22/4 12:12

What happened to Pogi's head?

Emanuel Pogatetz eats Transformer toys in vehicle mode and poos them out transformed into a robot.

Max_Headroom Posted on 22/4 12:16

What happened to Pogi's head?

Emanuel Pogatetz once held a lion in a headlock for a fortnight.

ferencpuskas Posted on 22/4 12:19

What happened to Pogi's head?

Emanuel Pogatetz refuses to acknowledge the existence of the colour pink, instead calling it "very light red".

sean_boro Posted on 22/4 12:21

What happened to Pogi's head?

Emanuel Pogatetz doesn't consider it sex if the woman lives.

the_broken_fridge Posted on 22/4 12:26

What happened to Pogi's head?

Pogatetz only kicks you into next week so that he can kick you again. Harder.

Max_Headroom Posted on 22/4 12:29

What happened to Pogi's head?

Emanuel Pogatetz carved the Alps with his fists.

Max_Headroom Posted on 22/4 12:31

What happened to Pogi's head?

Britney Spears shaved her hair off after seeing Pogatetz's goal against the Mackems on YouTube.

Goal_Scrounger Posted on 22/4 12:31

What happened to Pogi's head?

Think of the most gorgeous woman you can imagine.

Pogi has had her.

Twice.

Today.

sean_boro Posted on 22/4 12:33

What happened to Pogi's head?

When Emanuel Pogatetz's wife burned the turkey one Christmas, he said, "Don't worry about it, honey," and went into his garden. He came back five minutes later with a live turkey, ate it whole, and when he threw it up a few seconds later, it was fully cooked and came with cranberry sauce. When his wife asked him how he had done it, he head-butted her.

Durham_Red Posted on 22/4 12:34

What happened to Pogi's head?

Pogi once arm wrestled Superman. The stipulations were the loser had to wear his underwear on the outside of his pants.

jd1973 Posted on 22/4 12:34

What happened to Pogi's head?

Emanuel Pogatetz saved the world from destruction by heading clear a seven mile wide asteroid that was heading for Earth. Whilst doing this, he held his breath for 17 minutes in deep space after taking off his helmet.

He is currently in training to volley the Earth an extra 10,000 miles away from the Sun to counteract global warming.

(This is classified information I received from a source at NASA).

Mattyk50 Posted on 22/4 12:35

What happened to Pogi's head?

Emanuel Pogatetz owns the greatest poker face of all-time. It helped him win the 1993 world series of poker despite him holding just a joker, a 2 of clubs, a 7 of spades, a green number 4 from Uno, and a Monopoly 'get out of jail free' card.

Mattyk50 Posted on 22/4 12:37

What happened to Pogi's head?

In an average living room there are 1,242 objects Emanuel Pogatetz could use to kill you, including the room itself.

Durham_Red Posted on 22/4 12:37

What happened to Pogi's head?

There are two hands that can beat a royal flush. Pogi's right hand and Pogi's left hand.

Mattyk50 Posted on 22/4 12:41

What happened to Pogi's head?

Emanuel Pogatetz has counted to infinity. Twice.

sean_boro Posted on 22/4 12:41

What happened to Pogi's head?

Emanuel Pogatetz has two speeds: walk and kill.

Coluka Posted on 22/4 12:42

What happened to Pogi's head?

Emanuel Pogatetz can eat three Shredded Wheat at breakfast.

And he can also knock the skin off rice pudding.

And when he walks down the street, heads turn. He only uses one hand to do it too.

Mattyk50 Posted on 22/4 12:43

What happened to Pogi's head?

There is no theory of evolution, just a list of creatures Emanuel Pogatetz allows to live.

sean_boro Posted on 22/4 12:44

What happened to Pogi's head?

When Emanuel Pogatetz goes to donate blood, he declines the syringe, and instead requests a handgun and a bucket.

Emanuel Pogatetz wasn't born, he was unleashed.

jd1973 Posted on 22/4 12:48

What happened to Pogi's head?

Emanuel Pogatetz is a time traveller and collects items and people for his own personal museum and theme park, whilst delivering his own sense of justice around the world.

So far he has:

Killed off the dinosaurs.
Was on the Grassy Knoll.
Arranged for Fat Freddie to take control of Newcastle.
Fathered the next King of England.
Lord Lucan, Glenn Miller, Shergar, Elvis, the Colossus of Rhodes, El Dorado and Atlantis are in his museum.

Michael_Debeve Posted on 22/4 12:53

What happened to Pogi's head?

MacGyver can build an airplane out of gum and paper clips, but Emanuel Pogatetz can kill him and take it.

flabby66 Posted on 22/4 12:54

What happened to Pogi's head?

Mohammed moved the mountain because Pogi instructed him to do so.

Michael_Debeve Posted on 22/4 12:55

What happened to Pogi's head?

Emanuel Pogatetz does not sleep. He waits.

Durham_Red Posted on 22/4 12:58

What happened to Pogi's head?

Emanuel Pogatetz wasn't born, he was unleashed.

Michael_Debeve Posted on 22/4 13:03

What happened to Pogi's head?

A study showed the leading causes of death in Austria are: 1. Heart disease, 2. Emanuel Pogatetz. 3. Cancer.

tacker Posted on 22/4 13:20

What happened to Pogi's head?

And Thread of the Year goes to...

sean_boro Posted on 22/4 13:50

What happened to Pogi's head?

Emanuel Pogatetz sold his soul to the Devil for his rugged good looks and unparalleled martial arts ability. Shortly after the transaction was finalised, Pogga roundhouse kicked the Devil in the face and took his soul back. The Devil, who appreciates irony, couldn't stay mad and admitted he should have seen it coming. They now play poker every Tuesday.

Michael_Debeve Posted on 22/4 14:07

What happened to Pogi's head?

Emanuel Pogatetz never did homework when he was a kid. The teachers knew better than to assign Emanuel Pogatetz homework.

Michael_Debeve Posted on 22/4 14:08

What happened to Pogi's head?

The secret to eternal life is an IOU note from Emanuel Pogatetz.

Michael_Debeve Posted on 22/4 14:10

What happened to Pogi's head?

Emanuel Pogatetz can take a number 2 standing up.

Michael_Debeve Posted on 22/4 14:10

What happened to Pogi's head?

It is impossible to be raped by Emanuel Pogatetz because that would mean you did not want it to happen.

shortandbald Posted on 22/4 14:15

What happened to Pogi's head?

When the new authorities in Graz, Austria, built their new stadium they wanted to name it The Emanuel Pogatetz Stadium. Having seen the plans Emanuel Pogatetz declined, saying the place looked too girly and that it should be named after one of Austria's more effeminate celebrities...

Mr_Incident Posted on 22/4 14:23

What happened to Pogi's head?

Emanuel Pogatetz may contain traces of nuts.

Durham_Red Posted on 22/4 14:26

What happened to Pogi's head?

Pogi makes onions cry.

Michael_Debeve Posted on 22/4 14:29

What happened to Pogi's head?

The truth is, Emanuel Pogatetz has been dead for over a thousand years... but the Grim Reaper is too scared to tell him.

shortandbald Posted on 22/4 14:36

What happened to Pogi's head?

On the First Day Pog created the Earth, and he saw what he had done and he was pleased.

The_Commisar Posted on 22/4 14:42

What happened to Pogi's head?

On a Sunday Emanuel Pogatetz helps out at Teesside Airport by kick starting the 747s.

Max_Headroom Posted on 22/4 14:42

What happened to Pogi's head?

Emanuel Pogatetz is the reason aliens haven't invaded and enslaved the Earth yet.

Michael_Debeve Posted on 22/4 14:48

What happened to Pogi's head?

Emanuel Pogatetz screams his own name during sex.

Michael_Debeve Posted on 22/4 14:50

What happened to Pogi's head?

Emanuel Pogatetz was born with an evil twin but as soon as they exited the womb, Emanuel Pogatetz killed his twin with a powerful head-butt to the chest and claimed, "There can only be one Mad Dog."

Mr_Incident Posted on 22/4 14:52

What happened to Pogi's head?

When he looks at himself in a mirror, he sees Michael Heseltine, naked.

scoea Posted on 22/4 14:58

What happened to Pogi's head?

Pogatetz signs his contracts in his own blood, which is both cold and black.

shortandbald Posted on 22/4 15:18

What happened to Pogi's head?

There is very little crime in Austria because parents tell their kids when they are young that if they are naughty Emanuel Pogatetz will come and get them.

danboro0902 Posted on 22/4 15:23

What happened to Pogi's head?

Great thread. I'll give it a whirl...

Pogatetz purposely breaks his own bones so when fully healed they become stronger.

Nuge Posted on 22/4 15:47

What happened to Pogi's head?

Every year, towards the end of December, Emanuel Pogatetz dresses in a red and white costume and flies around the world delivering gifts to the world's children.

Manu was frustrated by the Old Man's bullshit when he received cinders one year. He has been extinguished.

shortandbald Posted on 22/4 15:49

What happened to Pogi's head?

That particular year he had Cinders, both her sisters and the prince too for good measure.

Michael_Debeve Posted on 22/4 16:13

What happened to Pogi's head?

Emanuel Pogatetz finished The Never Ending Story. Twice.

Michael_Debeve Posted on 22/4 16:13

What happened to Pogi's head?

Emanuel Pogatetz took a maths test and put down "violence" for every answer and got a perfect score. Emanuel Pogatetz solves all his problems with violence.

XXLshirts_fit_all Posted on 22/4 16:17

What happened to Pogi's head?

At a very young age Pogi became one of Maggie Thatcher's best advisors. At a time when she was considering becoming more compassionate, he told her to stand firm and not turn. He also saw an opportunity whereby he got her to lay waste to a large area of land near the Tees and give financial incentives to a young haulier in the area.

He instructed that an alter should be built where he could grow up and display himself as the greatest centre back ever and be worshipped by a small but very difficult to please population and forever be remembered as such.

It only went wrong when Woody turned up!

Disclaimer - some of the above is wrong, he isn't the greatest centre back Boro have ever had, Mogga is!

BoroMutt Posted on 22/4 16:17

What happened to Pogi's head?

Emanuel Pogatetz doesn't have nipples; he has handholds for the ladies to grab hold of.

tacker Posted on 22/4 16:38

What happened to Pogi's head?

Emanuel Pogatetz's brain works just like that of the 'Terminator'. When he sees an opponent, the small microchip placed in the back of his head gives him a choice of which death he will use on said opponent.

More often than not, his choice is usually 'decapitate'.

Michael_Debeve Posted on 22/4 16:51

What happened to Pogi's head?

Emanuel Pogatetz answered 50 Cent's 21 Questions with one answer, a swift head-butt to the chest.

Michael_Debeve Posted on 22/4 16:54

What happened to Pogi's head?

Emanuel Pogatetz does not own a house, he walks into random houses and people move.

`Michael_Debeve Posted on 22/4 17:08

What happened to Pogi's head?

Emanuel Pogatetz's calendar goes straight from March 31st to April 2nd. Nobody fools Mad Dog.

Michael_Debeve Posted on 22/4 17:10

What happened to Pogi's head?

Once Mad Dog pops, he CAN stop.

Take that, Pringles.

The_Commisar Posted on 22/4 17:22

What happened to Pogi's head?

Mad Dog uses The Stig as his bitch.

sean_boro Posted on 22/4 18:43

What happened to Pogi's head?

Most people put their trousers on one leg at a time. Emanuel Pogatetz does both legs at once.

Freddy_Guarin Posted on 22/4 18:50

What happened to Pogi's head?

Emanuel Pogatetz eats wasps for breakfast.

TOPIC

MESSAGE

POST

REGISTER

Emanuel Pogatetz's calendar goes straight from March 31st to April 2nd. Nobody fools Mad Dog.

simmo649 Posted on 22/4 19:25

What happened to Pogi's head?

Superman wears Pogatetz pyjamas.

Beelzeebub Posted on 22/4 19:34

What happened to Pogi's head?

Chuck Norris has to ask for Emanuel Pogatetz's permission to go to the toilet.

micky_k86 Posted on 22/4 19:58

What happened to Pogi's head?

Pogatetz once shot down a plane by looking into the sky, pointing his index finger at it and saying "bang".

micky_k86 Posted on 22/4 20:02

What happened to Pogi's head?

Pogatetz is suing C5, claiming "Law and Order" are trademarked names for his left and right legs.

johnsmithsno2 Posted on 22/4 20:26

What happened to Pogi's head?

'Manuel' labour was actually named after Pogatetz.

ferencpuskas Posted on 22/4 20:34

What happened to Pogi's head?

Emanuel Pogatetz's sperm are the size of tadpoles.

southstandstud86 Posted on 22/4 20:39

What happened to Pogi's head?

Some kids piss in the snow, Emanuel Pogatetz pisses into concrete.

dooderooni Posted on 22/4 20:42

What happened to Pogi's head?

Emanuel Pogatetz has a 10 star NCAP rating.

dooderooni Posted on 22/4 20:46

What happened to Pogi's head?

As a small child, Pogo went to Ireland on a family holiday.

Whilst sat in a quiet country pub, the hungry young Mad Dog confessed that "he could eat a horse."

Police are still looking for Shergar to this day.

sean_boro Posted on 22/4 20:46

What happened to Pogi's head?

That's surely too safe for the Pogmonster.

dooderooni Posted on 22/4 20:48

What happened to Pogi's head?

Sean, you should see the state of the concrete blocks when he crashes into them at 30mph and they enter his 'crumple zone'.

moxzin87 Posted on 22/4 20:50

What happened to Pogi's head?

When Emanuel Pogatetz sends in his taxes, he sends blank forms and includes only a picture of himself, crouched and ready to attack. Pogatetz has never had to pay taxes.

dooderooni Posted on 22/4 20:52

What happened to Pogi's head?

Cat's eyes look the other way when Manu burns rubber in the Pogmobile.

scoea Posted on 22/4 20:52

What happened to Pogi's head?

Pogatetz is both a rock and a hard place.

moxzin87 Posted on 22/4 20:54

What happened to Pogi's head?

Pogatetz doesn't wear a watch; HE decides what time it is.

TheWolfMansWhiskers Posted on 22/4 20:57

What happened to Pogi's head?

Solar flares are the effects of Emanuel Pogatetz using the sun as a punch bag when training for the UFC. He is also credited with punching the universe and creating black holes.

SmogOverOrmesby Posted on 22/4 20:58

What happened to Pogi's head?

When the bogeyman goes to bed, he checks his closet for Pogatetz.

moxzin87 Posted on 22/4 21:02

What happened to Pogi's head?

Pogatetz doesn't do press ups, he pushes the world down.

bodysausage Posted on 22/4 21:05

What happened to Pogi's head?

I think he must have collided with a Manchester United player.

scoea Posted on 22/4 21:07

What happened to Pogi's head?

Pogatetz doesn't shave his head. His skin just stops letting the hair through.

TheBoroBoss61 Posted on 22/4 22:58

What happened to Pogi's head?

A census taker tried to test Pogatetz once. He ate his liver with fava beans and a nice Chianti.

jd1973 Posted on 22/4 23:17

What happened to Pogi's head?

Emanuel Pogatetz decides every day whether the Sun rises or not.

Be afraid, very afraid.

10hazza Posted on 22/4 23:37

What happened to Pogi's head?

There's no such thing as tornadoes, Pogatetz just doesn't like trailer parks.

10hazza Posted on 22/4 23:58

What happened to Pogi's head?

Once, the Romans crossed Pogatetz... once.

shortandbald Posted on 23/4 0:02

What happened to Pogi's head?

Yeah, and he got his revenge by pushing Venice a few feet underwater.

10hazza Posted on 23/4 0:04

What happened to Pogi's head?

Great white whales worldwide invested in cages since Pogatetz decided to go for a swim.

micky_k86 Posted on 23/4 0:07

What happened to Pogi's head?

There is no such thing as performance enhancing drugs, only people Pogi has breathed on.

timfrancoll Posted on 23/4 0:21

What happened to Pogi's head?

Mad Dog has left more back doors swinging off their hinges than the drug squad.

sean_boro Posted on 23/4 10:08

What happened to Pogi's head?

Outer space exists because it is afraid to be on the same planet as Emanuel Pogatetz.

tacker Posted on 23/4 10:36

What happened to Pogi's head?

However, Pogatetz has a feminine side which he showed when directing and starring in the mid-'90s cheese-tastic porn series 'Emmanuelle'. Obviously named after him, but with a feminine twist.

His penis is huge.

BoroTommo Posted on 23/4 11:22

What happened to Pogi's head?

Pogatetz is constantly on standby, employed by the Northern Hemisphere to counteract THAT situation when 1 billion Chinamen jump up at the exact same time.

flabby66 Posted on 23/4 11:35

What happened to Pogi's head?

Pogi isn't hung like a horse, horses are hung like Pogi.

London_Boro Posted on 23/4 11:52

What happened to Pogi's head?

Pogatetz does not have an alarm clock, he keeps Keith Moon, Jimi Hendrix and Jim Morrison by his bedside to wake him up with a rendition of 'Gonna Fly Now' from Rocky every morning at 8:30 am.

TheBoroBoss61 Posted on 23/4 11:53

What happened to Pogi's head?

Emanuel Pogatetz is the man Keyser Soze fears.

dooderooni Posted on 23/4 11:57

What happened to Pogi's head?

Pogi penned the lyrics to 'Bad' as a laugh but when Michael Jackson found out who he'd nicked the song from he suddenly developed a 'skin complaint'!

danboro0902 Posted on 23/4 12:55

What happened to Pogi's head?

It is all revealed in an interview on the MFC website... where only Pogatetz asks the questions!

Max_Headroom Posted on 23/4 13:40

What happened to Pogi's head?

Pogatetz's carbon footprint is the Grand Canyon.

XXLshirts_fit_all Posted on 23/4 13:55

What happened to Pogi's head?

Everyone thought that life's building block was carbon, when in fact carbon is derived from Pogi's sweat! Fact!!

Chris_Riggots_Head Posted on 23/4 13:59

What happened to Pogi's head?

Emanuel Pogatetz is the REAL Keyser Soze.

Michael_Debeve Posted on 23/4 14:50

What happened to Pogi's head?

There are no such things as lesbians. Just women who haven't met Emanuel Pogatetz.

shortandbald Posted on 23/4 15:14

What happened to Pogi's head?

Emanuel Pogatetz IS Austria's nuclear deterrent.

borotiger Posted on 23/4 17:41

What happened to Pogi's head?

I can't believe nobody knows what happened to Pogi's head. He met Jack Bauer at Old Trafford on Saturday... there was a meeting of the minds.

Pogi's summer job is... Jack Bauer's body double... 24/7.

TOPIC

MESSAGE

POST

REGISTER

Pogi isn't hung like a horse, horses are hung like Pogi.

The_Commisar Posted on 23/4 17:54

What happened to Pogi's head?

Nothing can kill Captain Scarlet.

Then again… he hasn't met the Pog yet.

Mat_Evans Posted on 23/4 17:54

What happened to Pogi's head?

Once a grizzly bear threatened to eat Emanuel Pogatetz. Poga showed the bear his fist and the bear proceeded to eat himself, because it would be the less painful way to die.

Mat_Evans Posted on 23/4 17:56

What happened to Pogi's head?

Emanuel Pogatetz CAN touch MC Hammer.

Mat_Evans Posted on 23/4 17:57

What happened to Pogi's head?

Emanuel Pogatetz drinks napalm to quell his heartburn.

tommy_wheelie Posted on 23/4 18:39

What happened to Pogi's head?

Pogi is Luke Skywalker's real father.

KrivoyRog Posted on 23/4 19:43

What happened to Pogi's head?

Pogatetz fears nowt, 'cept for one thing.

Mrs Pogatetz.

thescruffyboy Posted on 24/4 13:27

What happened to Pogi's head?

Emanuel Pogatetz ate my parents.

Nisko Posted on 24/4 13:50

What happened to Pogi's head?

Jack Bauer takes 24 hours to stop terrorists. Emanuel Pogatetz took over the world in 24 minutes, but he got bored of it and decided to give it back.

Wakey_Boro_Fan Posted on 24/4 13:56

What happened to Pogi's head?

Emanuel Pogatetz doesn't believe in wasting money on carpets. His floor is lined with broken glass from the bottles of beer he uses to bathe in. He walks on it bare foot.

BoroPigeon Posted on 25/4 0:49

What happened to Pogi's head?

In the beginning was the word - and the word was Pog.

A_New_Era Posted on 26/4 15:36

What happened to Pogi's head?

Jonathan Woodgate signed his new contract as he wanted four more years in the showers with Emanuel Pogatetz. Everyone wants showers with Emanuel Pogatetz.

Max_Headroom Posted on 26/4 15:38

What happened to Pogi's head?

George Boateng ate one of Pogatetz's McCoys crisps at lunch while the man wasn't looking and now he is making an escape before Pogi finds out. Once Malcolm Christie took a bite out of Pogi's Greggs sausage roll. When Pogi found out he broke his legs and threw him in a dungeon for a year - hence the injuries and beard.

BoroTommo Posted on 26/4 15:41

What happened to Pogi's head?

Pogatetz can rip a whole Yellow Pages in half with one hand. The Chinese Yellow Pages!

shaun_84 Posted on 26/4 16:10

What happened to Pogi's head?

In fact, Pogatetz once ate China, and stopped at Thailand for seconds.

UndercoverElephant Posted on 26/4 16:25

What happened to Pogi's head?

Emanuel Pogatetz was not born, he was sculpted out of granite by the finest craftsmen. As they struck the last blow with a hammer and chisel, a bolt of lightning was seen to strike the granite man-beast, giving him life. His first act upon gaining life was to rip out the eyes of said craftsmen.

There can be only one Pog.

craigmfc Posted on 26/4 16:30

What happened to Pogi's head?

Emanuel Pogatetz ate my dog and shagged my missus.

samglish Posted on 26/4 16:42

What happened to Pogi's head?

Pogatetz is what Willis was talking about.

shortandbald Posted on 26/4 16:44

What happened to Pogi's head?

Emanuel Pogatetz ate Freddie Starr's Hamster.

key_toenail Posted on 26/4 16:50

What happened to Pogi's head?

Emanuel Pogatetz pulls his eyes out of his sockets and looks round corners with them in his hand when spying on people.

Max_Headroom Posted on 26/4 16:54

What happened to Pogi's head?

Emanuel Pogatetz is 'the something down there' in Trap Door.

richardofyork Posted on 26/4 18:12

What happened to Pogi's head?

Emanuel Pogatetz is the Eighth Deadly Sin.

willie_shafter2 Posted on 26/4 18:16

What happened to Pogi's head?

Emanuel Pogatetz once had a fight with Ben Grimm (Fantastic 4). Now Emanuel Pogatetz has a lovely rockery in his back garden.

LLPJ Posted on 26/4 18:25

What happened to Pogi's head?

You can get better than a Kwik Fit Fitter, Pogi is the man to trust.

UndercoverElephant Posted on 27/4 9:17

What happened to Pogi's head?

Emanuel Pogatetz cannot only eat three Shredded Wheat, but some mornings has a fourth.

Mat_Evans Posted on 30/4 17:03

What happened to Pogi's head?

Pogatetz is the reason Lord Lucan disappeared.

YouAreBoateng7 Posted on 30/4 17:30

What happened to Pogi's head?

Pogatetz killed the Grim Reaper with one bat.

scoea Posted on 30/4 18:00

What happened to Pogi's head?

Pogatetz does not eat. He devours.

TOPIC

MESSAGE

POST

REGISTER

In fine print on the last page of the Guinness Book of World Records, it notes that all world records are held by Emanuel Pogatetz and those listed in the book are simply the closest anyone else has ever gotten.

Cyrus2006 Posted on 30/4 19:03

What happened to Pogi's head?

There are no disabled people. Only people who have met Emanuel Pogatetz.

LLPJ Posted on 30/4 19:08

What happened to Pogi's head?

Pogatetz scores 190 every time he plays darts.

slightlymad22 Posted on 30/4 19:36

What happened to Pogi's head?

Pogi has already been to Mars; that's why there are no signs of life there.

Captain_Moonlight Posted on 30/4 19:37

What happened to Pogi's head?

"On the First Day Pog created the Earth, and he saw what he had done and he was pleased."

"On the Second Day he created light." He did all the First Day's work IN THE DARK.

slightlymad22 Posted on 30/4 19:39

What happened to Pogi's head?

Pogi is 1/8th Cherokee. This has nothing to do with ancestry, the man ate a f***ing Indian.

In fine print on the last page of the Guinness Book of World Records, it notes that all world records are held by Emanuel Pogatetz and those listed in the book are simply the closest anyone else has ever gotten.

The Great Wall of China was originally created to keep Emanuel Pogatetz out. It failed miserably.

Emanuel Pogatetz made Ellen DeGeneres straight.

Captain_Moonlight Posted on 30/4 19:41

What happened to Pogi's head?

John McClane from Die Hard is based upon Pogi, as is He-Man and Captain Ivan Drago from Rocky IV, who didn't get beaten in the original script.

Captain_Moonlight Posted on 30/4 19:47

What happened to Pogi's head?

Pogi can eat two whole packets of crackers without a drink or breath.

slightlymad22 Posted on 30/4 19:49

What happened to Pogi's head?

Mad Dog sent Jesus a birthday card on December 25th and it wasn't Jesus' birthday. Jesus was too scared to correct Mad Dog and to this day December 25th is known as Jesus' birthday.

Mad Dog once broke the land speed record on a bicycle that was missing its chain and the back tyre.

If Pogi is late, time better slow the f*** down.

A disabled parking sign does not signify that this spot is for disabled people. It is actually a warning that the spot belongs to Emanuel Pogatetz and that you will be handicapped if you park there.

Mad Dog ordered a Big Mac at Burger King, and got one.

If paper beats rock, rock beats scissors, and scissors beats paper, what beats all three at the same time? Answer: Emanuel Pogatetz.

Although it is not common knowledge, there are actually three sides to the Force: the light side, the dark side and Emanuel Pogatetz.

When Emanuel Pogatetz was denied a Bacon McMuffin at McDonalds because it was 10:35, he kicked the store so hard it became a KFC.

slightlymad22 Posted on 30/4 20:00

What happened to Pogi's head?

If you want a list of Mad Dog's enemies, just check the extinct species list.

One time while sparring with Wolverine, Mad Dog accidentally lost his left testicle. You might be familiar with it to this very day by its technical term: Jupiter.

Mad Dog once walked down the street with a massive erection. There were no survivors.

When you open a can of whupass, Mad Dog jumps out.

Mad Dog once ate three 72 oz. steaks in one hour. He spent the first 45 minutes having sex with his waitress.

Aliens do exist. They're just waiting for Mad Dog to die before they attack.

There are no races, only countries of people Mad Dog has beaten to different shades of black and blue.

The show Survivor had the original premise of putting people on an island with Emanuel Pogatetz. There were no survivors and the pilot episode tape has been burned.

Mad Dog is the reason why Wally is hiding.

Emanuel Pogatetz can often be seen wearing white socks with black shoes and black pants. No one has DARED call him on it. Ever.

The last man who made eye contact with Emanuel Pogatetz was Ray Charles.

slightlymad22 Posted on 30/4 20:14

What happened to Pogi's head?

Mad Dog beat a wall at tennis. A f***ing WALL.

Mad Dog is so scary that his hair is afraid to grow.

Mad Dog never takes showers. Instead, whenever he's dirty, he points to himself and shouts, "CLEAN!"

Mad Dog scared the black out of Michael Jackson.

Emanuel Pogatetz once won the Olympics. All of them.

A diamond is the hardest element found on Earth. A scientist will swear to that fact, until - in the very near future - he meets the wrong end of Mad Dog's fist.

Mad Dog has scared the s**t out of so many players over his brilliant life that most club doctors now classify him as a laxative.

He was hired for the role of Mason Dixon in Rocky Balboa. However, while filming the big fight scene, Mad Dog punched Sylvester Stallone so hard, Sly spoke clearly for a week. He lost interest when he found out he wasn't really going to beat anyone up.

To make sure he was born tough, Mad Dog's mother would punch her womb between shots of vodka.

Chuck Norris and Vin Diesel are actually the names Mad Dog has given to his testicles. The ability of his balls to make movies has saved Mad Dog the bother of earning a living himself for the past 20 years. You can find him having a kick about on a Saturday at the Riverside Stadium to cure the boredom.

paul_yarm_red Posted on 30/4 22:24

What happened to Pogi's head?

Al Gore has recently admitted that all that piffle about global warming is actually attributed to Emanuel Pogatetz's rage.

Max_Headroom Posted on 1/5 16:17

What happened to Pogi's head?

Who forgot to tell the ref that goals by Pogatetz count double at the weekend? Poggy will now hunt down the man in black. Be afraid.

Winston_Spangler Posted on 1/5 16:39

What happened to Pogi's head?

Emanuel Pogatetz is harder than my dad.

Slasher1975 Posted on 1/5 16:42

What happened to Pogi's head?

Emanuel Pogatetz is everyone's dad.

Mat_Evans Posted on 1/5 16:49

What happened to Pogi's head?

Pogatetz's best round of golf is 17.

gibson Posted on 1/5 16:57

What happened to Pogi's head?

Pogi is used in the Highlands, in head-butting contests with stags, to see if they are 'up for it.'

salt_boro Posted on 1/5 17:18

What happened to Pogi's head?

Kevin Davies will check Pog's career from now on and will become injured the week before each of the fixtures when he is to face the Boro unless Pog is suspended.

the_arc Posted on 1/5 17:58

What happened to Pogi's head?

Mad Dogatetz slams shut revolving doors!

Michael_Debeve Posted on 7/5 15:15

What happened to Pogi's head?

Emanuel Pogatetz is that good, that not even Freddy Shepherd would sack him and the Jawdees wouldn't dare to boo him.

Nuge Posted on 25/5 19:49

What happened to Pogi's head?

Manu Pogatetz knows where Wally is at all times.

the_broken_fridge Posted on 26/5 15:14

What happened to Pogi's head?

Mad Dog once won a game of Connect 4 in three moves.

theduke615 Posted on 26/5 19:08

What happened to Pogi's head?

Emanuel Pogatetz is so hard, Jonathan Woodgate has hired him as his new bodyguard.

dtooth89 Posted on 3/6 0:36

What happened to Pogi's head?

Pogatetz CAN believe it's not butter!

dtooth89 Posted on 3/6 0:38

What happened to Pogi's head?

The question 'what happens when an unstoppable force meets an immovable object' was answered when Pogatetz punched himself in the face to psyche himself up before a match!

EDDIE62 Posted on 19/6 17:27

What happened to Pogi's head?

Pogatetz can do a wheelie on a unicycle.

EIO_EIO_EIO Posted on 19/6 17:34

What happened to Pogi's head?

Emanuel Pogatetz can eat a FULL pork parmo + salad + chips!

The_Commisar Posted on 19/6 17:35

What happened to Pogi's head?

Viagra takes Pogatetz when it needs to get a stiffy.

LLPJ Posted on 19/6 17:36

What happened to Pogi's head?

The Devil has got those horns on his head 'cos Pogatetz shoved his last pitchfork that far up his ass.

Max_Headroom Posted on 19/6 17:36

What happened to Pogi's head?

It pleases Emanuel Pogatetz that this thread has been hoofed.

Emanuel Pogatetz is the FMTTM Admin.

parmoandstella Posted on 19/6 17:38

What happened to Pogi's head?

Poggy was the first man on the Moon, but he became sick of the fuss so he said it was some other bloke.

LLPJ Posted on 19/6 17:41

What happened to Pogi's head?

Pogatetz is the meaning of life, and also the cause of death.

parmoandstella Posted on 19/6 17:45

What happened to Pogi's head?

Christmas is not to celebrate the birth of Jesus Christ, it is to celebrate the birth of Emanuel Pogatetz.

boro_lad_1991 Posted on 19/6 18:00

What happened to Pogi's head?

If Pogi jumps in the water, he does not get wet - the water gets Pogatetzed.

Mr_Unsavoury Posted on 19/6 18:20

What happened to Pogi's head?

Emanuel Pogatetz does not eat steak, he eats whole limbs.

ravastwin Posted on 19/6 18:22

What happened to Pogi's head?

A kid once said to the Pog "bet you can't eat a Fruit Pastille without chewing it". At that, he ate the kid then the Fruit Pastille factory. Nobody dares the Pog!

youngbill Posted on 19/6 18:26

What happened to Pogi's head?

Pogi's toenail clippings are used to drill into diamonds.

Frankieq Posted on 19/6 19:35

What happened to Pogi's head?

Pogi hoofs threads subconsciously.

parmoandstella Posted on 19/6 23:40

What happened to Pogi's head?

History is wrong... it was not Adam and Eve... it was Emanuel Pogatetz.

BoroTommo Posted on 4/7 15:44

What happened to Pogi's head?

Robert Huth today confirmed, "I am looking forward to the new season, and will be proud to sit on the bench whilst my hero Manu Pogatetz plays harder, faster and better than me. He told me to say that."

Michael_Debeve Posted on 4/7 15:55

What happened to Pogi's head?

Pogatetz is good.

TheYak87 Posted on 6/7 11:39

What happened to Pogi's head?

Emanuel Pogatetz donates blood to the Red Cross, just not his own.

scobba Posted on 6/7 13:30

What happened to Pogi's head?

Pogi sleeps with a light on. Not because he's scared of the dark but because the dark is scared of him.

TOPIC

MESSAGE

POST

REGISTER

If Pogi jumps in the water, he does not get wet - the water gets Pogatetzed.

thedoors Posted on 21/7 14:28

What happened to Pogi's head?

Pogatetz = mass x acceleration.

downing_4_england Posted on 21/7 14:38

What happened to Pogi's head?

Jesus Christ did not walk on water. Pogatetz roundhouse kicked him across a lake.

shortandbald Posted on 13/8 0:46

What happened to Pogi's head?

Emanuel Pogatetz doesn't like this board any more...

IT HAS TO GO.

Mat_Evans Posted on 13/8 0:49

What happened to Pogi's head?

This is my favourite ever Fly Me post... but if it wasn't, Pog would drive round my house and actually cut off my right index finger and use it to type in that it WAS my favourite ever thread... God bless Manu Pogatetz!

shortandbald Posted on 13/8 0:54

What happened to Pogi's head?

Mine too, Matt. That's why I hoofed it for old time's sake. Plus someone had to otherwise the repercussions if it hadn't, when Pogi found out, didn't bear thinking about. By doing it myself I hope to guarantee immunity from Pogi's wrath come Judgement Day.

Mat_Evans Posted on 13/8 0:58

What happened to Pogi's head?

shortandbald, there's no such thing as "immunity from Pogi's wrath."

shortandbald Posted on 13/8 1:00

What happened to Pogi's head?

No, but by staying on his good side I'm hoping for a quick and painless end.

Full_Clip Posted on 13/8 9:05

What happened to Pogi's head?

Pogi went to "The running of the bulls" and the bulls ran the other way.

Some_Strange_Gadgie Posted on 13/8 9:13

What happened to Pogi's head?

Pogi's sperm count is so high, women have to chew before they can swallow.

tmcadam Posted on 18/9 19:13

What happened to Pogi's head?

There is no such thing as email, it gets to Pogi and he runs it to the other person.

tmcadam Posted on 18/9 19:14

What happened to Pogi's head?

He once kicked a football so hard, the leather ripped off and killed a goat six miles away.

tmcadam Posted on 18/9 19:18

What happened to Pogi's head?

Pogi does not drive, he imagines he is somewhere else and the laws of existence put him there out of fear.

wayvvee_dayvee Posted on 18/9 19:24

What happened to Pogi's head?

The Bermuda Triangle used to be a square but Pogi kicked a corner off it.

When the bogeyman goes to sleep at night he checks under the bed for Pogi.

He's that fast he can run around the Earth and rabbit punch himself.

tmcadam Posted on 18/9 19:30

What happened to Pogi's head?

Pogatetz destroyed China once, as he resents anything smaller than his penis. He then rebuilt it as he found something else smaller. We once had two suns...

Boro_Owl Posted on 18/9 19:35

What happened to Pogi's head?

Pogatetz once lost both his legs. He walked it off.

Boro_Owl Posted on 18/9 20:01

What happened to Pogi's head?

Pogatetz cuts diamonds with his little finger. Then he eats them.

Boro_Owl Posted on 18/9 20:06

What happened to Pogi's head?

In Star Wars, fear leads to anger, anger leads to hate and hate leads to Emanuel Pogatetz.

Johnny_Briggs Posted on 18/9 20:07

What happened to Pogi's head?

Pogi doesn't understand why some doors say "pull". All doors open when pushed.

Boro_Owl Posted on 18/9 20:22

What happened to Pogi's head?

The Flash once challenged Mad Dog to a race. Mad Dog kicked his head off.

parmoandstella Posted on 24/10 21:55

What happened to Pogi's head?

The world's ice isn't melting because of global warming, it is trying to get away from Emanuel Pogatetz.

parmoandstella Posted on 24/10 21:59

What happened to Pogi's head?

Pogi doesn't have to go to the toilet, the toilet has to go to Emanuel Pogatetz.

Chapter Three
The Enigma of Allens West

Teesside Urban Legends

TOPIC

MESSAGE

POST

REGISTER

TOPIC - The Enigma of Allens West

Previous | Next | New Topic | Top Of Board

Who was Allen
and what was
he west of? Is
it Mr Allen
West's own
private
station?

uncle_harry Posted on 21/4 18:17

The Enigma of Allens West

I went past it on the train. No one ever gets on or off. Is there an Allens East, North or South. Who was Allen and what was he west of? Is it Mr Allen West's own private station?

sossage Posted on 21/4 18:18

re: The Enigma of Allens West

There is a restaurant in Connecticut called Allen's East. Does that help?

Archie_Stanton1 Posted on 21/4 18:19

re: The Enigma of Allens West

It was built in the '60s for the old Royal Navy stores depot, which was next to it. That closed about 10 years ago and is now a logistics centre. I presume the station survives to serve the part of Eaglescliffe that's near it. I've no idea where the name comes from though.

dicky_rooks Posted on 21/4 18:43

re: The Enigma of Allens West

Is it the same guy who invented the key?

Derby_Red Posted on 21/4 19:02

re: The Enigma of Allens West

And furthermore, Allens West fact spotters, I once read that the ticket for Allens West to Eaglescliffe (a journey of yards, rather than miles) is the most expensive ticket per mile on the rail network. Get that, eh?

And yes, it was built as a halt for the Royal Navy depot, I think. Dunno where all the other Allens are though...

Mind you, I think the bigger Enigma is Teesside Airport Station. The amount of trains that used to not stop there, thus not providing a useful service just after a flight had landed was a bit silly. Was it one of those ploys to get the halt shut? (Why?)

And while we're at it, Eaglescliffe is called Eaglescliffe and not Egglescliffe like the nearby village coz when the railway came they spelt Egglescliffe Junction wrong.

Derby_Red Posted on 21/4 19:06

re: The Enigma of Allens West

And if that's not a thread killer, I don't know what is...

OPEO Posted on 21/4 19:22

re: The Enigma of Allens West

Threads on here are made of hardy matter and are not that easy to kill off! Allen was a near neighbour of Fred the landscape gardener, but that's another story.

JoeLaidlaw Posted on 21/4 19:30

re: The Enigma of Allens West

Who had a brother called John, who was a fisherman.

jamesiegang Posted on 21/4 19:34

re: The Enigma of Allens West

What about Uncle Bruce, who played Batman on telly?

Valer Posted on 21/4 19:34

re: The Enigma of Allens West

"And while we're at it, Eaglescliffe is called Eaglescliffe and not Egglescliffe like the nearby village coz when the railway came they spelt Egglescliffe Junction wrong. Ner."

Why is the secondary school called Egglescliffe when it's nowhere near the village?

littlejimmy Posted on 21/4 19:37

re: The Enigma of Allens West

I've always wanted to change the second "L" to an "I" in order to confuse any invading interstellar warriors who may choose to use the great British rail network. Who knows what they'd make of Transpennine Express coffee.

speckyget Posted on 21/4 19:40

re: The Enigma of Allens West

Allens West Fact Spotters. I'm off to start a band. That's all there is to it.

stuartd75 Posted on 21/4 19:50

re: The Enigma of Allens West

Sadly (very sadly, actually), I am very excited by this thread. For years I used to travel on the train from Cumbria for every Boro home match and every Saturday I used to go through this station and I have never seen anyone get on or off there. A couple of weeks ago I travelled up from London for the Basel game and turned to my mates and said "I'll bet you a tenner nobody gets on or off at Allens West." Of course, someone did...

Valer Posted on 21/4 19:53

re: The Enigma of Allens West

Plenty of people get on and off at Allens West - me for one, Keith Lamb for two; it's the nearest station to his home, and that of Steve McClaren (though I haven't seen him there). It's also nearer to Yarm than Yarm Station (work that one out!) and therefore the nearest station for many of our players (including Matty Bates). Dean Gordon used to live on the estate next to Allens West, while Zenden used to live two minutes up the road.

uncle_harry Posted on 21/4 20:32

re: The Enigma of Allens West

Allens West - busier than Times Square. Who'da thowt it? Is it west of someone called Allen? Or is Allen living west of the station?

Valer Posted on 21/4 20:45

re: The Enigma of Allens West

Matty Bates used to go to Egglescliffe school - and Hayley McQueen. Bet they both hung around Allens West Station.

10hickton Posted on 21/4 21:05

re: The Enigma of Allens West

Derby_Red, so how come Egglescliffe Comprehensive School is in Eaglescliffe?

Jimmy_Boy Posted on 21/4 21:16

re: The Enigma of Allens West

As an Eaglescliffe resident for many years and having attended Egglescliffe School, I can say with some confidence that the reason for the difference in spelling is because... of local legend. The village above Yarm is called Egglescliffe and apparently it's all down to the misspelling of Egglescliffe when the now Eaglescliffe was being built. So that's cleared that up then.

Valer Posted on 21/4 23:02

re: The Enigma of Allens West

You'd think the school would have known how to spell it!

uncle_harry Posted on 22/4 9:35

re: The Enigma of Allens West

Nearer to Yarm than Yarm Station? I didn't know there was a Yarm Station!

Corcaigh_the_Cat Posted on 22/4 9:43

re: The Enigma of Allens West

I read that the station is earmarked for closure. Along with a few others along the line!

stockton_smoggie Posted on 22/4 9:44

re: The Enigma of Allens West

Dunno much about the station, but the bloody level crossing. 'Level' - that's a laugh. It's knackering my suspension on me car.

Jimmy_Boy Posted on 22/4 10:00

re: The Enigma of Allens West

Yarm Station and Allens West are on different lines. You can't go from Yarm to Allens West. You'd have to go down to Thornaby and change. They are both roughly the same distance from Yarm High Street.

Allens West is on the edge of "new" Eaglescliffe next to the old MoD stores. Eaglescliffe Station is in "old" Eaglescliffe, off Yarm Road, not far from Preston Park. Yarm Station is on Green Lane, opposite Conyers School. This is the road that leads to Tall Trees.

Boro290204 Posted on 22/4 10:11

re: The Enigma of Allens West

Didn't he have a brother called Fred, who married Rose and moved to Gloucester?

uncle_harry Posted on 22/4 11:22

re: The Enigma of Allens West

You can't go to Yarm from Allens West? This country is turning to cack before our eyes.

nopsfc Posted on 22/4 11:36

re: The Enigma of Allens West

I can let you all know that from Allens West you can link through by train to Graz in Austria. This I know because 3 of us did it in February 2005 to see the Boro.

Perry_Combover Posted on 22/4 11:45

re: The Enigma of Allens West

From Graz, you can get the train to Moscow, then the Trans-Siberian railway right through to Vladivostock. From there, it's a relatively easy hop down to Bangkok for example. So basically you can get from Allens West to Bangkok via the medium of rail transport.

uncle_harry Posted on 22/4 12:01

re: The Enigma of Allens West

"So basically you can get from Allens West to Bangkok via the medium of rail transport"

...but not Yarm.

Paulinho Posted on 22/4 12:19

re: The Enigma of Allens West

I once got off at Allens West! I was going out with a girl who lived in Eaglescliffe. I got the bus into town, from Hemlington, and then the train to Allens West for a bit of 13-year old snogging in her bedroom. Jeez, that was 22 years ago. Happy days, mind.

Boro_Gadgie Posted on 22/4 12:21

re: The Enigma of Allens West

As someone who used to work at MoD Eaglescliffe, I too am very excited by this thread. Before I could drive (though some would say "what do you mean, before?"), I got the train from Boro and used the station regularly.

There is an area of land with a cottage adjacent to the station, between the railway line and the old MoD depot. I believe the cottage is called Allens West Cottage and that the station was named after the cottage. Presumably the land belonged to someone called Allen and possibly he had more than one cottage, this one being the furthest west.

The_DiasBoro Posted on 22/4 12:45

re: The Enigma of Allens West

In fact the name is a corruption of Aliens West because the MoD site actually houses the UK's very own downed flying saucer. Not many people know this.

TOPIC

MESSAGE

POST

REGISTER

Right, if there's a Northallerton, where is Southallerton? Or indeed Allerton?

piggy_nichol Posted on 22/4 13:39

re: The Enigma of Allens West

When I was a kid, I wasn't as good a person as I am now and was travelling by train, perhaps from Stockton to Darlington. I only bought a ticket to Allens West and pretended to be asleep for the rest of the journey. It was 13p instead of 18p. Odd how you remember the price but not where the train was going to.

I'd always thought that's what Allens West was for, to save kids who would rather buy an extra packet of football stickers 5p on their train fare.

ayresomeangel365 Posted on 22/4 15:07

re: The Enigma of Allens West

In 1631 a bloke called Ralph Allanson owned approx 320 acres of land and a fishery on the Tees. The land covered Egglescliffe, Aislaby and surrounding land. This would locate the station at the west side of his manor. Therefore, I reckon there's a good chance the name comes from there. Just my theory after a bit of research. Best I could come up with. Someone's gonna prove me wrong, I'm sure.

uncle_harry Posted on 22/4 16:47

re: The Enigma of Allens West

This board is great sometimes.

7_The_Informer Posted on 22/4 17:14

re: The Enigma of Allens West

Just checked on Google maps and I live merely 27.3 miles from the Allen's East restaurant, in Stratford, CT. Maybe I will have to go and pay it a visit. Though, therein lies the Enigma. Why is the restaurant Allen's East and the train station Allens West?

AwesomeSwells Posted on 22/4 18:52

re: The Enigma of Allens West

Truly an Enigma. Come to think of it, the many times I came up from the Smoke and changed at Darlo and went through there, I too can't recall anyone getting on or off. It felt to me the furthest place from home I'd ever been and yet I was 15 minutes away. Can anyone think of any other 'Enigma' places?

janplanner Posted on 22/4 21:35

re: The Enigma of Allens West

It's a very long way from Bridge of Allen.

tony_block19 Posted on 22/4 21:44

re: The Enigma of Allens West

"Dean Gordon used to live on the estate next to Allens West."

Aye, he did. I lived in his old house. He left me an old Boro jacket with two 50p's in the pocket, you know!!

Allens West is a legendary station. We should never be rid of it. I use it regularly, going to and from Boro matches, and also my girlfriend gets off when coming from Darlington. Long live Allens West!

OPEO Posted on 23/4 7:45

re: The Enigma of Allens West

Right, if there's a Northallerton, where is Southallerton? Or indeed Allerton?

Maccarone_Is_Me Posted on 24/4 8:28

re: The Enigma of Allens West

The old Yarm Station is at the north end of the viaduct under Aislaby Road. I always wanted to walk along the viaduct but never had the bottle to do it.

Maccarone_Is_Me Posted on 24/4 8:30

re: The Enigma of Allens West

There's Allerton Bywater and Chapel Allerton around Leeds. And there's an Allerton Hall off the A1.

Leedsclive Posted on 24/4 8:33

re: The Enigma of Allens West

Another interesting fact (stretching the use of the word 'interesting') is that Allens West is a private station, as it's owned by MoD. Like British Steel Redcar's stop (if that's still open), you are technically trespassing if you get off without having official business there.

gibson Posted on 24/4 8:36

re: The Enigma of Allens West

Great Heck and Little Heck are near Snaith, East Yorks. Don't know where Flipping Heck is, though.

Capybara Posted on 24/4 8:38

re: The Enigma of Allens West

Derby_Red, the Teesside Airport service is what is known as a 'parliamentary' service, in that it exists purely because the authorities don't want to go through all the procedures needed to close the service. I believe one train a week stops there. A couple of seasons ago we had a nonsense kick-off - 12:45 on a Saturday, I believe - and I was on that week's service that stopped at the airport. I was amazed to see some people actually get on the train.

Other 'parliamentary' services include Enfield to Stratford via the Seven Sisters-South Tottenham curve, which has one service at about 5:20 in the morning, and the Fridays only Stockport-Stalybridge via Reddish service.

spiderbaby Posted on 24/4 8:47

re: The Enigma of Allens West

Just looked it up on our copy of the Domesday Book Yorkshire 1086 AD and can't find any reference to it, so it must've come into existence after then. So not as old as you think! Could be they spelt it wrong, as they did many times, as Stokesley was Stoxsly and Loftus Lofthouse. So maybe it was Aliens West and taken off the map...

janplanner Posted on 24/4 9:12

re: The Enigma of Allens West

But Allens West is north of the Tees and therefore in Durham, so it wouldn't be in the Yorkshire Domesday Book.

T4Tomo Posted on 24/4 9:33

re: The Enigma of Allens West

I love threads like these. I'd like to correct the assertion that to travel from Yarm to Allens West you'd have to change at Thornaby. Changing at Eaglescliffe is the obvious choice.

I'd also point out that while it is indeed a very short rail journey between Allens West and Eaglescliffe (it is the equivalent of Leicester Square to Covent Garden on the Piccadilly line), it's actually quite a long walk between the two as you have to take a long route around to get over the Yarm railway line.

I might hop onto the platform for a couple of seconds and hop back in when I pop up for the game on Thursday, just to say I've been there, like.

Maccarone_Is_Me Posted on 24/4 9:41

re: The Enigma of Allens West

You don't have to walk the long way round. Isn't there a tunnel under the railway at the bottom of Albert Road going over to that new estate?

The_Commisar Posted on 24/4 10:10

re: The Enigma of Allens West

I once got off the train at Allens West when it didn't stop there. Got the train from Newcastle to Boro at 5.30am.

"Allens West, please" I said.

"We don't stop there," came the reply.

"Eh?"

"Hang on, I'll have a word with the driver."

"OK, we won't stop but we will slow down for you."

Great. Door opens and I accelerate from 0 to 15mph in two steps. Great fun. Not!

spiderbaby Posted on 24/4 10:51

re: The Enigma of Allens West

Found out more re Allens West Domesday Book. Seems that Durham wasn't included in't book for the following reason:
"Durham (with Northumberland) was not included in the Domesday survey and Chaplais argued that its bishop, William of St Calais (1081-96), was the ideal person to be made responsible for writing up the Domesday Book because he had no personal interest in its findings."

So that clears up that argument.

ayresomeangel365 Posted on 24/4 12:52

re: The Enigma of Allens West

Round about the same time that Ralph Allenson owned the land in 1631, a rich man owned the adjoining manor, a chap called Mr Urlay...hence Urlay Nook! There u go. Wonder where the nook came from?

Archie_Stanton1 Posted on 24/4 17:04

re: The Enigma of Allens West

In my train-spotting days, I was good mates with a signalman who worked at Urlay Nook signal box. He'd let me signal the trains whilst he read the paper. I've changed the signals for Allens West many a time. Beat that!

OPEO Posted on 24/4 17:43

re: The Enigma of Allens West

At any time of day or night you will spot a spotter on the bridge over the marshalling yards at Teesside Park. Loonies.

jayno Posted on 24/4 17:46

re: The Enigma of Allens West

My brother works the signals at Allens West. What a boring job.

OooOo Posted on 24/4 18:03

re: The Enigma of Allens West

I am confused about the stuff about Egglescliffe being misspelled as Eaglescliffe. I mean Eaglescliffe makes sense as eagles sit on cliffs and stuff but have you ever seen an Eggle sitting on a cliff? And what is an Eggle anyway? And should it be Eggle's Cliff?

Cobain_94 Posted on 24/4 18:05

re: The Enigma of Allens West

I was thinking similarly as I passed through it on the way back from Darlo. I'd never heard of it. I don't think it actually exists.

HarrysDaffodil Posted on 24/4 21:06

re: The Enigma of Allens West

The 'Eggle' bit of Egglescliffe comes from 'ecclesial', ie church-like, because it translates to 'church on the cliff' and refers to St John's Church, which looks down over the River Tees and Yarm. Apparently.

Geek.

Cobain_94 Posted on 24/4 23:50 re:

The Enigma of Allens West

I hadn't heard of Allens West until a few months ago and I don't know anyone that's ever been there or lives there. Maybe people go there never to return.

Capybara Posted on 25/4 9:10

re: The Enigma of Allens West

Does anyone know the yardage and the coinage required?

T4Tomo Posted on 25/4 9:24

re: The Enigma of Allens West

£1.05 single. Pass on the yardage.

Capybara Posted on 25/4 9:29

re: The Enigma of Allens West

In that case, Wikipedia is wrong. If you include the London Underground as part of the rail network, that is. The cheapest single fare is three quid these days if you don't have an Oyster card. Which makes Leicester Square to Covent Garden a whopping £15 a mile, I reckon.

gravy_boat Posted on 25/4 9:52

re: The Enigma of Allens West

I've got off the train at Allens West loads of times. I used to pester my Gran to walk up there with me every summer holiday when I was a kid. We'd get one of those big, flat round mince pies from the butchers at Orchard shops on the way home.

In fact, I got off there only about 3 weeks ago. But that was only because we'd been drinking all day in Boro and got the train back to Eaglescliffe. Unfortunately, when we got to Eaglescliffe, we tried to get off the wrong side of the train, so it started moving again before we could get off. I was just grateful we weren't spending the night in Darlo.

littlejimmy Posted on 25/4 10:14

re: The Enigma of Allens West

I propose the formation of an Allens West Appreciation Society. We should have a monthly meeting at the station. Imagine how freaked out people on passing trains will be to see actual people at the station. I'll bring the egg sandwiches.

Kilburn Posted on 25/4 10:46 re:

The Enigma of Allens West

It is 944 metres between the two stations.

TOPIC

MESSAGE

POST

REGISTER

Who could have imagined how big a place Allens West played in people's lives?

Capybara Posted on 25/4 10:51

re: The Enigma of Allens West

Excellent work, Mr K. A snip at only £1.79 per mile, by my calculations. The Heathrow Express is more expensive than that (I think).

rilodog Posted on 25/4 16:54

re: The Enigma of Allens West

Allens West still has a station. Stockton, the birthplace of railways, has no railway station. What is going on there then?

T4Tomo Posted on 25/4 17:34

re: The Enigma of Allens West

rilodog - since when?

Poster adds link to Northern Rail website for Stockton Station.

rilodog Posted on 25/4 18:54

re: The Enigma of Allens West

T4Tomo, you call that a station? It is a half way house for the homeless.

ayresomeangel365 Posted on 25/4 18:54

re: The Enigma of Allens West

To totally ignore the town's only serious claim to fame bewilders and disgusts me. It's such a golden opportunity to transform the town into something decent. Steam is such a massive worldwide attraction. Look at Grosmont, for instance. They might wake up one day but I doubt it.

uncle_harry Posted on 26/4 8:19

re: The Enigma of Allens West

Who could have imagined how big a place Allens West played in people's lives? The Allens West Appreciation Society will need a number of symbols and artifacts. Boro have a lion. What should the AWAS have?

T4Tomo Posted on 26/4 8:57

re: The Enigma of Allens West

Apologies, rilodog, clearly I've touched a nerve. I've never been to Stockton so wouldn't know what the station is like. Grosmont is very nice but Stockton should have more to shout about in terms of railway heritage if nothing else.

Derby_Red Posted on 26/4 9:05

re: The Enigma of Allens West

As for Stockton, there were plans by a heritage group in the late '80s to create a museum/steam railway centre on what was the old Stockton sheds just north of the station. Quite ambitious but nothing more elaborate than what Waterman did at Crewe. A shame really, that.

littlejimmy Posted on 26/4 9:12

re: The Enigma of Allens West

I'd suggest either a classic grey ET holding a compass or... a duck in plus fours.

jax_1 Posted on 26/4 9:46

re: The Enigma of Allens West

Bit of a long shot but I'm sure one of you will know the answer. When travelling twixt Middlesbrough and York, you pass a railway carriage restaurant. Does anyone have any idea where exactly this is?

Secondly, on that same journey, is it only me that still smiles every time I see that stuffed/toy dog in the window of the house near Thirsk?

littlejimmy Posted on 26/4 9:52

re: The Enigma of Allens West

Jax, it's called The Sidings and is in Shipton By Beningbrough, which is on the A19, just this side of York. It has some bedrooms and is quite a good restaurant. You sit in the carriages themselves and it's all very authentic.

Capybara Posted on 26/4 9:54

re: The Enigma of Allens West

Except you don't go along.

Now, this stuffed dog. Where do I look for that? Haven't noticed it before.

jax_1 Posted on 26/4 9:56

re: The Enigma of Allens West

Thanks, Jimmy. It's puzzled me for a while, has that. Though I didn't think it looked big enough to have bedrooms. It's only 2 or 3 carriages long, isn't it?

littlejimmy Posted on 26/4 9:58

re: The Enigma of Allens West

There are a few carriages and a building or two. I think they only have a couple of bedrooms.

AwesomeSwells Posted on 26/4 10:00

re: The Enigma of Allens West

I'm up for AWAS. It'll get cult like Twin Peaks and X-Files. How about for the first meeting we do the most expensive train ride in the UK?

jax_1 Posted on 26/4 10:01

re: The Enigma of Allens West

There is a house, just before Thirsk, I think. It's very close to the track so you can't miss it - and in one of the bedrooms, there is a dog stood on the windowsill. I thought it was real for ages.

Capybara Posted on 26/4 10:12

re: The Enigma of Allens West

I'm pretty intimate with that line so I'm guessing it's on the right hand side as I usually sit on the left, for some reason. Going north, that is.

littlejimmy Posted on 26/4 10:16

re: The Enigma of Allens West

Ah, yes. No, the carriages don't actually move. I was thinking they should employ people to shake them while you're sat in there eating.

jax_1 Posted on 26/4 10:17

re: The Enigma of Allens West

If travelling facing oncoming trains, heading to York, it's on your right hand side, Capy. I'm sorry, I have no idea which direction that is.

The_Mighty_LC Posted on 26/4 10:19

re: The Enigma of Allens West

I'll be going through Allens West tomorrow evening on the way to the match (having left London at 1530 from doing a full day's work beforehand), and then on Friday morning on the way home (travelling from 0900 onwards, straight back to work in west London. Finish at 2300, go home for a few hours' kip, then back up again at 0415). Oh yes, Boro fans are worn out at the moment...

The_Bozza_Rogue Posted on 26/4 11:12

re: The Enigma of Allens West

I used to use Allens West every week for about 10 years. I used to get the train to school (Egglescliffe) from Dinsdale (Middleton St George). Half the time you wouldn't have to pay. I also used it to get to Yarm for a night out, on those occasions when my mum wouldn't give me a lift.

CleveleysSmoggie Posted on 26/4 11:18

re: The Enigma of Allens West

I'm coming by train tomorrow, so I will be looking out for the dog. What is it called? (Allen?) Is it on the East or West side of the track? (West?) And finally, is it North or South of Thirsk?

jax_1 Posted on 26/4 15:11

re: The Enigma of Allens West

It's between Thirsk and Middlesbrough and you can call it Allen if you wish. It's stuffed so it ain't gonna argue.

uncle_harry Posted on 26/4 17:48

re: The Enigma of Allens West

Perhaps we should have someone called 'Allen' - 'Mr Allen eg Ray Allen' or a Mr West, or indeed a Mr Allen West - on a flag in profile like the Queen is on stamps and money.

PapaJohn Posted on 26/4 19:19

re: The Enigma of Allens West

When Allens West was the station for the Royal Naval spares parts staff only, local residents had to apply for a special pass to use the trains which occasionally stopped there. I know this cos me mam had one. I could also hear the announcements at the station from my old bedroom.

uncle_harry Posted on 26/4 20:19

re: The Enigma of Allens West

Cuts in the budget for railway signage means that the station is rumoured to be renamed 'Al's W' next year! The resistance starts here at the virtual home of the Allens West Appreciation Society.

T4Tomo Posted on 27/4 9:14

re: The Enigma of Allens West

I'm a bit gutted as I'm on the 14.00 out of King's Cross today but changing at Darlo (and only having to wait 10 mins in Darlo, which is a bonus).

I might hop out for a second at Allens West just to say I've been on the platform. However, as I'm not doing the York-Boro bit I won't get to see the Stuffed Dog of Thirsk. Same route back as well, so I am well miffed.

Capybara Posted on 27/4 9:17

re: The Enigma of Allens West

You'll still be going through Thirsk, though, albeit at about 100mph faster than if you are on the York-Middlesbrough train.

Capybara Posted on 3/5 9:21

re: The Enigma of Allens West

Just outside Waterloo station in London, I observed the other day, is a piece of line-side equipment which says 'Allenwest Brentford' on it.

uncle_harry Posted on 21/6 19:49

re: The Enigma of Allens West

Allens West update - date line 19:44 - 21/06/06.

Allens West is, I confirm, in fine fettle, relatively litter free apart from a rogue wrapper on platform one (possibly a Kit Kat Chunky). As I was paying my respects from my carriage seat, I received what can only be described as 'the finger' from a youth. One of two possibilities spring to mind:

1. He is proposing the gesture as the Allens West Appreciation Society Salute ("Allens West, railway's number one station") or 2. He was one of the Dinsdale posse trying to infiltrate their rivals' station. The Dinsdale lot think they're it with their fancy galvanised steel shelter.

jax_1 Posted on 21/6 21:58

re: The Enigma of Allens West

I'd have thought he was saluting you and your new title, your Lordship.

uncle_harry Posted on 21/6 23:01

re: The Enigma of Allens West

Do you know, that's what I thought too. I think he was a bit confused because he called me a 'count'. I put him right though. I told him I'm an Earl.

PapaJohn Posted on 31/7 14:00

re: The Enigma of Allens West

I took the train from Liverpool Lime Street, changed at York and Darlington and arrived at Allens West in one piece about 4.5 hours after departure and 35 quid in spending. My ticket said Liverpool to Allens West!

The platform was tidy but for a young bloke on crutches having a somewhat close liaison with a young lady, similar to what I saw in Amsterdam a year or so back. Is there such a thing as 'station dogging'?

ayresomeangel365 Posted on 31/7 18:03

re: The Enigma of Allens West

Three cheers for Allens West! What an Enigma - the jewel of the north.

ayresomeangel365 Posted on 31/7 18:40

re: The Enigma of Allens West

Would never have happened in George Stephenson's time. Their heads would have been on the end of pikes on Yarm viaduct.

ayresomeangel365 Posted on 26/8 21:25

re: The Enigma of Allens West

Allens West could soon be servicing a major 600-plus housing estate if the planners get their way. The old MoD site has been sold off to a development company of which our friend John Prescott's son has an interest. Could this be Allens West's chance of fame? Moving on to bigger and better things, no more the Enigma?

uncle_harry Posted on 10/9 15:02

re: The Enigma of Allens West

Good news on the Allens West front, it looked in fine fettle on Friday. The Hawthorne bush was in fine fettle and the Kit Kat Chunky wrapper had been removed.

As for Dinsdale Station, is this what Robert Louis Stephenson invented The Rocket for? I think not.

George1507 Posted on 10/9 16:09

re: The Enigma of Allens West

Although the shelters at Dinsdale are somewhat utilitarian, they are still better than what was there before, ie nothing. Years ago, there was a long building on the bridge over the track which housed an office and a ticket office. The clock hadn't worked for years - it always said 3.25. The building was demolished, as is the way of things, to make way for nothing in particular. There is a bike track there now, I think.

The platforms at Dinsdale are about 150 yards long. I can only assume that express trains were expected to run through there at some time. The current one-coach train looks very silly on a platform of that length. The drivers usually stop at the start or end of the platform to ensure everyone has to walk to the train.

Mind you, compared to Teesside Airport station – sorry, Durham Tees Valley – sorry, Durham Airport station - Dinsdale is like Grand Central.

Bessie Posted on 10/9 20:50

re: The Enigma of Allens West

Allens West today.

Poster shows link to photograph of Allens West Station.

ayresomeangel365 Posted on 10/9 21:01

re: The Enigma of Allens West

That's not a very grand sign for such a historical S and D landmark is it? Will have to lobby the local council chap and see if he can be persuaded to arrange something more in keeping with the famous Enigma that is AW.

JoJon Posted on 11/9 9:57

re: The Enigma of Allens West

The day this thread originally appeared I was driving in Brighton, musing on the memories sparked off by the thread - I used to have a girlfriend who worked at the Admiralty who got the train to Allens West from Stockton every day - when I saw this opposite me at the traffic lights.

Poster attaches link to website about Allen West, an electrical engineering firm that was once the biggest employer in Brighton and Hove.

uncle_harry Posted on 11/9 19:54

re: The Enigma of Allens West

And people say the universe is just a bunch of chaotic stuff. How can you read that last post and still believe that?

ayresomeangel365 Posted on 11/9 20:04

re: The Enigma of Allens West

Sheesh... there's romance for you. Such Enigmatic power of coincidence, JJ. Maybe you should find your lost love and marry her on the platform at AW! We'll have a party!

littlejimmy Posted on 12/9 12:08

re: The Enigma of Allens West

There are no railways at all in the United Arab Emirates. Call me sad, but I miss trains and railway stations.

janplanner Posted on 12/9 12:16

re: The Enigma of Allens West

Wouldn't a railway bridge further down the Tees be great? Hartlepool to Middlesbrough in one leap.

ayresomeangel365 Posted on 12/9 12:51

re: The Enigma of Allens West

The original plan was to build a railway bridge over the Tees into Boro but it was deemed too expensive. To save costs, the line was diverted inland through Eaglescliffe etc. To stick one up the railway bosses, the big wigs of Boro sanctioned the building of the Tranny and Newport bridges to show them what we could do! Just think, if Boro had become a main line station we might have become a city. Eaglescliffe Station was huge - three or four platforms and associated buildings.

jiltedjiff Posted on 12/9 13:52

re: The Enigma of Allens West

Middlesbrough was Yorkshire's first ever passenger railway station - preceding the Leeds-Thirsk line by several months. That was due to it being an extension of the Stockton and Darlington.

jiltedjiff Posted on 15/9 14:06

re: The Enigma of Allens West

Something to delight uncle_harry - rush hour at Allens West! Yesterday evening because of a lightning strike at Leeds there were no Trans-Pennine services getting through to York so I had to get a Virgin train from York to Darlo. The five to five from Darlo to Saltburn was delayed till almost 5.15 and the one before that had not run so there were about three trainloads on it. There must have been over two dozen got off at Allens West - and even more than that got on. Must have been the busiest it's ever been.

Lelgie10 Posted on 6/2 9:22

re: The Enigma of Allens West

Poster attaches following information from a railway magazine:

"Allens West Station at Egglescliffe, Stockton on Tees was built in 1943 by the London and North Eastern Railway as a private halt for workers at a nearby Admiralty Depot. It was given up by the Ministry of Defence in 1971 though it had been available for public use for some time before. It is served by a Saltburn-Bishop Auckland Service. The site of the station is of interest as here was the Yarm halt of the Stockton and Darlington Railway until 1862. The Yarm goods branch also left the main S and D line here and it terminated at a depot in Egglescliffe across the river from Yarm, which was closed in 1871."

The question raised is how did the station get its name? Enquiries in the Yarm/Egglescliffe area have failed to elicit any answers.

Capybara Posted on 6/2 9:36

re: The Enigma of Allens West

Excellent stuff that. It answers a few questions. In particular, why it was built during the war. In general, very few (if any) railway stations were built during the war. It's the reason, for instance, why the Northern Line in London wasn't extended as had been planned before the war; all construction stopped when the war started and the money wasn't there afterwards to continue the project.

But it doesn't answer the main question, obviously. And if that is Allens West, is there, and where is, Allens East?

Jon2977 Posted on 22/3 13:04

re: The Enigma of Allens West

Allens West is one of those places you are not sure why it exists. It's on the edge of another world, bit like Loftus and out that way.

uncle_harry Posted on 23/3 17:45

re: The Enigma of Allens West

It seems our musings have stirred the region's movers and shakers.

Poster attaches link to a new website allenswest.co.uk created by JG Land & Estates, which has bought the site of the old Eaglescliffe Logistics Centre and renamed it Allens West.

Capybara Posted on 23/3 17:48

re: The Enigma of Allens West

And they are naming the PLACE after the STATION.

ayresomeangel365 Posted on 23/3 17:56

re: The Enigma of Allens West

Allens West, soon to be the thriving hub of a new metropolis - the King's Cross of the north-east, a phoenix rising from the ashes of the S and D. What a grand old lady she is!

PapaJohn Posted on 10/4 10:27

re: The Enigma of Allens West

Read the 'leaflet' from the planning exhibition and it appears it's gonna be a huge development. Looks very impressive. I reckon it will happen but my folks reckon there is a lot of local opposition, regarding lack of skools, roads etc. Could be Eaglescliffe's own Ingleby Barracks.

uncle_harry Posted on 16/6 12:45

re: The Enigma of Allens West

Capybara was nominated for a CBE for his services to this thread. Rumour has it that he turned it down in protest about the decision not to install a vending machine on the platform that would dispense Dairy Crunches, Bar Sixes and Waifas (Plain).

The Allens West Appreciation Society salutes him.

Chapter Four
Southgate is Ignorant of Boro's Traditions

Teesside Urban Legends

TOPIC

MESSAGE

POST

REGISTER

TOPIC - Southgate is Ignorant of Boro's traditions

Previous | Next | New Topic | Top Of Board

We prefer managers who mock us, patronise us with spin and hyperbole and convince us that you know nowt about football if it's not on paper. Southgate out!

Boro_Gadgie Posted on 22/1 11:59

Southgate is Ignorant of Boro's traditions

Not content with being the only Boro skipper to lift a major trophy, under his management we have now won THREE games in January. Does he not know that we never win for about two months after Christmas?

SOUTHGATE OUT!

Moody41 Posted on 22/1 12:03

re: Southgate is Ignorant of Boro's traditions

We also picked up seven points over Xmas out of a possible 12. Does he not know Boro never win games over the Xmas period?

TheSmogMonster Posted on 22/1 13:12

re: Southgate is Ignorant of Boro's traditions

He's also trying to get Boro playing attractive, attacking football, whilst having a solid defence.

It's one or the other Gareth, sort it out!

joseph99 Posted on 22/1 13:29

re: Southgate is Ignorant of Boro's traditions

We prefer managers who mock us, patronise us with spin and hyperbole and convince us that you know nowt about football if it's not on paper. Southgate out!

Proctors_Perm Posted on 22/1 13:30

re: Southgate is Ignorant of Boro's traditions

And another thing, why isn't his head turned about the Newcastle job?

Cogeur_le_Conq Posted on 22/1 13:31

re: Southgate is Ignorant of Boro's traditions

What's all this business of signing players a week before the deadline?

Doesn't he know we always wait until 11:55pm on the night of Janurary 31st before we put any bids in?

sad_man Posted on 22/1 13:43

re: Southgate is ignorant of Boro's tradition

Bloody A-typical Boro!

joseph99 Posted on 22/1 14:00

re: Southgate is ignorant of Boro's tradition

What on earth is Southgate playing at, scoring five goals in a home game against a top six team? What the hell is wrong in playing for a conservative 0-0 draw with only one up front? And what's even worse, Southgate is not playing players out of their natural positions... sack him!

andybarca Posted on 22/1 14:20

re: Southgate is ignorant of Boro's tradition

And winning on New Years' Day. Did he not take all the lads out on New Years' Eve? Fancy planning for a match the next day.

FestasVest Posted on 22/1 14:25

re: Southgate is ignorant of Boro's tradition

And what does Southgate think he's doing NOT taking up an assistant coaching role with the England squad, allowing him to concentrate 100% on the Boro?

See what happens, Mr Gibson, when you employ a bloody amateur?!

boro59 Posted on 22/1 15:42

re: Southgate is Ignorant of Boro's traditions

And he has not got the coaching badges. GET RID!!

grantus Posted on 22/1 15:46

re: Southgate is Ignorant of Boro's traditions

That lousy son of a bitch even has the audacity to let over-the-hill players go out on loan to save us some money.

Someone should pay the lout a little visit.

joseph99 Posted on 22/1 16:05

re: Southgate is Ignorant of Boro's traditions

How the fook can players perform without a Sports Psychologist?

old_archery_ground Posted on 22/1 16:09

re: Southgate is ignorant of Boro's tradition

And the cheeky fooker thinks it's clever to send the scouts on these long distance flights to ridiculous places like Korea!

What's wrong with old Don topping up his tan in Spain like usual and bringing back reports of the usually average players costing millions?

If I were in Don's shoes now, I'd be banging his door down.

sambaDTR Posted on 22/1 16:49

re: Southgate is ignorant of Boro's tradition

The worse thing is he has the cheek to send out an attacking team and boringly win 5-1 rather than wait until we are 3-0 down, play with four attackers and have an exciting 4-3, which is what we are all used to.

wheatmann Posted on 22/1 16:57

re: Southgate is ignorant of Boro's tradition

When exactly is he going to sign Juninho?!

joseph99 Posted on 22/1 16:58

re: Southgate is ignorant of Boro's tradition

When's the big fall out with Lamb and the board?

riverboat_captain Posted on 22/1 17:09

re: Southgate is ignorant of Boro's tradition

And has anybody seen him pissed in Yarm?

I didn't think so!

Bernies_right_boot Posted on 22/1 17:38

re: Southgate is ignorant of Boro's tradition

According to Southgate, we are yet to put in a MAGNIFICENT performance or show TREMENDOUS character yet. Give the lads the credit they deserve man!

post_edit Posted on 22/1 17:43

re: Southgate is ignorant of Boro's tradition

Next thing you know, people will be flooding back to watch the games. How on earth will I be able to chop and change my seat in the East Stand Upper when this happens? Damned inconsiderate if you ask me. Bah humbug!

SOUTHGATE OUT!

borogrape Posted on 22/1 19:12

re: Southgate is Ignorant of Boro's traditions

Quite possibly the most enjoyable post I have ever seen. Thank you for making an old fart giggle!

sambaDTR Posted on 23/1 0:29

re: Southgate is ignorant of Boro's tradition

And he's too content with being the Boro manager. He should forget about the Premier League and pick the best sides for the cups so he can get his mug on the telly and get the England job.

B_Hills Posted on 23/1 8:52

re: Southgate is ignorant of Boro's tradition

Doesn't he realise that by playing this attacking, entertaining football all he will do is have supporters flocking back. Have a word Gibbo!

Spoff_MFC Posted on 23/1 8:58

re: Southgate is ignorant of Boro's tradition

His teeth are not white enough for him to be the Boro manager.

OUT OUT OUT!!

Boro_2006 Posted on 23/1 9:10

re: Southgate is Ignorant of Boro's traditions

How dare the man have the audacity to get rid of "Mr Defence" Steve Round! And then dare to provide us with something good to watch! There's no need for this. Who's up for throwing their season ticket at him next game? Get rid - the man is a fool.

boro59 Posted on 23/1 10:58

re: Southgate is Ignorant of Boro's traditions

Should have listened to Barnwell from the League Managers Association. They know best. In fact, I seem to remember Fat Sam speaking against his appointment.

The_DiasBoro Posted on 23/1 11:04

re: Southgate is Ignorant of Boro's traditions

He has the cheek to ask overseas players that no-one's heard of to come and do a trial before signing them. Real managers take one look at the video, have a drink with the agent and do a deal.

B_Hills Posted on 23/1 11:33

re: Southgate is Ignorant of Boro's traditions

Doesn't he realise that by getting us back into Europe, we will have to endure all those comeback nights again... No not for me, it's just not good enough... He has to go!

joseph99 Posted on 23/1 12:43

re: Southgate is Ignorant of Boro's traditions

Whatever next? Fans leaving after the game, laughing, joking, talking about the events of the match as they sip their pints in the Nops, Browns etc. Too much joviality - we all much prefer deadly silence and a dread of returning to the stadium.

JoJon Posted on 23/1 13:09

re: Southgate is ignorant of Boro's tradition

And what's all this passing lark, eh?! Defenders passing the ball like a bunch of fairies. Big Jack'd soon sort 'em out.

The_Needle_Threader Posted on 23/1 13:18

re: Southgate is ignorant of Boro's tradition

Can't be doing with this play two up front lark. They can score out of nothing, how are we going to get a solid 0-0 playing like that? And signing a world class defender on loan to check his fitness is shocking managerial behaviour. You can tell he hasn't got the badges.

Amateur!!

TOPIC

MESSAGE

POST

REGISTER

If he gets manager of the month we're all gonna look like teacher's pet!

bernies_cigs Posted on 23/1 13:27

re: Southgate is ignorant of Boro's tradition

I'm not having this - if we don't put in a bid for Douala, Zenden, Geremi or Juninho immediately then I'm ripping up my season ticket and stuffing it down his tank top/suit combo.

If we dont revert to 5-4-1 then I'm off to support the Leeds Durties.

He'll be selling Massimo, Mendi and Parlour next ffs!

SOUTHGATE OUT!!

Boro_Forever Posted on 23/1 13:34

re: Southgate is ignorant of Boro's tradition

How dare he! The bloody cheek of the man, looking all passionate about the club. Does he not realise he is only supposed to use us as a stepping stone?

thegate Posted on 23/1 14:26

re: Southgate is Ignorant of Boro's traditions

Everyone knows a good manager has to sit in the stands for the first half. Us fans paid good money for those phones that connect to the dug out. What a doyle!

Boro_Gadgie Posted on 23/1 14:49

re: Southgate is Ignorant of Boro's traditions

Even when we win, he still says there are things that we still need to improve on. Is he ever happy? Whinging git!

And why didn't he describe the home performances against Pompey and Blackburn as "magnificent"? After these games and the home game with Liverpool, he looked like he was getting it right. He never made any mention of the tremendous character and attitude we showed during these games.

If we carry on like this, then I might have to renew my season ticket in the summer, which will cost me 360 bloody quid! How am I supposed to be able to afford a holiday as well?

JoJon Posted on 23/1 15:06

re: Southgate is ignorant of Boro's tradition

And there he is in every post-match interview, talking sense, fresh as a daisy, not a slurred word or a bleary eye or even a whiff of a hangover. What's the matter with these people? Don't they drink? I bet he doesn't even have a drag on a gasper at half-time.

Gah! What I'd give for a proper manager.

Boro_Gadgie Posted on 23/1 15:10

re: Southgate is ignorant of Boro's tradition

Gibson needs to get it sorted. Southgate doesn't patronise us with the same old clichés or tell us we need educating. I think he showed his true colours when he admitted that he wanted us to play entertaining and attacking football. Does he not know that we don't like the word "entertainment"?

Southgate out, Round in!

grantus Posted on 23/1 15:29

re: Southgate is ignorant of Boro's tradition

If nobody throws their season ticket at him in the next two weeks I will be very annoyed. This is not acceptable!

joseph99 Posted on 23/1 15:29

re: Southgate is Ignorant of Boro's traditions

Look 'ere, Southgate! The Riverside is normally a safe haven for boo-boys and we congregate there for a good fooking whinge. What do you suggest we do now?

Jonny_Greenings_sock Posted on 23/1 19:26

re: Southgate is Ignorant of Boro's traditions

How dare he play inexperienced youngsters like Downing, Cattermole and Taylor over quality, passionate, reliable veterans like Ray Parlour and Mendieta?

Southgate needs educating. Bet he doesn't even have a copy of the video where the geese fly.

Jonny_Greenings_sock Posted on 23/1 19:29

re: Southgate is Ignorant of Boro's traditions

And seriously, how dare he sign a player who hasn't previously scored against us in the UEFA Cup.

Funtime_Franckie Posted on 23/1 19:32

re: Southgate is Ignorant of Boro's traditions

And it's the middle of bloody January and he still hasn't brought in a geriatric Cockney wide boy with a tendency to release ropey singles to get him out of the clarts!!

Southgate OUT!!

Vidyak Posted on 23/1 19:55

re: Southgate is Ignorant of Boro's traditions

It's a disgrace that he promotes someone like Colin Cooper too and let's him wear his training gear as well.

Out!

Funtime_Franckie Posted on 23/1 19:57

re: Southgate is Ignorant of Boro's traditions

And there's only seven days left to sign Michael Ricketts.

Get yer finger out Gareth!!!

joseph99 Posted on 24/1 9:52

re: Southgate is Ignorant of Boro's traditions

No notebook and scribe? Fooking amateur. And why don't your disciples clutch their Prozone reference books in their hands whilst we are turning teams like Bolton over? Clearly clueless.

Woodymfc Posted on 24/1 9:59

re: Southgate is ignorant of Boro's tradition

I like ginger hair.
SOUTHGATE OUT

chorleygeorge Posted on 24/1 10:05

re: Southgate is ignorant of Boro's tradition

He either buys Francois Grenet on a long-term contract or I'm off to support Newcastle. Now there's a proper good club.

The_Needle_Threader Posted on 24/1 11:57

re: Southgate is ignorant of Boro's tradition

He keeps making something called "substitutions", which means when the game is won he rests players and brings on fringe players for a run-out and bit of fitness. What's all that about? The "tremendous" one didn't do that and he had badges.

Fancy changing a winning team with 20, 15 or 10 mins to go so we can start with the same 11 next week!

Shocking!

Boro85 Posted on 24/1 12:04

re: Southgate is ignorant of Boro's tradition

And while we're on about it, what's all this same formation, same team lark about, eh? What are we supposed to talk about in the pub when we already know what team we're gonna put out? Some of the best conversations were about which striker was going to play right wing this week!

Anyway, the players are too overworked playing week in week out? What happened to rotating them for God's sake? They'll get tired!

JLinardi Posted on 24/1 12:07

re: Southgate is ignorant of Boro's tradition

One other thing here, Viduka got two goals against Bolton. Two F***ING GOALS and he wasn't even brought off!

What was he thinking letting a striker try and get a hat-trick? We'll have less of that.

Woodymfc Posted on 25/1 7:51

re: Southgate is Ignorant of Boro's traditions

Southgate should learn to tell lies. All these interviews with his honest, straight-to-the point answers.
Come on, Gibbo, boot him out. His relationship with players and fans is non-existent.

holgateoldskool Posted on 25/1 9:06

re: Southgate is Ignorant of Boro's traditions

And another thing - what's this caper about promoting from within? Another ex-player and local lad, Coops. Why can't he bring in somebody else we've never heard of? Surround himself with yes men? Cheeky git!

Cogeur_le_Conq Posted on 25/1 9:09

re: Southgate is Ignorant of Boro's traditions

How comes he's not using the transfer window to take a hard earned third holiday since the season started?

How else is he going to spot Brazilians playing beach footie?

joseph99 Posted on 25/1 9:09

re: Southgate is Ignorant of Boro's traditions

Why doesn't Southgate cocoon himself with an entourage of "yes-men" cronies such as cone-men, pyschologists and a plethora of assistants who are renowned to be complete charlatans in the game? Now we hear that he has Cooper as his Number Two. Doesn't Southgate have any mates he can give a job too? Speaks volumes for me. Out of his depth...

Max_Headroom Posted on 25/1 9:19

re: Southgate is Ignorant of Boro's traditions

AND!! What's with the sudden lack of team meetings and seminars on the FA approved way to take corners? Where have they gone, eh? Why should our players be enjoying work and playing football, while we're all slaving away like idiots?

Christ on a toboggan, Southgate!

He even has the audacity to abandon the regulation quiff. In front of the fans!

Woodymfc Posted on 25/1 9:23

re: Southgate is Ignorant of Boro's traditions

Cheeky Bu**er waved at the fans on Saturday.
Just who does he think he is? One of us?

joseph99 Posted on 25/1 9:25

re: Southgate is Ignorant of Boro's traditions

I hope he has learnt something from his predecessor: I hope he remembers to dictate to his players in the closing minutes against an average Premiership team with the scores level to waste time at one of our corners. He needs to instil into our players a mantra that the opposition are more dangerous than us... otherwise he will fail.

Spoff_MFC Posted on 25/1 9:26

re: Southgate is Ignorant of Boro's traditions

I for one will be boycotting matches until my Boro return.

Go South and close the Gate.

holgateoldskool Posted on 25/1 9:33

re: Southgate is Ignorant of Boro's traditions

Next thing you'll see is him sending the Boro out with a game plan to dictate the pattern of play. How dare he!

borobuddah Posted on 25/1 9:52

re: Southgate is ignorant of Boro's tradition

He forgot to tell George to punch the air three times when we win.

Woodymfc Posted on 25/1 10:00

re: Southgate is Ignorant of Boro's traditions

AAAAAND!
It's no wonder our fans are turning up in smaller numbers these days - 16 goals we've scored in January. All those Pig Bag celebrations are tiring us out. Have Southgate and Co got no consideration for us?

Funtime_Franckie Posted on 25/1 10:25

re: Southgate is Ignorant of Boro's traditions

And we've even started beating teams that we are supposed to beat, like Charlton and Sheffield Utd.

Christ!! What is the man playing at?!

Boro85 Posted on 25/1 10:29

re: Southgate is Ignorant of Boro's traditions

Tying Lee Dong-Gook to a short term deal in case he's a flop? What's that all about? We should have him on huge wages and a five-year contract. Then at least if he's rubbish he'll still be happy! Booo!

Southgate man FFS!! Don't you know some bloke is stood in the North Stand with a season ticket to throw. He can't wait forever.

The_Commisar Posted on 25/1 12:34

re: Southgate is Ignorant of Boro's traditions

Southgate man FFS!! Don't you know some bloke is stood in the North Stand with a season ticket to throw. He can't wait forever.

AlphaGeeK Posted on 25/1 13:57

re: Southgate is ignorant of Boro's tradition

1: Winning three League games in a row.
2: Not throwing his water bottles down in the technical area.

Go now man, FFS!

eweyboro Posted on 25/1 14:08

re: Southgate is Ignorant of Boro's traditions

Plus we're actually defending set-pieces now, with men on both posts. Everyone knows the back post automatically takes care of itself, every time. This nonsense will never catch on.

Not to mention letting aged, overpaid wasters leave the club, rather than enjoying a backslapping last payday. Who knows when we'll need someone to amble gently into an opposition's midfield and give the ball away?

And what's this I hear about signing foreign players who we haven't faced in the UEFA Cup? I'll give him bloody Dong.

bernies_cigs Posted on 25/1 14:14

re: Southgate is Ignorant of Boro's traditions

This has to be the worst week in Boro's history. Reckless football against Bolton and now Ugo, Mendi, Maccarone and Parlour are all being shown the door when we have a difficult cup tie ahead.

FFS Southgate, sort it out or there will be CLARET everywhere.

SmogontheThames Posted on 25/1 14:40

re: Southgate is Ignorant of Boro's traditions

OW, Southgate! I hope you have taken the opportunity to read all these posts and then shamefully hang your head in shame, man. And close the door on your way out, will ya!!

Boro_Gadgie Posted on 25/1 15:02

re: Southgate is Ignorant of Boro's traditions

And what's all this playing a settled side about? It's no fun for us fans trying to guess the team any more. It must be boring as hell for the players as well. He should rest players more often otherwise they might, just might, get tired at having to play more than once a fortnight.

Not to mention playing people in their right positions too. Where's the fun in that for us supporters? It used to be enjoyable to see how an ageing, barely adequate central midfielder with no pace would perform as a winger.

XXLshirts_fit_all Posted on 25/1 15:02

re: Southgate is Ignorant of Boro's traditions

WHEN WILL HE reorganise the backroom staff into a more forward thinking revolutionary system used by sporting giants like the Russian women's volleyball team? We need separate coaches for each position whereby the whole team don't actually learn to play as a cohesive unit.

We also need an assistant manager who can motivate the players and fill them with confidence. He should have no footballing experience and a dodgy website that advertises his world-renowned courses.

And ffs get a cookery badge!!

The Gate should do the honourable thing and walk now! I never wanted a man who had such a deep respect amongst the fans and staff to take over and put that respect and our club in jeopardy. Things can only go wrong if we don't act now!

Boro_Gadgie Posted on 25/1 15:05

re: Southgate is Ignorant of Boro's traditions

And not employing a basketball coach as assistant manager. What's all that about?!

the_arc Posted on 25/1 16:03

re: Southgate is Ignorant of Boro's traditions

What about the goal difference? How can Southgate justify the fact that not only is it not in double figures, it's not even negative. It was a disgrace we didn't take off both forwards on Saturday after the first goal and sit with ten on the edge of the box desperately trying to hack the ball away for 85 minutes.

scoea Posted on 25/1 16:08

re: Southgate is ignorant of Boro's tradition

It's his growing popularity I am upset about. How can our manager be popular? It's a disgrace, he needs to shape up or ship out. I suppose what he really should do is win a cup or qualify for Europe via the League or get to the UEFA Cup Final. That would send his popularity plummeting.

Woodymfc Posted on 25/1 16:11

re: Southgate is Ignorant of Boro's traditions

We should all march on the pitch before the Arsenal game and throw our season tickets at him and that creepy mate of his.

Pinkers Posted on 25/1 16:20

re: Southgate is Ignorant of Boro's traditions

And what's all this about players staying in the team on merit? That Andrew Taylor's been brilliant, but is he out the side when Arca's fit? Is he bollox. This kind of thing will give ALL the squad players a real incentive to play well! Disgraceful.

And don't get me started on this letting two strikers build a partnership... where is that getting us? I'll tell you - 16 goals in five games. I don't go to see goals and attacking football!! Get Maccarone on the right wing in a 4-5-1 ffs!

Southgate out!

scoea Posted on 25/1 16:54

re: Southgate is ignorant of Boro's tradition

You watch, before you know it he'll be playing left backs in the centre of midfield and central midfielders on the right wing...

Briney Posted on 25/1 16:55

re: Southgate is Ignorant of Boro's traditions

Next he will be trying to sort the crowds, ticket office and commercial dept out. Who does he think he is? He's trying to run the show, I reckon.

At this rate, he'll be asking to come to the next meeting of the Twe12th Man, sucking up to the fans trying not to get the sack. It gives me the creeps.

Yet I warned him off at some posh NE football awards do, don't be getting fancy and forward thinking on us. Us Chicken Run lads don't go in for all that.

borobuddah Posted on 25/1 17:12

re: Southgate is Ignorant of Boro's traditions

If he gets manager of the month we're all gonna look like teacher's pet!

B_Hills Posted on 25/1 18:23

re: Southgate is Ignorant of Boro's traditions

And about this Academy nonsense. Don't you understand, Gareth, that by playing three, four, five home grown players, you are destroying the very soul of the Academy?

It was designed for us to bring sub-standard, average youngsters through who we could loan out to lower division teams before we give them frees to Hartlepool, Darlington, York, Billingham etc. What are you playing at by bringing these young internationals through a youth system? Don't you realise everyone will soon copy us and it will end in tears.

Stop now! Southgate out!

grantus Posted on 25/1 22:57

re: Southgate is Ignorant of Boro's traditions

I am utterly disgusted that we are not using the first half of each game to contain, defend and analyse the opposition in preparation for the 'real' match, which we all know doesn't start until second half kick-off.

Attacking football from the first minute is negligent, careless and will drive the supporters from the terraces and into the Dundas Arcade on Saturday afternoons.

Gibson, have a word!

joseph99 Posted on 26/1 7:30

re: Southgate is Ignorant of Boro's traditions

And when Southgate decides to play certain team members out of their position they usually do well (eg Arca) - what's all this about? Listen, Southgate, in this area we've been reared on square pegs and round holes. Just ask Bernie.

And all this making the beautiful game simplistic, let me tell you it is not - it's about reading and writing good tactical books and over-coaching with shackles.

Keyboard_Worrier Posted on 31/1 0:28

re: Southgate is Ignorant of Boro's traditions

What is all this trying to win the game in the last 15 minutes all about when we should be just settling for the point? The bloke is clueless. Keep it in the corners and no attacking at last minute corners. The bloke knows nowt.

Funtime_Franckie Posted on 31/1 10:47

re: Southgate is Ignorant of Boro's traditions

Not once have I seen Southgate make a "tactical" substitution which has made four teammates play out of position and result in the team completely losing shape.

The bloke hasn't got a bloody clue.

Boro_Gadgie Posted on 5/2 14:46

re: Southgate is Ignorant of Boro's traditions

And why no panic buys during January? Not even a reserve team midfielder from a Championship club. As for saying the players were disappointed at only getting a draw v Arsenal, just don't get me started...

B_Hills Posted on 6/2 8:41

re: Southgate is Ignorant of Boro's traditions

And why did he not consult with Robbo before the Arsenal game? Isn't he aware that they always come here and give us a good spanking, usually by as many as five goals? I'm getting a bit fed up with all this teamwork and 100% effort. This is not what Boro fans expect.

borobuddah Posted on 28/2 17:22

re: Southgate is Ignorant of Boro's traditions

What did he think he was doing last night?

Running on the pitch and doing a clenched fist salute to the away end?

Needs to calm down, he's far too over emotional to be a manager.

He should learn off John Neal, Stan Anderson, Robbo and them, keep a sour face on and say nowt when the press are about.

He's turned out to be a worse spiv than wor Tel - you wouldn't see him running around like a nob 'ed.

Out!

B_Hills Posted on 28/2 19:17

re: Southgate is Ignorant of Boro's traditions

And look, we usually get beat at Sid James' Park... So let's not be sending out an attack-minded team full of inspiration and fight. It is normal for us to keep our heads down as the Jawdees laugh at us for the next couple of weeks!

erimus73 Posted on 28/2 20:33

re: Southgate is ignorant of Boro's tradition

Why, why, why hasn't he yet turned our wage barrier upside down and not signed ageing 'Boksic' style players who would not play for us if not for the excessive cash thrown at them? Where are the half truths and cheesy grins when we have been beaten 7-0? I share your amazement at our Christmas consistency. The red book is now in the bin. How dare this non ex-Man United man ignore our traditions.

sambaDTR Posted on 28/2 23:47

re: Southgate is ignorant of Boro's tradition

I'm sorry but this guy has to go. I was so sure we would get knocked out. I was expecting to go to the Coro, drown my sorrows and be miserable like all the other Boro supporters but I found myself happy and enjoying myself. Come on, that's not what a Boro Boy is used to! How the hell did Boateng run up, curve his run and put a perfect penalty in the bottom corner when he can't normally hit a barn door? Not to mention Rochemback and Xavier looking like world beaters in the last penalty shoot out. That's nine different penalty takers in the last two rounds. HOWAY. NO WAY!

EireBoro Posted on 1/3 1:34

re: Southgate is ignorant of Boro's tradition

Isn't he aware we haven't got a journeyman midfielder from France in the squad? What sort of preparation is that for an FA Cup tie with United? What if we need to chase the game in the closing stages?

Sort it out, Gareth!!

borobadge Posted on 4/3 11:28

re: Southgate is ignorant of Boro's tradition

And he won't let the Skunks score against us...

Come on Gareth, man, have a heart and know your place!

TOPIC

MESSAGE

POST

REGISTER

There's only one answer to these disgraceful failures. He'll have to go and get his coaching badges.

illuminati Posted on 4/3 11:41

re: Southgate is ignorant of Boro's tradition

Why the heck is he defending our corner and mocking the Geordies?

Does he not realise that he should have been fluttering his eyelids at Freddy Shepherd at every given opportunity?

Gareth obviously learnt nothing from his predecessor!

Out!!

zaphod Posted on 4/3 11:48

re: Southgate is ignorant of Boro's tradition

There's only one answer to these disgraceful failures. He'll have to go and get his coaching badges.

OverTheTopAussie Posted on 4/3 13:28

re: Southgate is ignorant of Boro's tradition

4-4-2? Bloooody 4-4-2 away?!

shakes head in disbelief

joseph99 Posted on 4/3 13:39

re: Southgate is Ignorant of Boro's traditions

Using tiredness as an excuse against a fired-up rival and only managing a point when the same players have played and been victorious in a strenuous mid-week match?

Proper managers play the tiredness card when the team has been chopped, tinkered and unbalanced with lots of fresh legs who escaped any mid-week match but fail to put in a good performance and then lose.

Get shot of Southgate - he's too honest.

joseph99 Posted on 8/3 7:29

re: Southgate is Ignorant of Boro's traditions

Southgate has to go! He's created bedlam for the ticket office - long queues and even DEMAND. And just look what's happening now... tickets for a game against Man U have now become golden and are sold out within minutes. There are even tickets appearing on ebay. WE KNOW WE NEVER SELL THE GROUND OUT, EVEN FOR A SEMI-FINAL!

BobUpndown Posted on 8/3 8:32

re: Southgate is ignorant of Boro's tradition

I'm sick of his talking sense to the media. I want a return to hyperbole and platitudes mixed with repetitive uber-adjectives!

Bully_Boy Posted on 17/3 0:13

re: Southgate is ignorant of Boro's tradition

Just watched his interview on Radio Cleveland. What's this idiot doing trying to answer questions honestly without putting up a smokescreen of an answer?

Also what's this about him liking Parmos? Doesn't he know it should be an US V THEM situation like what happens up at Newcastle? What will we achieve by being united as a club?

BOOOOOOOOOOOOOOO - Get rid before we become successful.

Mat_Evans Posted on 17/3 0:30

re: Southgate is ignorant of Boro's tradition

I tell yer what... I've had enough of him telling these primadonnas (ala Mr Rochemback) that they should be knuckling down and working hard to get back in the team. Doesn't he know that they only come here for the money?

Boro_Gadgie Posted on 13/4 11:09

re: Southgate is Ignorant of Boro's traditions

And refusing to let the season fizzle out once we're just about safe. Anyone knows we should have played out a boring 1-1 or 0-0 draw v Watford, but the way we played, we could have had seven or eight.

BoroinCheadle Posted on 5/5 21:11

re: Southgate is ignorant of Boro's tradition

What the hell does Southgate think he's doing?

Doesn't he realise that the Geordies always finish up higher in the league than Boro?

Cock of the North indeed.

Get it sorted, Southgate - make sure we blow it against Fulham next week.

coruscant Posted on 14/6 21:33

re: Southgate is ignorant of Boro's tradition

Southgate is clueless. Why oh why is he trying to sign players before the 31st of August? Doesn't he realise that if he gets players in early that they stand a chance of gelling with their team mates early?!

That's NOT how Boro does things. I demand last-minute panic buys at 23.58pm on Aug 31st

BOOOOOOOOO...

andybarca Posted on 14/6 21:38

re: Southgate is ignorant of Boro's tradition

And what is he doing signing young, hungry players with pace when he should be moving for experienced over thirty-year-olds on long term deals?

Chapter Five
Call My (Boro) Bluff

Teesside Urban Legends

TOPIC

MESSAGE

POST

REGISTER

TOPIC - Call My (Boro) Bluff

Previous | Next | New Topic | Top Of Board

A Rochemback is a large variant of the Stickleback. Not as nimble, it clumps about in the middle of the pond, looking to get involved.

KrivoyRog Posted on 8/10 6:13

Call my (Boro) Bluff

Roger Roginson here with a new series of "Call my (Boro) Bluff"
There are three definitions but which one is the right one? Let's play...

Ping! The first word is... DORIVA and here are the choices:

1. A Doriva is a dance similar to the Brazilian samba but less exciting. If a disc jockey wants to get the party finished, he will often stick on a Doriva and everyone just buggers off home.

2. The Dorivas are tiny pixie people who live far, far away and are never ever seen... apart from match days.

3. GM's new light van model to replace the Vauxhall Turgido has been named the Vauxhall Doriva. It is said to be a tough little van and does its job unfussily. Yet, strangely, some observers slag it off without ever giving it a road test. Consumption is low, passing can be a problem.

So, three definitions but which one is the true one?

KrivoyRog Posted on 8/10 6:22

re: Call my (Boro) Bluff

Ping! Next word is... a BESWICK.

1. A Beswick is an ornamental hat stand. Many houses have one but they are rarely used.

2. A person unhappy with the bill in a restaurant may say to the waiter, "Look, Pepe, get me the manager NOW, not some Beswick!"

3. Beswick is a small hamlet in rural Gloucestershire; quiet, sleepy, undisturbed, it just sits there.

KrivoyRog Posted on 8/10 6:37

re: Call my (Boro) Bluff

Ping! Ooh, it's a long 'un ... a ROCHEMBACK.

1. A Rochemback is a large variant of the Stickleback. Not as nimble, it clumps about in the middle of the pond, looking to get involved.

2. A Lesser-Spotted Rochemback bird is native to Brazil; white plumage and a distinctive squealing call. It has one rectangular yellow area on just one wing, which, when flustered, it waves at it all about it.

3. El Rochemback was a legendary bullfighter, who teased the adoring crowds by pretending he could not hit the bull but in reality, he was cunning and soon got the crowds behind him when his aim became true. His record season was 15 bulls, bettered only by El Lampardoni and Don Gerrardo.

WilmslowRed Posted on 8/10 9:42

re: Call my (Boro) Bluff

Ping! The next word, is VIDUKA.

1. Viduka is a supposedly ancient Japanese number puzzle, where figures have to be arranged in a grid to show a combination adding up to 40,000. This is repeated each week but the puzzle can be completed with minimal effort every time.

2. A 'Viduka' is a Serbo-Croat insult, meaning a lazy wastrel, who acts as a parasite on the group to which he belongs. An example of the word in use I heard two weeks ago would be two 'gadgies' sat at a football match - one says to the other, "That bloody 'Viduka', he has done nothing all day. I don't know what he is here for. Do you know, Albert?"

3. Gypsy Rose 'Viduka' was a 19th Century Romany who placed a curse on an area of Birmingham just south of the City Centre which in later years came to be known as 'St. Andrews.' The curse has unknown properties, but manifests itself once in a blue moon when Birmingham City find an opposing footballer will be in the form of his life and score two amazing goals in one game - then fail to trouble goalkeepers for the rest of the season.

Other Romany women that are thought to have placed similar curses on an area in the TS1 postcode over the years are Mary Claridge, Eunice Di Matteo, Agnes The entire Sunderland team, O'Grady (a particularly devastating manifestation of this curse is thought to have occurred recently) and Frances 'Yakubu' (although this last curse is thought to have recently been lifted.)

KrivoyRog Posted on 8/10 10:27

re: Call my (Boro) Bluff

Ping! Ooh, a BOKSIC.

1. Simple, this one. BOKSIC translates literally from Croatian to English as Box of Tricks. Indeed.

2. A Boksic is a wrestling hold. Those of you familiar with the great Les Kellett will know his speciality was the half-Boksic and, if it were offered, the deadly full-Boksic, which no-one ever got out from. Basically, it choked its victim and yet, surprisingly, required little effort.

3. The Boksic is the name given to a European wind that blows strongly across the Balkans and Italy before heading north and eventually petering out over a small town in north-east England.

OPEO Posted on 8/10 11:47

re: Call my (Boro) Bluff

Dong! JUNINHO.

1. A South American imp, rather like our fairy. It flits and flies and dances rings around its enemies, the penguins.

2. A small gigolo that frequents suburban toy town.

3. A vision, a dream, an unreality that people hold dearly and to some an impossible hope.

dooderooni Posted on 8/10 11:49

re: Call my (Boro) Bluff

Ping! A RAVANELLI.

1. A Ravanelli is an old Italian word used to describe a much-travelled troubadour. Famed for his ability to accompany small urchins when they danced about the place, the Ravanelli was often found to be lacking when it came to being gracious towards his hosts.

2. The Ravanelli is a very rarely spied bird these days but in its heyday its beautiful white plumage was seen the length and breadth of the country. A timid creature by nature, it was often seen trying to hide its plumage from the onlooking crowds.

3. A Ravanelli is an expression of orgasmic pleasure often favoured by Latin lovers. While it can be used if scoring away from home it is far more likely to be expressed on home territory or, strangely, down by the riverside.

You_lookin_at_liburd Posted on 8/10 13:21

re: Call my (Boro) Bluff

Ping! The next word is DAVENPORT.

1. A large sofa usually convertible into a bed, often confused with a Chesterfield, which is an overstuffed Davenport with upright armrests.

2. A city of eastern Iowa on the Mississippi River opposite Moline and Rock Island, Illinois. It grew rapidly after the first railroad bridge across the Mississippi was completed in 1856 and has a population of 97,700.

3. A shot-shy, overpriced, under-talented excuse for a striker who couldn't hit a cow's arse with a spade, costing £750,000 more than he could ever hope to be worth, who later found his level in lower league football with Sunderland.

CrazyL Posted on 8/10 14:16

re: Call my (Boro) Bluff

Ping! SLAVEN.

1. The bitter-tasting rind of the pomegranate fruit.

2. Ancient, foul tasting, East European broth, or tincture, brewed by Romany apothecaries for the treatment of severe depression. The principal constituents are derived from the bone marrow, and bile duct, of the recently deceased.

3. Physiological term for a reflex verbal out-burst with almost negligible latency. The speed of the (often irate) response has been calculated, in vitro, as less than one nanosecond and is characterized by its ability to bypass all of the higher (cognitive and rational) brain centres.

borobadge Posted on 8/10 14:33

re: Call my (Boro) Bluff

Ping! SPRAGGON.

1. A nut and thread fitting for an early Penny Farthing bicycle wheel.

2. An early type of coffee bean brought to these shores by the Danes, soaked in cow's milk for three days then diluted with three drops of freshly drawn blood taken before 08:30 in the morning and served in a cow's horn.

3. A world famous undercover detective from Peru, who went on to write the Spraggon Mysteries published in 104 countries, but none of them ever in English.

WilmslowRed Posted on 8/10 14:53

re: Call my (Boro) Bluff

Ping! And the next word is... BROWNLEE.

1. A 'Brownlee' refers to a military strategy first employed in the American Civil War by General Arthur P. Brownlee of the Confederate Army. His strategy, which bears his name to this day, was to ignore all evidence of the superior firepower of opposing armies and instil a belief of inevitable victory in his troops through constant praise for their abilities, however limited. General Brownlee died in battle (his first), aged 22, in 1845.

2. "Ere mate, got any Brownlees?" - a common phrase heard in the pubs and clubs of Britain. An illegal, Class A drug that gives users a sense of euphoria and excitability, which has an unfortunate comedown feeling where the user experiences a sense of doom and negative foreboding for up to an hour after the drug wears off - usually accompanied by random idiotic voices in their head.

3. Brownlee's Syndrome - an unfortunate medical condition closely associated to the better-known Tourette's Syndrome. The sufferers feel compelled to involuntarily pepper their speech with phrases such as "Bradley's The Jewellers, Cleveland's leading independent jewellers," "Great news - Boro are only 15 places off a Champions League place," and "Shut it, you whinging Scots pillock." Sadly, there is no known cure and to avoid contagion, people are advised to avoid certain radio broadcasts on Saturday afternoons.

borobadge Posted on 8/10 15:00

re: Call my (Boro) Bluff

Ping! SUGRUE.

1. A very early Irish prototype of rocking chair, made with recycled timber from the depths of an Irish bog... t'was black in colour, most didn't survive as when times were hard the chair went on the fire.

2. A form of Polynesian matting, similar in style to what can be seen on the ultra modern floor of Islington apartments. Sea-grass Sugrue flooring didn't take off in Europe due to its inability to repel smells.

3. A Scottish wild fowl, very rare in numbers and sightings, much rarer than the other Scottish low flying bird, the delightfully named Grouse.

TOPIC

MESSAGE

POST

REGISTER

Rioch - mid-1980's slang for a journey to the moon.

The_Commisar Posted on 8/10 15:45

re: Call my (Boro) Bluff

Ping! A PALLISTER.

1. The most difficult element of a castle's defences, usually tall, unyielding and difficult to get over through or round. "M'lord, the natives are attempting to storm the Pallister." "Don't worry; they'll be there until Christmas trying to break it down."

2. An ailment that travels from one element of the body to the other, before settling for residence just above the gluttonous maximus. "Dear God, that Pallister was knacking my arm this morning and now it's settled in just above my big toe. Bleeding knacks, it does."

3. A once popular friend who emigrated, returns home and winds you up by eating you out of house and home and drinking all your beer and you catch him with his hands down your mums underwear. "You're becoming a bleeding Pallister. SOD OFF!"

borobadge Posted on 8/10 16:01

re: Call my (Boro) Bluff

Ping! VIDMAR.

1. An Israeli sex aid, battery-free, made of finely whittled cedar wood and immersed in oils from the fig. I know you thought that there wasn't such a thing, but believe me the device is called a Vidmar...

2. Scouse slang, often used by a young urban Liverpudlian dressed by catalogue. Just as his parents are set to leave for the local hubcap and pools social club, the youngster can be heard to wallow... "Anee chance of a vid, ma?"

3. A fish found in the darker depths of the Med, slightly oily, but - and here's the surprise - also slightly salty... magnificent with chips... but hard to catch in season and it doesn't stay in the same place for long.

Grrreds Posted on 8/10 16:18

re: Call my (Boro) Bluff

Ping! RIOCH.

1. A youth leader, who specialises in gathering together groups of bleached blonde youngsters, persuading them that they can conquer the world and then beating them to a pulp when they don't.

2. A native of the British Isles which speaks perfect Middle-English with an unfailing ability in persuading the inhabitants of Scotland he is one of their own, all the time wearing a blazer and slacks.

3. Mid-1980's slang for a journey to the moon.

boro74 Posted on 8/10 23:45

re: Call my (Boro) Bluff

Ping! A PHILSTAMP.

1. Somebody who is incredibly lucky, and for no apparent reason gets a highly paid job, doing what he enjoys doing, even though he's not very good at it.

2. A northern anachronism for a pork pie.

3. A unit for measuring wide backsides.

mcbrid Posted on 9/10 8:15

re: Call my (Boro) Bluff

Ping! A FESTA is:

1. A medical term to describe a deformation of the right knee as in "Henry's corner has hit Festa and gone in."

2. An Italian word meaning 'someone holding grudges against rat-faced sub-humanoids wearing red and white stripes.' This condition is characterised by reflex jerking actions of the right elbow or an uncontrollable desire to eject substances from the mouth at great speed in the general direction of aforementioned little bar$teward. Fortunately, both conditions are considered highly desirable in certain parts of the North East.

3. A pasta dish, which has completely dried out - as in "That Festa is really fcukin hard."

borobadge Posted on 9/10 22:25

re: Call my (Boro) Bluff

Ping! BOAM.

1. A very posh word, often used to describe a self-exploding device.

2. When sailing through Europe's choppy waters one should never be without one's Boam. It can save a life if you fall in t'water, for a Boam is a float that fits in to one's underwear, and can be situated just beneath one's sack, or close to Ebbett's Bridge.

3. A word familiar to the medical profession. When one's leg is in a splint you will often hear a doctor say "The leg was badly damaged but he will survive as the Boam was still intact." The Boam is a small sack of leg oil situated in between the kneecap and the lower leg bone fitting.

mcbrid Posted on 9/10 23:43

re: Call my (Boro) Bluff

Ping! MOWBRAY

1. Noun. A unit of hardness on the scale of 0 to 1 as in 'Phil Whelan is not even a tenth of Mowbray.'

2. Verb. To Mowbray… to yearn constantly for a lost one's return as in "I wish Gibbo would tell SMc to fcukoff and get mowbrayin."

3. Noun. A sheepshagger.

KrivoyRog Posted on 10/10 8:14

re: Call my (Boro) Bluff

Ping! Aah, now then, BRANCO. Over to the panel:

1. A Branco is a mythological half-man, half-lard, wing-backed trophy collector characterised by its fixation in shooting from 45 yards. Beware if your club is approached by one of its agents.

2. The Bucking Branco is a fairground ride with a difference. You go onto your hands and knees and a fat bloke climbs on… and stays for two seasons. No-one can get him off.

3. Branco is a legendary figure in Brazilian folklore. Considered to be the finest full back of his generation, he helped his country win the World Cup. He set off on the gold trail to the place they call 'Meedelsbro' and was last heard of on a small radio station in Cuba where he hosts 'El trio legendaros' alongside Stan Collymore and an unknown Belgian sweeper.

OPEO Posted on 10/10 20:30

re: Call my (Boro) Bluff

Ping! A BLACKMORE.

1. This was to the Claymore what a needle is to a spear. A very feeble attempt at sword making by the late Bravetart.

2. To Blackmore, a term usually heard in tanning salons. First you turn orange then you go black more.

3. Blackmore. To offer one's services to an old friend even though you know you can only ever be a shadow of your former self.

dundeejock Posted on 10/10 21:50

re: Call my (Boro) Bluff

Ping! The next word is CURTIS. Over to the panel:

1. Having the CURTIS is having the ability to pick out individuals in large crowds. To show that you have this ability you have to wave at these individuals.

2. A CURTIS is someone who is able to adopt a nationality other than that of their birth - see also Slaven, Lawrenson and Elliott.

3. CURTIS is an incurable disease leading to severe nose bleeding. The cause of this disease is venturing too far from one's normal surroundings. Other symptoms are colour blindness and loss of strength (especially in legs).

littlejimmy Posted on 10/10 22:05

re: Call my (Boro) Bluff

Ping! The next word is McCLAREN.

1. McClaren Syndrome - an incredibly rare genetic disorder, which turns your hair a shiny, strawberry blonde and makes your teeth incredibly sparkly, white and large.

2. McClaren's Law - a much-neglected law of financial, retail and sports management whereby everything must be described as "Magnificent," whatever state it is in.

3. Doing a McClaren - having unprecedented success in a field where all others have failed, bringing unheard of ventures into never-seen-before places, but ultimately still being unpopular with large sections of the population.

borobadge Posted on 10/10 22:21

re: Call my Boro Bluff

Ping! MURDOCH.

1. In the country pile, villas and indeed even the larger town houses of the finest homes in the country, it's not unusual to find a Murdoch, for it is a rather grand and finely designed four-seater settee, made from the finest upholstery, timber and webbing that the human hand can find and design. A Murdoch - quality at its best.

2. A bright mountain flower found only on the lower slopes of the Cairngorm mountains in Scotland, traditionally appears green in colour for nine months of the year and then in a 24 hour burst of sublime change, turns red overnight, a sweet, sweet touch.

3. An ancient art known only to a few, passed down from elder to son of a chosen one, very mystical I know, but it is the wondrous sight of placing a cased football through a 30, 40 or even if required (and only the finest artisans of this craft can attempt it) dare I say a 50 yard pass on to a silver sixpence piece. The word for such a movement, a kick, a pass, a controlled movement of that cased leather ball is… a MURDOCH.

CrazyL Posted on 11/10 10:24

re: Call my (Boro) Bluff

Ping! The next word is… HASSELBAINK.

1. Brutal and bloodthirsty, 18th century witch finder general. The Hasselbaink established missions across 'Godless' swathes of rural Bavaria preaching extreme fundamental Presbyterianism to terrified peasant populations. Even the slightest deviation from the frugal tenets of the creed resulted in the hapless perpetrator being tried as a witch or warlock. If found guilty, the Hasselbaink would exact torturous penance and was known to have feasted frequently upon the fricasseed testicles of young males who had displeased 'The Lord.'

2. Earliest known prototype of the modern day handheld rocket launcher, developed for use in The Great War of 1914-18. The Hasselbaink was loosely derived from the original Blunderbuss but possessed around about 100 times the ballistic power. Unfortunately, the extra weight required rendered it a cumbersome, and unwieldy, weapon with compromised accuracy. This led to its rapid succession by the lighter, and more dynamic, Yakubu 7.5.

3. Hasselbaink (homos humilitus). Small, dark-coloured flower closely related with the better-known Shrinking Violet. Blossoms spectacularly, if sporadically, before lying perfectly dormant, often for weeks on end.

dorivasdad Posted on 11/10 12:50

re: Call my (Boro) Bluff

Ping! The next word is GEORDIE.

1. Would like to be known as a Magpie, but is unable to claim any silverware.

2. A Geordie thinks he is loved by everyone.

3. A Geordie is a result of a liaison between a Jock and a pig.

Boro_Gadgie Posted on 11/10 13:08

re: Call my (Boro) Bluff

Ping! Aahh, the next word is QUEUDRUE.

1. Queudrue, or as it is pronounced by those who have been taking Brownlies, "Kwerdrer", is a word of French origin (though some suggest Irish) meaning to dive into a situation recklessly without giving any thought for the consequences either for oneself or others.

2. To Queudrue is an expression which originates from the Napoleonic wars, meaning to defend defiantly, though with the attitude of "they shall not pass at any price," then preceding to launch an aggressive counter-attack.

3. Queudrue is a French adjective that describes those who despite their good intentions are indisciplined. Often you hear Frenchmen use the phrase "Il est tres Queudrue," meaning he is very indisciplined.

littlejimmy Posted on 11/10 13:10

re: Call my (Boro) Bluff

This stuff is gold. It should be published.

Boro_Gadgie Posted on 11/10 17:15

re: Call my (Boro) Bluff

This has got to be the best original idea for a thread in ages.

Well done, KR!

TOPIC

MESSAGE

POST

REGISTER

Souness - a Scottish word for a member of a secret society who enters enemy neighbour territory and wreaks uncontrolled havoc on their supplies and morale.

bodysausage Posted on 11/10 18:21

re: Call my (Boro) Bluff

Ping! RICKETTS

1. The condition of being large and not very mobile; increased body weight caused by excessive accumulation of fat, often exacerbated by lack of exercise and an inability to get up off the floor. A Ricketts can sometimes be tempted into a brief flurry of action by the rustle of a Mars bar wrapper or a phone call from his agent, but a proper Ricketts will remain dormant under all but the most trying circumstances.

2. A card game for from two to four players in which the score is kept by inserting small pegs into a large voodoo doll.

3. Waste matter eliminated from the bowels; excrement.

CrazyL Posted on 11/10 19:16

re: Call my (Boro) Bluff

Ping! POGATETZ.

1. Composite noun made popular in mid-Eighties Teutonic youth culture. The Pogatetz was a manic, shapeless dance which combined the established 'Pogo' with traditional heavy metal 'headbanging' and was most often observed at German/Austrian electro-rock Oompagh band crossover gigs e.g. The Scorpions, Opus. The dance was, for a short time, banned by the authorities thanks to the complete disregard felt by the participants for the health and well being of their fellow 'Pogatetzers.'

2. An incredibly rare neurological/ocular condition where by the individual eyes are able to function independently of one another, whilst still registering the two sets of visual stimuli perfectly within the brain. Only a handful of people worldwide are known to have 'Pogatetz vision', the ability to literally look, menacingly, in two different directions at the same time.

3. Highly trained Japanese Ninja warriors believe that they are practiced enough in their art to sense impending attack and danger, even before it happens. In Russia a similar phenomenon is observed whereby individuals are able to sense and even feel, extreme pain in advance of any actual physical trauma being suffered. The name given, by research psychologists, to this 'sixth sense' is The Pogatetz.

Jonny_Greenings_sock Posted on 12/10 0:16

re: Call my (Boro) Bluff

Dammit, I wanted to do Pogatetz.

Pong! EMERSON

1. An 'Emerson' is a colloquial term native to the North Yorkshire region used to describe an exotic young secretary who starts work in a failing business, promising visions of previously unimagined sensual bliss, but which proves to be a false and ultimately dispiriting fantasy. Such Emersons can be easily identified by a distinct hip wiggle and a minging cousin.

2. Noun used by electricians and other engineers to describe a new technological innovation in their field which works fantastically well for two months, then indescribably becomes ineffectual and, indeed, invisible eg: "Could have sworn I put a new washer on this tap in March, it's properly Emersoned."

3. Migratory species of South American buffalo, known to vanish at the first sound of samba drums.

Grrreds Posted on 12/10 0:53

re: Call my (Boro) Bluff

Ping! SOUNESS

1. A Scottish word for a member of a secret society who enters enemy neighbour territory and wreaks uncontrolled havoc on their supplies and morale.

2. An intermediary used for diffusing aggressive confrontations between work colleagues.

3. A puppet being controlled by a once great, but now seriously weakened and boring, but nevertheless all-powerful subordinate.

Chapter Six
The Inbox of
Gareth Southgate

Teesside Urban Legends

TOPIC

MESSAGE

POST

REGISTER

Bill was wondering whether you've read 'Focused for Soccer' yet. He said you should hang onto it, as it'll be worth a fortune when we win the World Cup.

TOPIC - The Inbox of Gareth Southgate

Previous | Next | New Topic | Top Of Board

When Boro endured bad runs in April 2007 and again in November of the same year, message board users went into overdrive when they humorously imagined the emails that would be dropping into Gareth Southgate's inbox. Here's the best of their posts...

Eddie_Catflap Posted on 5/4 10:59

The Inbox of Gareth Southgate

To: Gareth@mfc.co.uk
From: Smac@thefa.com

Hiya there, how are you? Keeping my desk tidy I hope. You should see my new one. Magnificent doesn't do it justice, although Sven left some dubious stains on it. I tell you, took me ages to shift them. Eventually I wiped on a bit of that toothpaste I mentioned to you before. You know, the stuff my surgeon recommended? Took them straight out. It's great stuff.

Bill was wondering whether you've read 'Focused for Soccer' yet. He said you should hang onto it, as it'll be worth a fortune when we win the World Cup (between you and me, I've seen copies going for 50p down at Oxfam). It's that sort of positive thinking (even when the facts say something completely different) that got me where I am today though, so it's good advice.

Anyway, I was just wondering if you could give me a bit of advice. Remember when we were getting beat in those UEFA games last season, and looked like we were going to go out? How could you forget? Well, thanks again for suggesting that we went with 4 strikers in an all out attack. Steve Round wanted to play 6 across the middle, remember? LOL! And then that little baldy fella scored, what character! I was thinking the other week that I needed a hero to get the press off my back and gave him a call up. Anyway, I thought it was the one who plays for Everton now, but it isn't, is it? I couldn't believe it when he got on the plane to Israel the other week and it was some other slaphead. I don't think anyone sussed me out though, so mum's the word. Anyway, I was wondering if the other one is still at the Boro? What was his name, is he English?

boksic Posted on 5/4 11:23

re: The Inbox of Gareth Southgate

To: Gareth@mfc.co.uk
From: Woody@unemployedgoalkeepers.co.uk

Nord

I keep ringing your home number but Alison always says you are busy. Has your boss said whether I can have the goalie coaching job yet?

Cheers.

The_Lizards_Jumpers Posted on 5/4 11:52

re: The Inbox of Gareth Southgate

To: Gareth@mfc.co.uk
From: Headmaster@Southgatesoldschool.co.uk

Gareth,

Really appreciate the exposure you've given to our school since you became manager, what with your insistence on wearing your old school jumper and tie. We've never been so well represented on telly since I got caught in that compromising position with that girl from the 6th form.

Kind Regards.

Eddie_Catflap Posted on 5/4 12:10

re: The Inbox of Gareth Southgate

To: Gareth@mfc.co.uk
From: Osvaldo Giroldo Senior
Cc: Gibbo@mfc.co.uk; Lamby@mfc.co.uk

What do you mean, no thanks? Have you seen your midfield lately?

captain5 Posted on 5/4 12:15

re: The Inbox of Gareth Southgate

To: Gareth@mfc.co.uk
From: chrisc@ffc.co.uk

Hi Mate,

Any chance I could stay at yours for a while?

Have you done a security sweep of the place?

Thanks.

bandito Posted on 5/4 12:54

re: The Inbox of Gareth Southgate

To: Gareth@mfc.co.uk
From: JasonEuell@mfc.co.uk

Hi Gareth, I feel really guilty telling you this but I actually lied on my CV. I've never been a professional footballer. Hope you don't think bad of me.

Apologies once again.

Jase x

Eddie_Catflap Posted on 5/4 13:54

re: The Inbox of Gareth Southgate

To: Gareth@mfc.co.uk
From bids@ebay.co.uk

OUTBID NOTICE

You no longer have the current highest bid for item #300096970915 FA COACHING BADGES (GENUINE, GOOD CONDITION)

mf_c Posted on 5/4 13:56

re: The Inbox of Gareth Southgate

To: Gareth Southgate <gareth@mfc.co.uk>
From: Alex Ferguson <rednosedalky@mufc.co.uk>

Gareth,

To stop making you and your players look silly next time we play I'll tell you now we are getting our penalty in the 49th minute.

Alex

key_toenail Posted on 5/4 14:15

re: The Inbox of Gareth Southgate

To: Gareth@mfc.co.uk
From: a.shearer@nufc

Hard luck horse face, I outbid you for the FA coaching badges.

Boro_Gadgie Posted on 5/4 14:22

re: The Inbox of Gareth Southgate

To: Gareth@mfc.co.uk
From: S.Round@hotmail.com

I am a fully qualified holder of the UEFA pro licence coaching badge with experience of coaching in the Premiership, UEFA Cup and international level. After taking a brief break from coaching at Premiership level for 5 years, I am currently looking to return to this.

I hope you will give my CV your consideration and I look forward to hearing from you.

Thanks

Steve

Boro_Gadgie Posted on 5/4 14:25

re: The Inbox of Gareth Southgate

To: S.Round@hotmail.com
From: Gareth@mfc.co.uk

Steve

Thank you for your application. Unfortunately, we do not have any suitable vacancies at the moment, but we will keep your CV on file and if I ever decide to implement an 8-1-1 formation, I will be in touch.

Yours sincerely

Gareth

PS Good luck with your search for employment.

Boro_Gadgie Posted on 5/4 14:34

re: The Inbox of Gareth Southgate

To: A.Shearer@nufc.co.uk
From: Gareth@mfc.co.uk

So, how many trophies did you win in your 10 years at Newcastle?

Eddie_Catflap Posted on 27/11 14:40

The in box of Gareth Southgate

Alright there, Gareth.

Sorry to bother you when you've a lot on your plate, but you couldn't do me a favour could you and send me the dimensions of your office? I'm getting something very similarly sized in my new job apparently and just wanted to make sure I could get all my stuff in.

Cheers

Paul Jewell

PS Have you got a decent view out of your window?

Brick_Tamland Posted on 27/11 14:43

re: The inbox of Gareth Southgate

Gaffer,

Sorry I wasn't at training today. When I return I will fire this team into the top 6. To infinity and beyond!

Luv 'n' hugs

Mids

TOPIC

MESSAGE

POST

REGISTER

Ping-pong
after
playtime?

Eddie_Catflap Posted on 27/11 14:47

re: The inbox of Gareth Southgate

Dear Mr Southgate

As requested, we have searched our database for experienced coaches who may be in a position to offer advice on a consultancy basis. Please find attached the CVs of two very suitable candidates - both available immediately. I'll ring you later to see what you think.

Regards

Helen Barwick
SweetFA Coaching Recruitment Ltd

Attachments: SMcClaren.CV; BBeswick.CV

onthemap Posted on 27/11 14:48

re: The inbox of Gareth Southgate

Can't make le training today boss, ma amstring az popped out again. If we are on le tele on Samedi a will be ok for alf an ower.

Ali

onthemap Posted on 27/11 14:53

re: The inbox of Gareth Southgate

Herr Southgate,

Vy af we got ze French nincompoop at ze front line?

Gott im Himmell.

Emanuel

mattrich Posted on 27/11 14:53

re: The inbox of Gareth Southgate

Hi boss, can't make Reading on Saturday, I'm DJing on the night at Purple Onion and won't get back in time. Jinky said he would stand in for me if it's OK with you? Later – Stewy.

Turner_86 Posted on 27/11 14:55

re: The inbox of Gareth Southgate

Dear Gareth,

We hear you may be looking for work quite soon. We'd be more than happy to offer you something.

Your good friends at...

Pizza Hut.

PS Are your cooking skills any better than your acting?

Brick_Tamland Posted on 27/11 15:00

re: The inbox of Gareth Southgate

Gareth-San,

Ping-pong after playtime?

Dong

rat_out Posted on 27/11 15:11

re: The inbox of Gareth Southgate

Agent Southgate,

Nearly half way through the season now and you're going strong. Told you Gibson wouldn't have the bottle to sack you! The fans are starting to catch on a bit though so maybe you should announce a spectacular signing or something. I hear Boro fans are good at falling for that one. Anyway keep up the good work, you'll be rock bottom with no way back soon enough.

Regards,

Agent N. Quinn and Agent M. Ashley

slaven Posted on 27/11 15:20

re: The inbox of Gareth Southgate

Keep your chin up, Gareth.

You have my support.

Results will come.

rat_out Posted on 27/11 15:21

re: The inbox of Gareth Southgate

Slaven, stop joking around will you, this is a serious thread.

Boro_2006 Posted on 27/11 15:28

re: The inbox of Gareth Southgate

Dear Gareth,

Could you pop up to my office please. I'm still having trouble with this fax machine. I need to send a fax urgently to a Mr Venables in Spain about a possible vacancy we have coming up at the club soon. Oh, and bring some Kleenex would ya, there's a love!

Keith

mackey69 Posted on 27/11 15:32

re: The inbox of Gareth Southgate

Now then Gaz,

Sorry I wasn't at training today. I was out on the lash in Onyx last night, and when I got to Europa I had an argument with the guy at the till. The prat made me pay for my parmo and when I said "Don't you know who I am?" he replied "You're Kirk from Corrie, aren't ya?"

Cattermole

fatknackerlardarse Posted on 27/11 15:34

re: The inbox of Gareth Southgate

Hello Mr Southgate,

Are you sure you still want to go ahead with the reconstructive surgery to your nasal passages?

We have had a long discussion about this and feel it may be better to delay the surgery until your results start improving, otherwise we fear that the nose area may suffer more damage from season tickets.

Yours

Ivor Nosedone.
Chief Plastic Surgeon.
Hurworth Clinic.

Grrreds Posted on 27/11 15:37

re: The inbox of Gareth Southgate

Gareth,

I've unearthed another gem for you.

Stevie Wonder
(Chief Scout, Far East).

Jonny_Greenings_sock Posted on 27/11 15:38

re: The inbox of Gareth Southgate

Nord,

Thanks for the three points mate.

Arsene, Alex, Rafa, Avram, Mark, Harry, Sven, David, Martin, Gary, Alex, Lawrie, Sam, Steve, Roy, Paul, Alan and Juande.

Boro_2006 Posted on 27/11 15:40

re: The inbox of Gareth Southgate

Universal Studios
Hollywood
California
USA

Mr Southgate,

It has come to our attention here at Universal that you may be at a loose end soon. We are planning a sequel to the Borat Movie and wondered if you would fancy some stunt double work?

Awaiting your reply.

S Spielberg

bororeddaz Posted on 27/11 15:43

re: The inbox of Gareth Southgate

Gareth

I was concerned, but not worried, at your scoreline at the weekend. It seemed that you were unlucky and there were some magnificent performances from some of the younger players.

I have attached the address and contact details of my orthodontic surgeon that you asked for. We should get together over Christmas as I'm guessing we'll both be free.

Yours magnificently,

Ginger

Boro_2006 Posted on 27/11 15:45

re: The inbox of Gareth Southgate

Dear Gareth,

Many thanks for your letter regarding what you really wanted.

Unfortunately, we don't make the show any more and even if we did, Jesus Christ himself couldn't make that happen.

Best Wishes for the future

Jim'll Fix It Former Office
BBC TV Centre
Wood Lane
LONDON

Jonny_Greenings_sock Posted on 27/11 15:46

re: The inbox of Gareth Southgate

Gareth,

Here's a voucher attached worth £100. Go and get yourself a drink.

Woody

Archie_Stanton1 Posted on 27/11 15:47

re: The inbox of Gareth Southgate

Gareth,

Yerv no bought enuff playerz.
I sayz that at the start o the season.

Bernie

You thinka Donga Gook suitable replacement fora mia? You a liar and stinky managera.

Bukowski_MFC Posted on 27/11 15:48

re: The inbox of Gareth Southgate

You thinka Donga Gook suitable replacement fora mia? You a liar and stinky managera.

Hugs,

Massimo xxx

Eddie_Catflap Posted on 27/11 15:49

re: The inbox of Gareth Southgate

Sorry, but Steve Gibson rejected your friend invite on Facebook.

Billy Davies added you as a friend on Facebook. We need you to confirm that you are, in fact, friends with Billy Davies.

Sammy Lee added you as a friend on Facebook. We need you to confirm that you are, in fact, friends with Sammy Lee.

To confirm these friend requests, follow the link below:
http://www.facebook.com/n/?reqs.php

Thanks,

The Facebook Team

Boro_2006 Posted on 27/11 15:50

re: The inbox of Gareth Southgate

Gareth,

Your dinner's in the dog.

Love The Missus x

SuperBokSupper Posted on 27/11 15:50

re: The inbox of Gareth Southgate

Hi All,

Just an invite to this year's Xmas do at The Purple Onion down the Boro. It's on Friday 14th December (we've only got Derby away the next day).

Superstar DJ Stewie Downing will be spinning the discs so it should be a good do. Players only night this one so don't tell the Gaffer.

Cheers

George Boateng
Club Captain

SuperBokSupper Posted on 27/11 15:52

re: The inbox of Gareth Southgate

Gaffer,

Please delete the last email I sent u.

Eez impotant.

George

Manila Posted on 27/11 15:53

re: The inbox of Gareth Southgate

Yo boss,

Am confused. You pulled me out of a Championship team to play in a team that is heading for the Championship? Surely it would have been better gaining more experience getting out of it than going into it?

Jinky

Boro_2006 Posted on 27/11 15:54

re: The inbox of Gareth Southgate

Gareth,

I know how it is to be lonely and unliked. Join me. I have attached a flight voucher to Afghanistan. We will party! I have lots of funky ciggies and as many camels as you need (very pretty).

See you soon,

Osama

Bukowski_MFC Posted on 27/11 15:56

re: The inbox of Gareth Southgate

Please play me next game. I am Braveheart. The Turkish David Beckham. I love your club very much. Nice kebab for you. Chilli sauce.

Tuncay

SuperBokSupper Posted on 27/11 15:58

re: The inbox of Gareth Southgate

Deer Garef

I am steel ere you kno. Am I allowed to play weev ze beeger boys yet?

I am going bald through ze stress of eet all.

I will proper try dead ard an zat.

Gaizka
x

---

boro_mod Posted on 27/11 15:59

re: The inbox of Gareth Southgate

Mr Southgate,

Your book "Managering for Dumbies" has arrived for collection at Waterstones, Captain Cook Square.

Waterstones Store Manager

Jonny_Greenings_sock Posted on 27/11 15:59

re: The inbox of Gareth Southgate

Achtung, I hurt so bad.

Robert

0T_Kenny Posted on 27/11 16:01

re: The inbox of Gareth Southgate

G'day Gaffer,

I think some of the players aren't pulling their weight in the team, but I am right behind you.

Marco (Ned Kelly) Schwarzer

Dicky200006 Posted on 27/11 16:03

re: The inbox of Gareth Southgate

Hi Gareth

Thanks for your email. Unfortunately, even I can't get your team out of this. Good luck though.

Yours,

Santa

London_Boro Posted on 27/11 16:05

re: The inbox of Gareth Southgate

G'day Boss,

Just wondering how many flaming shots I've got to let in before you realise I want to jump in me ute and drive off into the distance to another club.

Strewth, what a flaming dingo.

Yours

Mark 'Skippy' Schwarzer

Manila Posted on 27/11 16:10

re: The inbox of Gareth Southgate

Are you wanting a bigger penis?

As seen on TV
Over 781, 000 Men around the world are already satisfied
Gain 2+ Inches In Length
Increase Your Penis Width (Girth) By upto 29%
100% Safe To Take, With NO Side Effects
No Pumps! No Surgery! No Exercises!

Eddie_Catflap Posted on 27/11 16:14

re: The inbox of Gareth Southgate

Gareth

Look, I know how many points we've got. I've seen the league table. Relax, man. I'm not going to give you the chop. So you can stop cutting up my newspapers, fix whatever you did to my web browser and bring back the remote for the tele.

Still - I got Keith to fax the FA for the weekend's results so I could check my coupon. Still cracks me up seeing him trying to use it. He was sweating like it was transfer deadline day.

Steve

The_Boro_Bugler Posted on 27/11 16:23

re: The inbox of Gareth Southgate

Dear Gareth,

I understand that things are not looking good... a bit of advice from a man in the know!

Under no circumstances resign, no matter how bad it gets. Even if the fans boo and players cry off sick, pretend to be positive.

Eventually they'll sack you, pay you compo (can you believe that?) and then you can buy a villa in Jamaica next door to me.

Rgds

Steve

Boro_2006 Posted on 27/11 16:27

re: The inbox of Gareth Southgate

Gareth,

If all fails mate just shout "WHEN IT'S A BATTLE FOOKIN BATTTTLE!"
It nearly worked for me...

Steve Bleasdale

If not, storm out in a huff.

Maybe now you have come to realise why we opposed your appointment. Things would have been different if you had actually earned your coaching diploma (or as you called it 'just a meaningless piece of paper').

Vincent75 Posted on 27/11 16:29

re: The inbox of Gareth Southgate

Dear Gareth,

Maybe now you have come to realise why we opposed your appointment. Things would have been different if you had actually earned your coaching diploma (or as you called it 'just a meaningless piece of paper').

I trust you will be able to partake in full-time studying after Christmas.

Regards

J. Barnwell
League Managers Association.

Boro_2006 Posted on 27/11 16:31

re: The inbox of Gareth Southgate

Gareth,

Thanks for taking the heat off me for a bit, mate. Roy says thanks too. Look forward to our clashes next season in the Fizzy Pop League.

Big Sam

mackey69 Posted on 27/11 16:32

re: The inbox of Gareth Southgate

Dear Gareth,

I've got a plan so cunning you could put a tail on it and call it a weasel.

Blackadder

Boro_2006 Posted on 27/11 16:35

re: The inbox of Gareth Southgate

The Premier League
LONDON

Dear Mr Southgate,

Congratulations! You have been voted Barclaycard Premiership Manager of the Month for November!

Only Kidding!

The lads at the Premier League office.

Proctors_Perm Posted on 27/11 16:43

re: The inbox of Gareth Southgate

You've been outbid on eBay item: PREMIER LEAGUE STRIKER, GUARANTEED 20 GOALS + IN SEASON!!!!!!
(330190221280)and#8207;
From: eBay (ebay@ebay.co.uk)

Sent: 27 November 2007 16:07:48
Reply-to: ebay@ebay.co.uk
To: southgate77@hootmail.com
eBay sent this message to Gareth Southgate (southgate77).
Your registered name is included to show this message originated from eBay. Learn more.
You've been outbid. Bid again now!

Dear southgate77,

There's a new highest bid on the following item, but there's still a chance to make the item yours.

PREMIER LEAGUE STRIKER, GUARANTEED 20 GOALS + IN SEASON!!!!!!

Current price:
£5,500,000.00
End time: 31-01-08 10:28:38 GMT
Your maximum bid: £25.00
View Item | Go to My eBay |

Wedgwood Posted on 27/11 16:47

re: The inbox of Gareth Southgate

Fantasy Premier League - Gameweek 14 Preview

Hi Gareth Southgate,

On Thursday the team selected for Middlesbrough was:

Schwarzer, Young, Woodgate, Huth (Ankle - doubtful), Pogatetz, Boateng (Captain), Arca (Knee - expected back Nov 30th), O'Neil, Downing, Mido (Groin injury), Aliadiere

With the following substitutes:

Jones, Rochemback, Tuncay, Cattermole.

The Gameweek 14 deadline is 24 Nov 11:30 (UK time).

You are currently ranked 1,345,273 out of 1,345,276 registered players.

Eddie_Catflap Posted on 27/11 17:03

re: The inbox of Gareth Southgate

Boss

You know you were saying you're that desperate for a striker, you'd even have that Nemeth back? Well I've got a slight confession.

I've been keeping him in my shed. Figured no-one would miss him once he left the club. He's a bit bewildered and confused, but what's new? I'll swap you him for Dong Gook.

Mad Dog

SidSnot Posted on 27/11 17:18

re: The inbox of Gareth Southgate

Boss,

F**k me. We didn't discuss this in the interview....

Gaz O

PS - 'Arry used to take us to the dogs for team building. Worked a treat. Best not tell Dong though....

Boro_2006 Posted on 27/11 17:18

re: The inbox of Gareth Southgate

Gareth,

We look forward to seeing you soon. Please bring with you your last payslip, p45, and some sort of identification, passport, household bill etc.

Yours Sincerely

Dept for Employment.

ExiledInStoke Posted on 29/11 12:06

re: The inbox of Gareth Southgate

Re £13million debt.

Dear Mr Southgate

Good news! We at Ocean Finance can help you consolidate your existing debts into one easy manageable monthly payment. This means that you may have £300,000 (that's right, £300,000) to spend in January!

Just think of all the luxuries you could buy with that sort of money - a relaxing holiday, a splendid detached home, or even Jason Euell.

We look forward to hearing from you soon.

Carol Vorderman

Chapter Seven
Best Away Day Stories Following The Boro

Teesside Urban Legends

TOPIC - Best Away Day Stories Following The Boro

Previous | Next | New Topic | Top Of Board

THRYLOS_MFC Posted on 9/11 13:36

Best Away Day Stories Following The Boro

What are your best away day tales following the Boro? Not just the away wins, but difficult journeys etc!

blotonthelandscape Posted on 9/11 13:38

re: Best Away Day Stories Following The Boro

Went to Joker five times, five victories, nice.

YoungAlf Posted on 9/11 13:41

re: Best Away Day Stories Following The Boro

Most annoying journey was on the way back from Fulham last season with the Boro coaches. Left on time, even though we were missing three people and everyone told the driver not to go. Got one hour into the journey only to have to turn back and get them (cos of the knob head driver. They were only teenagers.) Therefore we lost around three hours travel time and got back to Boro around 2am - and it was a 3pm kick off.

junouk Posted on 9/11 13:53

re: Best Away Day Stories Following The Boro

Wembley, Cardiff, Banik.

Coventry, watching Job and Boksic's first League game. We won easy but I thought my mate was driving home and he thought I was, so we ended up spending the night in Leamington Spa. Got loads of sh*** off the wife when I got home at lunchtime on the Sunday. But a great weekend and a great result.

YoungAlf Posted on 9/11 14:00

re: Best Away Day Stories Following The Boro

Best away day apart from Cardiff for me was probably one of my first away games - away to Palace in the Cup a few years back now. It was a surprise and I was supposed to be going skating but for some reason my dad never let me wear my Boro shirt. Anyway we were 2-0 down inside 7 mins and we came back to equalise with Barmby scoring. Got to meet all the players before the game including Phil Whelan (wot a player). Only problem was I had to sit in the Palace end and couldn't control myself when we equalised. Luckily I was with some hard Palace friends who told everyone to stay clear of me.

Then, to top it off, I heard that Boro were signing Juninho on the radio on the way home and he was coming over. I was gobsmacked after seeing him play in the Umbro Cup and thought they must have meant the old Brazilian right back, Jairzinho, lol.

Sidebar

Got loads of sh*** off the wife when I got home at lunchtime on the Sunday. But a great weekend and a great result.

wilfym Posted on 9/11 14:08

re: Best Away Day Stories Following The Boro

Got lost coming back from Cambridge in the Cup a few years ago and ended up on a pub crawl with locals in a hick village, then nearly killed myself getting out of a car for a piss as it was doing approx 90mph at the time... ahhh the memories!

Nedkat Posted on 9/11 14:12

re: Best Away Day Stories Following The Boro

Bloody Zenith Data Cup Final. Whoever it was who booked the Laurel and Hardy coach company needs a clip round the ear! Two drivers, ancient coach, which is now in a museum. When one was driving, the other was back seat driving. On the way back, after we had been beaten by Chelsea, the coach developed a problem. Damn thing would only get into first gear. So we're pottering up the A1 at around 6mph. I suggested we get off the A1 and find somewhere we can grab a pint whilst they call for a replacement coach. Nooooo!! Bad idea... The coach drivers want to continue on up the A1 at 6mph!!! Eventually... we ended up in Biggleswade, nice boozer and got back to the Boro after the sun was up next day!

Preston, 1974. I think there were 16,000 Boro fans who travelled to see the Boro that day. We had a great time. I was 16 and it was the summer of the Boro!

Cardiff. 8,000 mile round trip to see the Boro lift the Carling Cup. Worth every single penny!! Only wish we had travelled to Cardiff earlier and left a bit later. We did it all on the same day, and missed a lot of the celebrations. Great day though, to see all those Boro supporters mingling around the stadium and when Job's goal went in, I thought I'd died and gone to heaven!

Piquet2 Posted on 9/11 14:16

re: Best Away Day Stories Following The Boro

"Preston. 1974." I remember that game, Ned. It was rearranged after the original was postponed due to snow, if I remember right. Preston were managed by Bobby Charlton, I think we won 4-0. Bobby didn't last long after that season. We were all singing "Jackie's better than Bobby."

Great days.

tony_block19 Posted on 9/11 14:26

re: Best Away Day Stories Following The Boro

I went to most of the away games in the 1994/95 season and don't really remember them but the first game of the season, 1995 v Arsenal, my dad and I went down for the weekend to stay with friends. Remember me telling my dad off for drinking "mucky beer" lol. Loved that weekend, got to see the sights of London for the first time and see Nick Barmby put us in the lead. I must have been a right pain in the arse because it was unbelievably hot and I kept nagging my dad for a drink! Bless me.

PodgerC Posted on 9/11 14:32

re: Best Away Day Stories Following The Boro

In the heady old days of the 1987 Second Division campaign, three of us were sat in the pub after hours on Friday night and as more pints were drank, we decided to go to the away match at Plymouth the next day. Spent one hour (at one in the morning) phoning around to get a fourth person. Achieved that at about 2am.

Went home and went to bed. Aware of someone knocking on window next morning at 6am, four bedraggled souls set off on the road to Plymouth. One of the lads phoned his girlfriend from a service station on the M5 to say he probably wouldn't be out with her that night. She wasn't happy.

Had a blow-out on the M5 and had to have a tyre replaced in Gloucestershire (Ebley Tyre Centre, if my memory serves me correctly). Arrived at Plymouth in time for a quick bite to eat and a pint before going to the match. Driver had locking wheel nut confiscated as offensive weapon by Police jobsworth. Had to talk to an inspector to get it returned after the match.

Half time came and a group of Boro fans wandered in. One of our lot knew them and asked why they were late. It turned out they had just got there. They had set off and had turned left somewhere instead of right and only realised they were wrong when they saw a sign informing them they were twenty odd miles from Ipswich. They had to stop at a garage and nick a road atlas.

The match itself - Gary Hamilton scored the only goal and Dean Glover got sent off for an atrocity of a tackle that would have merited a twelve-match ban had it occurred nowadays.

Left Plymouth at 17:30 with the object of reaching home by last orders. Had a stop for petrol that would have done credit to a Formula One pit stop crew. Walked into pub at 22:40 after a ten-minute delay at Urlay Nook crossing.

freethenorton7 Posted on 9/11 14:40

re: Best Away Day Stories Following The Boro

Some of my best ones were:

Doncaster last game of season.

Barnsley last game.

Zenith Data - first Wembley trip.

Aston Villa in semi for ZDS - Mark Brennan!

Blackpool for weekend when in 3rd division.

Cardiff, of course.

Ostrava.

Many more but these spring to mind initially.

THRYLOS_MFC Posted on 9/11 15:31

re: Best Away Day Stories Following The Boro

PodgerC - The lads who got into Plymouth at half time were my mates (Wiffy and the lads). They had set off at 5am and ran out of petrol at Thirsk! They set off again and all except the driver didn't know the way and they ended up 10 miles from Ipswich!!! Then it was 100mph all the way to Plymouth to get there at half time and miss Gazza Hamilton's winning goal! I was there but laughed my tits off when we saw them! 1000 miles for 45 mins of football!

I remember going to see Boro v Palace and getting lost on the North Circular and having to get the Woolwich ferry across the Thames. We got to the "Palace ground", parked up and ran like f**k to the pub, only to find it was the Crystal Palace athletics stadium!

My best away games are just too numerous to mention, but 1) Wolves away FA Cup 6th round replay - lost 3-1 AET with about 10-12k Boro there and also 2) Wolves away promotion under Lennie.

andymfcok Posted on 9/11 15:55

re: Best Away Day Stories Following The Boro

Carlisle - first season after near liquidation. A few lads bought something a little stronger than lager from the wine shop before we set off. By the time we crossed the Bridge at Barnard Castle, one lad had stripped naked and had started running back over the bridge. We calmed him down and he was asleep as we parked in Carlisle, so we left him in the car. As we approached the ground, another lad tried to storm the gates and was promptly arrested. We won the game 1-0 and returned to the car to wake up our sleeping dog, who thought it was still before the match. He was a little disappointed to say the least and even more so when he realised he had wet himself.

Anyway, on to the police station to pick up our arrestee. Whilst waiting, we got some fish and chips, our streaker sighted some Carlisle fans wanting aggro, so he set off after them, only to get run over by a car. He wasn't too hurt and we again waited at the police station for our other mate. Suddenly the Carlisle fans appeared with a copper in tow. They pointed out our mate, who was having the day of his life. So just as one lad was getting released, another was being arrested. Another 2-hour wait and everyone out of nick, we finally set off home. Good day, good memories.

Jack_Russell Posted on 9/11 16:10

re: Best Away Day Stories Following The Boro

The Arsenal away game in the Cup last year sticks in the mind. Drove down there nice and early, got to Highbury about 4pm and could not find a place to park the car anywhere. All the housing estate roads had gates on so you could not drive down the street. And everywhere else you needed a permit to park or the Police advised I could not park there.

I drove around for 2 hours. I eventually parked on an industrial estate which was covered in deep wet mud, (we wished we had brought our wellies). Our clothes got covered. This industrial estate, where we ended up parking, turned out to be the place they are now building the new ground on.

A tip is DON'T EVER EVER DRIVE TO ARSENAL!!!

blotonthelandscape Posted on 9/11 16:20

re: Best Away Day Stories Following The Boro

Went to the Wolves Cup game in a removal van with numerous others. It was during the time of the carry outs. After boozing all morning, we set off at 2pm for Wolves with the carry outs. Learnt a very basic lesson in that you cannot piss out of a van at 70mph on a motorway. Somehow we found the ground and watched the game, then set off back. We were in Manchester at 1am, thinking we were in Leeds. Decided that the local nightclub was desperate for our company, unfortunately the bouncers were not as keen. Got home at 5.

TOPIC

MESSAGE

POST

REGISTER

Even though we didn't get to see the game, it was a cracking day out.

gibson Posted on 9/11 16:24

re: Best Away Day Stories Following The Boro

Cardiff (after we'd won!) I had a few shandies at the airport and some Bolton fans were giving it the massive whinge 'til some largish scaffolder type Boro fans rolled up and planted themselves beside them. They went a bit quiet then. I also saw Malcolm Christie at the airport, and shouted to him, "'ow's yer leg, Malc?" (I know, I know, I cringe even now!). He was obviously gutted. To his credit, he said it was coming along fine. My missus won't let me forget that one!

Another was at Reading, watching Gazza wind up their fans.

And recently, I thoroughly enjoyed the day at Blackburn. All the lads and lasses singing their hearts out 1/2 hour before kick off on the concourse and E-I-O-ing to all the Blackburn fans opposite the coaches. Class.

silly_sod Posted on 9/11 16:43

re: Best Away Day Stories Following The Boro

3 of us decided to go to a sold out game at Southampton full of beer at 10pm on the Friday night. Set off at 6am and stopped somewhere in the South Midlands for a bit of breakfast before making it to Southampton in time for the pubs opening. Had a few, went to the ground, couldn't get in, went to London, met mate, drank loads, fell over 3 times in the space of 5 minutes, drove home severely hung-over, realised we didn't even know what the score had been.

janplanner Posted on 9/11 16:50

re: Best Away Day Stories Following The Boro

Derby County in the FA Cup at the BBG. It felt like we ruled the world that day.

bandito Posted on 9/11 16:58

re: Best Away Day Stories Following The Boro

Letting a couple of stink bombs off on a bus full of Leeds fans and seeing one lad throw up was rather funny. We won 3-2 as well, which was extra sweet.

stocko_mfc Posted on 9/11 16:59

re: Best Away Day Stories Following The Boro

Charlton away, John Pickering's only game in charge, which we won 5-2. On the way out of London we passed a car full of Boro fans, from Derby I think. Anyway they flagged us down and asked us if we wanted to go for a drink and something to eat at a pub they knew in Grantham. We spent most of the night on the pool table and having a bit of banter with the locals as well as getting p***ed... great day/night.

THRYLOS_MFC Posted on 9/11 17:05

re: Best Away Day Stories Following The Boro

janplanner, that was such a significant day in Boro's history - getting past the FA Cup 6th Round - and another one I left off my list!

Another time, away to Bristol City, night match, about '87. Got arrested on the A19 (wrongful arrest, long story, but 12 hours in Stockton cells until the thick rossers realised they had f***ed up) but the funny part was that one of the lads, desperate to go, went in the boot (well, it's only a 540 miles round trip) and when we were being read our rights, there was a loud banging and screaming coming from the boot! The copper nearly shat himself when he saw the lad. By the way, we never got to the game...

My most expensive away game was the ZDS Cup in '90. I lived in Australia for 2 years and spent about £2000 to come home for the game and got my mug shot on the front page of the Gazette. "Boro fans home in on Wembley". Well, Andy Worhol said 15 minutes...

London_Boro Posted on 9/11 17:28

re: Best Away Day Stories Following The Boro

Away to Forest, can't remember the year, it may have been 11-12 years ago. Got a lift down with a bunch of lads in a mini-bus. We were told by the club that we could buy tickets at Forest. When we got there, they wouldn't let us in, to the delight of the Forest supporters looking from the concourse windows. So we turned round and headed home. We stopped in Mansfield for a quick pint on the way and ended up leaving, completely sh**faced at about 10:30 at night. One of the lads with us even managed to shag one of the locals in the pub toilet and from what I remember she was a bit tasty too!

Even though we didn't get to see the game, it was a cracking day out, we had a real laugh in the pub and the locals were great, loads of friendly banter and beers flowing all day.

redlion57 Posted on 9/11 18:36

re: Best Away Day Stories Following The Boro

Not the best but one, Coventry, New Year's Day 1980. Didn't realise me and a few mates were going until I got a phone call at 9am New Year's morning (we'd arranged it during the alcoholic haze that is New Year's Eve). Waiting at Normanby Top with some cans left over from the previous night when what should roll up? A furniture van!

We managed to get to the match somehow and on the way home we decided to stop off at what can only be described as one of the dodgiest pubs in Nottingham. Anyhow, we must have fitted in because they left us alone and one pint became two, two became three and next minute it was last orders!

We staggered back into the back of the van to find the drink we'd spilled on the way to the game had started to freeze, it was that cold. Driving home for what seemed an eternity (the van was sounding like a right bag of hammers), we suddenly stopped. The driver shouted that the van had broken down. One of the lads managed to look under the roller at the back and said "It's OK lads, we're in South Bank." Only we weren't, we'd broken down in Thirsk at about 3 in the morning! Went to the local bobbies to phone for some alternative transport home and the t**ts kicked us out in the cold until it came. Eventually got home about 6am.

Oh, and we got beat 2-0.

---

borobadge Posted on 9/11 18:36

re: Best Away Day Stories Following The Boro

Where do you start? Being a time served Boro fan, I could fill a book...

Bolton 1974 and the Boro fans chaired Bobby Murdoch from the coach to the ground entrance because the ground wasn't fit for him to walk on...

Preston away on the League Liner special train. 4-2 win and thousands of Boro. The police had to empty one end of Preston before the Boro could be allowed in. We got in and Boro fans were in 3 sides of the ground...

Hitchhiking in the snow overnight to Highbury, 0-0.

Hitchhiking overnight to Wolves... ended up in Coventry. Started to hitch back home at 14:30 and the van goes straight past the ground. "Hang on, mate, let us out here". Run to the ground, get in and we're getting beat 1-0 with 5 minutes gone...

QPR away and some loon throws a milk bottle full of petrol at us. It smashes against the wall and bursts into flames...

Stoke away and a Stoke fan tries to get in the Boro end... only we were all p***ing ourselves laughing as he was dressed as Elvis!

Leeds away and two blown up Santas have an air fight... only for the police to arrest them. Then a police dog decides to bite my shoulder so I'm walking around the pitch on me wat for treatment. I complain to a police chief, who informs me that I may well have infected HIS dog...

Bolton away and a copper says to me, "I'm watching you, man at C&A." I had bondage strides on and a mohair jumper!

Going on a school bus to Derby! Stopping at Thirsk on the way home... too many great weekends in Derby @ t.b.b.g. The Cup game was quality. Derby fans were most upset on the train back to London. One bloke never did see the funny side of me telling him that "this seat is reserved for the winners, mate!" I came back to London with Chris Powell, a real cool, nice guy...

The pre-season games in Holland 5-6 seasons ago were class as well and this season I went to Germany for the friendly with Hansa Rostock. That was quite an eye opener. Hamburg makes Amsterdam look like Scarborough...

I'm sure I can remember more... the craic and fun has been my fortunate experience and luck at being born a supporter of Middlesbrough FC...

It doesn't really matter what league you're in, it's the camaraderie and the friendships that are important when watching the Boro. The days of watching the lads during the Great Miners' Strike was something else... winning at Mansfield and singing "Arthur Scargill, Arthur Scargill, we'll support you ever more" to the non-striking Mansfield/Nottingham miners was a strange one but it didn't half upset 'em...

Hopefully, there are many more to come... it's a marathon, not a sprint and Boro are for life, not just for Christmas...

HolgateEnd Posted on 9/11 19:08

re: Best Away Day Stories Following The Boro

Flippin 'eck - what a post to start! I think everyone has so many memories of away games it's a struggle to think of the games you've been to, never mind which were the best.

When I was a kid (around mid-late '80s time) my old fella took me to Old Trafford. Don't remember the game at all - I was too excited and overawed as it was my first away game. Anyway, the train had been diverted through Liverpool on the way home and just as we got to the station, someone in our carriage shouted "duck" which we duly did before every single window on the train was bricked!

Of those I can remember, over the last few seasons we've had some good days out at Bolton and Everton though the result didn't always go well. Birmingham last season was quite good (though the game was s***e) as we'd won the Cup three days before and my voice was still hoarse! Anyway, I was at work when I got a phone call at 1pm.

"Hiya, what time do you finish work?"

"4 o'clock - why?"

"Fancy going to Birmingham?"

"Nah, I'm skint from Cardiff... oh well, f**k it, let's go... pick me up from mine at 3 then." And off I went to tell my boss there was an emergency and I had to get home...

Spurs and Arsenal (Carling Cup) last season were good, as was the obvious one - Cardiff. I'm just glad we decided to do Saturday to Monday instead of there and back in a day. The Gatekeeper was fantastic on the Saturday and the whole Sunday will never be forgotten!

stockton_red Posted on 9/11 19:28

re: Best Away Day Stories Following The Boro

Quite a few spring to mind but as a 17-year-old they don't stretch back too far. This season at Charlton, absolutely s***faced, fare-dodging on the train across London, a 2-1 win, an hour in a strip club outside King's Cross, more cans, even more s***faced on the train from Darlo to Thornaby, seeing a gay party in Teesdale, drink in Stockton, parmo and then getting home to collapse on the sofa. I love it.

I'm sure there are plenty of tales that could be told about MN4 motors.

Aaaaah, f*** it, you've twisted my arm. Let's go to Liverpool, boys!!!

captain5 Posted on 10/11 9:19

re: Best Away Day Stories Following The Boro

Tranmere away, last game of the season. "Uwe, Uwe, Giz a wave." Sat in the foot well of a car on the way there, got a very old coach back and went back via Castleford. Still not sure why this was, as I was living in Manchester at the time.

Stoke City, a few days before, but they were playing Bolton!! Bolton bottle it, Peter Shilton plays in goal and we get promoted. Get in there! Got a lift back to Manchester with a bloke from Boro in a Land Rover.

Notts County, same season. Train down for 11.00am start in Nottingham, was a 90-minute wait afterwards for the train, so decide to hitchhike. Great plan! Again, was back in Boro. Starting to realise where a lot of my money went when I was a student.

TOPIC

MESSAGE

POST

REGISTER

Don't remember the game at all - I was too excited and overawed as it was my first away game.

boros_moggy Posted on 10/11 10:46

re: Best Away Day Stories Following The Boro

So many, but these are the ones that spring to mind:

Hull 1970 - first ever away game, watched the Ayresome Angels taking the Hull end. Remember being able to walk all the way round the ground and the train station at one side.

Liverpool 1976. FA Cup Q-final - I was the last one let in the Boro end, mate behind me was locked out with loads more. It was that packed that I spent most of game on the stairs. Came out of ground, Scousers tried to rob me so ran off and found myself near Goodison where Everton v West Ham was on. Chased back by Everton. Jumped on any old coach home.

Pisa 1993 Anglo-Italian Cup - drove Ford Escort there and back - took forever. Impressive tower, bugger all else.

QPR FA Cup 2 Jan '82 - 5 of us in my Mini in snow gradually losing car electrics on way home. Desperate to get back to Coatham nightclub so drove the last 50 miles with no lights. Car finally conked out 200 yards from home. I believe Boro's first game on a plastic pitch? Drew 1-1 anyway.

Blackpool mid-Eighties. What a weekend! Best memories are of my mate's girlfriend trying to get on the pitch waving a vibrator just bought from a sex shop (after downing pints of white wine in our round). Got nose accidentally broken by Boro fan when it all kicked off in their Kop. Got treated pitchside whilst the match was going on.

Great thread. Have to stop, could go on forever.

extratomato Posted on 10/11 11:13

re: Best Away Day Stories Following The Boro

Oldham v Boro early '90s. Lennie Lawrence era, I think.

Four of us in this boozer with a wedding reception going on in one side. Couple of hundred other Boro in the other side of boozer with us watching TV and trying to get food ordered. After a few hours, the beer had taken effect and some Boro lads had started helping themselves to the food from under the hot lamps. One lot took a huge oven dish of lasagne from under the hot lamps and were busy tucking into it on their table.

There was horse racing on the TV and we were all betting on it. I was £5 down when my horse looked like it was about to win. All I remember is the TV going off and I believe someone was trying to nick it off the wall. My mates dragged me out, kicking and screaming, demanding my winnings. I soon calmed down when I got outside and saw the riot police taking positions about to go in.

I think we won as well. Joy.

tweedle Posted on 10/11 17:37

re: Best Away Day Stories Following The Boro

Too many to type, but:

Blackpool away 1986-1987 - thousands upon thousands of Boro wandering the streets and crammed into our two ends. It all kicked off - can still see one lad hanging upside down on a fence by his leg. He tried to get onto the pitch but got his leg caught - he was left dangling for a good couple of minutes. Oh, and the best headed goal I've ever seen by Sir Archie of Stephens.

Darlo away same season - again it kicks off (bit of a theme). Amongst all the scrapping and policemen, one Boro lad sits on the centre circle eating a pie!

Chester away 1986-1987. Torrential rain, open grassy knoll behind goal. Mud slides are created at half time. Chat to policeman before game who was anticipating trouble. Tells us that "Your boys put on an impressive display at Blackpool, I've seen the footage". He wasn't talking about the game.

Doncaster away 1986-1987 - sitting on 20 foot high fence for the whole game then surrounding the pitch with other Boro before the final whistle.

Bradford away play off first leg - 1987-1988. Sell spare ticket on A1 after advertising it for sale in back of car window. A Boro supporters' bus flashed us down. Police gave both drivers a fine! Following a Boro car through Bradford centre before game. Passengers leaning out of window, supping lager and spitting it at passers-by. Delightful. Buying my "England invasion of Germany - with support from Middlesbrough" T-Shirt. Cheering Trevor Senior.

Blackburn away - early '90s. Got over there and asked bobby for away car park. He smirks, "Sorry lads, the game has been called off, waterlogged pitch". About turn. Stop at Wetherby (where, funnily, I now live) and spend afternoon/night in pub. Driver drinks too many to drive home. Five of us cram into Fiesta for some kip. Driver wakes at 3:00 and takes us home.

THRYLOS_MFC Posted on 12/11 8:46

re: Best Away Day Stories Following The Boro

Shrewsbury away '86, for all the wrong reasons, but still very memorable!

Lionheart86 Posted on 12/11 10:18

re: Best Away Day Stories Following The Boro

Rochdale in the "Freight Rover Trophy" (I await correction on the exact comp), first time I'd witnessed Boro in a penalty shoot-out! Good laugh and to finish it off, MN4 and the Buck lads' minibus had all its tyres slashed (tee hee).

Obviously, Chelsea play-off in '88 and Plymouth, not sure of the year but late '80s and Hammy got the winner (great lad and a top player, who had to retire before his time). EIO!

THRYLOS_MFC Posted on 12/11 13:07

re: Best Away Day Stories Following The Boro

re Lionheart86 - it was FRT and, if I remember right, Gary Parkinson scored the winning pena to send the Boro fans wild behind the goal! We've come a long, long way...

Chapter Eight
Things People Still Call by Their Old Name

Teesside Urban Legends

Previous | Next | New Topic | Top Of Board

TOPIC

MESSAGE

POST

REGISTER

Had four manufacturers of carpet cleaners over the years. Although none have been HOOVER, they have all been called the hoover...

TOPIC - Things People Still Call by Their Old Name

trodbitch Posted on 22/3 10:04

Things People Still Call by Their Old Name

The ABC Cinema.

Wakey_Boro_Fan Posted on 22/3 10:05

re: Things People Still Call by Their Old Name

Pint of beer.

Quarter of sweets.

Fever_dog Posted on 22/3 10:06

re: Things People Still Call by Their Old Name

The Mobil garage, Marsh House Ave in Billog, even though it was BP. Knocked down now, like...

mufflar Posted on 22/3 10:07

re: Things People Still Call by Their Old Name

Marathons.

key_toenail Posted on 22/3 10:09

re: Things People Still Call by Their Old Name

Aruba in Redcar - still call it the Piper.

grantus Posted on 22/3 10:10

re: Things People Still Call by Their Old Name

What are Marathons called?

London Marathon, New York Marathon.

You're out of whack, bozo.

Automobile.

mufflar Posted on 22/3 10:11

re: Things People Still Call by Their Old Name

I still call CIF (the new collective European brand name for JIF) JIF!

We often have a laugh about that in my house...

PMSL!

Piquet2 Posted on 22/3 10:11

re: Things People Still Call by Their Old Name

"The ABC Cinema"... which was called The Elite.

TheYak87 Posted on 22/3 10:12

re: Things People Still Call by Their Old Name

Teesside Airport. And they always will.

trodbitch Posted on 22/3 10:13

re: Things People Still Call by Their Old Name

The Electricity Board.

johnsmithsno2 Posted on 22/3 10:14

re: Things People Still Call by Their Old Name

What about "pulling the chain" for flushing the loo and "dialling" a telephone number when there's no dial any more?

Oh, and The Gaumont.

speckyget Posted on 22/3 10:15

re: Things People Still Call by Their Old Name

This becomes a problem with new things that don't have an old name equivalent. I get round this by assigning random old names to my possessions - e.g. I refer to my iPod as 'the O Bus' and DVDs as 'Variety Bandbox'.

Works quite well.

mufflar Posted on 22/3 10:16

re: Things People Still Call by Their Old Name

I still call 118 118 by its old name of 192, but then, hilariously, I ACTUALLY dial 118 118...

I tell you, man, I ALWAYS LOL at that one!

trodbitch Posted on 22/3 10:16

re: Things People Still Call by Their Old Name

I've heard people say they are taping something onto their recordable DVDs.

mufflar Posted on 22/3 10:16

re: Things People Still Call by Their Old Name

iPOD = Walkman!

harryboro Posted on 22/3 10:20

re: Things People Still Call by Their Old Name

Had four manufacturers of carpet cleaners over the years. Although none have been HOOVER, they have all been called the hoover...

Ignore_Alien_Orders Posted on 22/3 10:22

re: Things People Still Call by Their Old Name

50p will always be ten bob to me.

onetoomany Posted on 22/3 10:28

re: Things People Still Call by Their Old Name

A 10 pence mix up will always be that. Even though a cola bottle and white mice cost 2p nowadays (probably).

flabby66 Posted on 22/3 10:31

re: Things People Still Call by Their Old Name

Opal Fruits.

YodaTheCoder Posted on 22/3 10:33

re: Things People Still Call by Their Old Name

Division 2.
Division 3.
Division 4 .

KENDAL Posted on 22/3 10:37

re: Things People Still Call by Their Old Name

Heard a word this morning that I've not heard since my schooldays... jamrag.

StevieT Posted on 22/3 10:39

re: Things People Still Call by Their Old Name

A band's new CD is still an 'album' to me. Bugger, I can remember when it was an LP.

Chokesondique Posted on 22/3 10:40

re: Things People Still Call by Their Old Name

For some bizarre old man reason, I still refer to DVD's as videos, despite not owning a VCR or any videos.

gerd_muller Posted on 22/3 10:46

re: Things People Still Call by Their Old Name

Can you take a photostat of this please? = photocopy.

Pass me the snowpake = Tippex.

Put the wireless on = radio.

Will you tape this for me? = set Sky + .

Azedarac Posted on 22/3 10:47

re: Things People Still Call by Their Old Name

Lorries instead of trucks.

gerd_muller Posted on 22/3 10:50

re: Things People Still Call by Their Old Name

British Rail.

The Water Board.

Fatsuma Posted on 22/3 11:01

re: Things People Still Call by Their Old Name

Opal Fruits. Although - I actually tend to call them Chimpy Chompies, because that was one of the names they had in the TV advert that announced Opal Fruits were now called "Starburst".

Gamblor Posted on 22/3 11:03

re: Things People Still Call by Their Old Name

Video for DVD as in films straight to video when they're on DVD.

north_stand Posted on 22/3 11:08

re: Things People Still Call by Their Old Name

NTL/Comcast, now Virgin Media - or Safeway rather than the Somerfield it became.

Azedarac Posted on 22/3 11:15

re: Things People Still Call by Their Old Name

You can spot people at work who aren't confident with computers because they talk about "surfing the web."

trodbitch Posted on 22/3 11:19

re: Things People Still Call by Their Old Name

They'll probably come up with a really witty name for it such as t'Internet.

Hapas Posted on 22/3 11:30

re: Things People Still Call by Their Old Name

I'm just off to FINE FARE.

B_Hills Posted on 22/3 11:56

re: Things People Still Call by Their Old Name

Up until she died a few years ago, my mam always called the area in Doggy where the Buccaneer is "Whitehouse Garage", even though I don't think there had been a garage there for 50 years.

grantus Posted on 22/3 12:19

re: Things People Still Call by Their Old Name

I call movies 'talkies' and like to go to the 'flicks' on occasions.

TOPIC

MESSAGE

POST

REGISTER

A night out in Middlesbrough would contain:

Flixx, Faulkner's, Billy Paul's, The Lord Raglan, The Shakespeare, The Welly, The Old Mint, The Royal Exchange, The Albert, 2B's, The Madison, Whicker's World, Henry's, The Zetland.

fastcakes Posted on 22/3 12:24

re: Things People Still Call by Their Old Name

The Monkey Tree.
Club Fiesta.
Bon Lea Pub.
Heads (Head Wrightsons).
The Plegs.
Cassie's Field.
The Airfield.
The Top House (Nellies).
Peppermint Park.
The Carlton Club (Hartlepool).
Bowes Wine Cellar.
Rockerfellers (Grangetown).
Redcar Jazz Club.
Teessider.
The Theatre.

bandito Posted on 22/3 12:25

re: Things People Still Call by Their Old Name

The Blue Bell garage.

KENDAL Posted on 22/3 12:26

re: Things People Still Call by Their Old Name

Do you still listen to The Hit Parade on a Sunday (Top 40)?

ayresomeangel365 Posted on 22/3 12:38

re: Things People Still Call by Their Old Name

The 'new' Holgate.

grantus Posted on 22/3 12:40

re: Things People Still Call by Their Old Name

The New Inn will always be the Tavern.

gerd_muller Posted on 22/3 12:49

re: Things People Still Call by Their Old Name

A night out in Middlesbrough would contain:

Flixx, Faulkner's, Billy Paul's, The Lord Raglan, The Shakespeare, The Welly, The Old Mint, The Royal Exchange, The Albert, 2B's, The Madison, Whicker's World, Henry's, The Zetland.

Natarli1 Posted on 22/3 14:09

re: Things People Still Call by Their Old Name

Pikelets! Not crumpets.

Azedarac Posted on 22/3 16:03

re: Things People Still Call by Their Old Name

Pikelets and crumpets are different, aren't they? I reckon a pikelet is flatter and less fluffy on the inside.

trodbitch Posted on 22/3 16:05

re: Things People Still Call by Their Old Name

You'd be right about that. Also, pikelets are sometimes square. No crumpets are square.

KENDAL Posted on 22/3 16:20

re: Things People Still Call by Their Old Name

Frankie Dees.

poolie_boro_fan Posted on 22/3 16:31

re: Things People Still Call by Their Old Name

Wimbledon… MK Dons.

borofan1986 Posted on 22/3 16:34

re: Things People Still Call by Their Old Name

I hate it when I hear people referring to the Riverside as 'The Cellnet' - honestly! It hasn't been called that for years.

borowally Posted on 22/3 16:34

re: Things People Still Call by Their Old Name

Andy Cole.

DrBuck Posted on 22/3 16:34

re: Things People Still Call by Their Old Name

North Eastern.
Talbot.
Cattlemarket
Three Tuns.
Spread Eagle.
White Hart.
Blue posts.
Green bushes.
Garrick.
Jockers.
Berni Inn.
Harveys.
etc, etc.

onthemap Posted on 22/3 16:45

re: Things People Still Call by Their Old Name

Lager turned magically into beer.

smoggyramone Posted on 22/3 16:51

re: Things People Still Call by Their Old Name

The Corporation - the Council.
The United - any bus that starts with a '2.'
The Palladium - there isn't one.
The A bus - the 24.
2B's? Rumours!

DoubleM69 Posted on 22/3 16:56

re: Things People Still Call by Their Old Name

The Mall, Stockton.

newholgate Posted on 22/3 18:51

re: Things People Still Call by Their Old Name

In Thornaby (don't know if this is true of anywhere else) people still call women by their maiden name instead of their married name, even if they've been married for years.

borobadge Posted on 22/3 19:18

re: Things People Still Call by Their Old Name

New name..................................correct name.

1. French fries ....chips.

2. Cigarettes...............................fags.

3. Cycle......................................bike.

4. Ketchup ....sauce.

5. Soccer ....foota'.

6. Snickers ....Marathon.

7. Holdall ....haversack.

8. Launderette............................bagwash.

9. People carrier ....transit.

10. Sexual intercourse................a shag.

11. Alcohol ....ale.

12. Fuel ....petrol.

13. Sunderland...........................shyte.

14. Designer stubble ....unshaven.

15 4 x 4 ....jeep.

16. Stand up comedian..............comic.

17. Health centre.......................the doctors.

18. Fizzy drinks ....pop.

19. Nineteen..............................Sunlun points.

Long_Live_Zombies Posted on 22/3 19:18

re: Things People Still Call by Their Old Name

Coming out of Redcar on the Trunk Road you pass Cowies on the right... well, you used to. FFS, they've knocked it down and built a new place.

smoggyramone Posted on 22/3 19:21

re: Things People Still Call by Their Old Name

Nice one, borobadge... I refuse to call it 'footy'.

In the town of my birth, it's called FOOTA!

mufflar Posted on 22/3 19:26

re: Things People Still Call by Their Old Name

"10. Sexual intercourse......................a shag."

This isn't a particularly new phrase, is it?

Ray_Jinghardon Posted on 22/3 19:38

re: Things People Still Call by Their Old Name

Hog's Head - L For Leather.

swordtrombonefish Posted on 22/3 19:43

re: Things People Still Call by Their Old Name

I still call a spade a spade, though I'm not sure it's PC.

I guess it should be called a manual garden rotavator or some such.

Stepper_T Posted on 22/3 20:06

re: Things People Still Call by Their Old Name

The Spastics Society.

thornabyred Posted on 22/3 20:22

re: Things People Still Call by Their Old Name

New H, it's only on the Brims estate.

thornabyred Posted on 22/3 20:23

re: Things People Still Call by Their Old Name

Brewery Bank and Pottery Bank in Thornaby.

thornabyred Posted on 22/3 20:25

re: Things People Still Call by Their Old Name

The Erimus and Wilderness, as the way out of Boro from Thornaby.

Chapter Nine
Should Women Be Allowed to Drive?

Teesside Urban Legends

TOPIC - Should Women Be Allowed to Drive?

MESSAGE

POST

REGISTER

If women actually used their rear view mirrors to look behind them, they would actually stop more and sort out the accident they have just caused.

Previous | Next | New Topic | Top Of Board

MarlonD Posted on 21/3 13:51

Should women be allowed to drive

...cars with bigger engines than 1.3 litres?

I think not.

bandito Posted on 21/3 13:52

re: Should Women Be Allowed to Drive?

Saw one filing her nails today in a Cayenne.

Smifter Posted on 21/3 13:52

re: Should Women Be Allowed to Drive?

I have to drive a 2.2 (I think) engine at work. It's a HUGE, high transit van, and I definitely do not think it is a good idea!

trodbitch Posted on 21/3 13:52

re: Should Women Be Allowed to Drive?

Why didn't you stop at the title?

runs

trodbitch Posted on 21/3 13:53

re: Should Women Be Allowed to Drive?

Smif, why do you say that? Do you think it's the driving position rather than the engine size?

OooOo Posted on 21/3 13:53

re: Should Women Be Allowed to Drive?

Women are safer drivers than men - fact. Hence their reduced insurance cost. Insurers are solely interested in money so they would not make insurance cheaper for women unless women were less likely to have an accident.

MarlonD Posted on 21/3 13:53

re: Should Women Be Allowed to Drive?

Very honourable of you, Smifter, to admit you lot aren't made for a bit of power.

(Also see Margaret Thatcher).

key_toenail Posted on 21/3 13:54

re: Should Women Be Allowed to Drive?

It will solve all congestion problems.

grabs trod's jacket and hangs on

Smifter Posted on 21/3 13:54

re: Should Women Be Allowed to Drive?

Well, I can't park it, and I can't reach either the clutch nor the handbrake. It's scary stuff!

Smifter Posted on 21/3 13:56

re: Should Women Be Allowed to Drive?

Marlon – it's very true, I am much better off in my normal 796cc car, thanks!

MarlonD Posted on 21/3 13:56

re: Should Women Be Allowed to Drive?

If women actually used their rear view mirrors to look behind them, they would actually stop more and sort out the accident they have just caused.

McCann_87 Posted on 21/3 13:57

re: Should Women Be Allowed to Drive?

OooOo - that's not a fact at all. I nearly crashed this morning because some stupid bint wasn't watching what she was doing and decided to try and ram someone in a van.

trodbitch Posted on 21/3 13:57

re: Should Women Be Allowed to Drive?

"Women are safer drivers than men - fact. Hence their reduced insurance cost."

Just to be an arsey sod (not like me, I know), it's actually because the cost of most men's insurance claims are higher rather than a direct indicator of the chance of having an accident.

captain5 Posted on 21/3 13:57

re: Should Women Be Allowed to Drive?

Have they got you out catching people now?

Sawadee_cap Posted on 21/3 13:58

re: Should Women Be Allowed to Drive?

Women should only be allowed to drive when taking men somewhere, ie to and from pub.

HAPPY DAYS, LAD!

MarlonD Posted on 21/3 13:58

re: Should Women Be Allowed to Drive?

Do camp blokes get cheaper insurance because they are more feminine?

KENDAL Posted on 21/3 13:58

re: Should Women Be Allowed to Drive?

My missus is a member of the IAM and is a much safer driver than me.

Shackman_99 Posted on 21/3 13:59

re: Should Women Be Allowed to Drive?

Isn't Iam cat food?

MsCurly Posted on 21/3 14:00

re: Should Women Be Allowed to Drive?

Oh, piss off.

MarlonD Posted on 21/3 14:03

re: Should Women Be Allowed to Drive?

Curls, I wasn't including you in the generalisation. Everybody knows you need at least 3.0 litres to pull your whammers along.

SouthernSmogette Posted on 21/3 14:03

re: Should Women Be Allowed to Drive?

I'm so glad about many things in life. A choice I made seven years ago being the operative one.

MsCurly Posted on 21/3 14:06

re: Should Women Be Allowed to Drive?

Once again, Marlon... piss off!

jeff_potato Posted on 21/3 14:06

re: Should Women Be Allowed to Drive?

One of my favourite dangerous pastimes is driving across Tesco's roundabout near South Shields.

Young lads have a tendency to stick Saxos and Clios in the merging outside lane, thinking they'll outpace a high spec BMW or Mercedes, whereas a lot of young girls simply driiiift across, completely oblivious to the braking, honking and light-flashing behind.

I think a lot of young drivers with powerful cars are simply unable to handle them. Apart from me of course, when I used to have a competently sized engine.

Miklosh Posted on 21/3 14:08

re: Should Women Be Allowed to Drive?

Smifter, do you have to use a booster seat and put blocks of wood on your feet to reach the pedals?

A_New_Era Posted on 21/3 14:09

re: Should Women Be Allowed to Drive?

"I'm so glad about many things in life. A choice I made seven years ago being the operative one."

Is this where we ask you what that choice was and you tell us some elaborate story about how you can drive safely?

MarlonD Posted on 21/3 14:09

re: Should Women Be Allowed to Drive?

Mr Potato - I have to go round that very roundabout every night. You are 100% correct with that description.

MarlonD Posted on 21/3 14:10

re: Should Women Be Allowed to Drive?

No, Esky. It's when she tells us about that visit to the specialist on Harley Street. Adam's apple and all that.

Miklosh Posted on 21/3 14:19

re: Should Women Be Allowed to Drive?

Not if they 'need' a people carrier or 4WD to take their one or two sprogs to school. What's wrong with a hatchback? You can fit two ankle biters in, no problem. Pretentious beehatches.

KENDAL Posted on 21/3 14:23

re: Should Women Be Allowed to Drive?

Because we live in a democracy and EVERYONE has a choice as to which vehicle they wish to drive.

Why do blokes buy 2L cars when a 1.6L would do adequately?

MarlonD Posted on 21/3 14:23

re: Should Women Be Allowed to Drive?

Because we know we can handle it?

colinfearon Posted on 21/3 14:23

re: Should Women Be Allowed to Drive?

MarlonD - I cannot believe you asked such a stupid question.

Of course they should not be allowed to drive.

bandito Posted on 21/3 14:24

re: Should Women Be Allowed to Drive?

One thing is for certain, they shouldn't be allowed at cash points.

MarlonD Posted on 21/3 14:24

re: Should Women Be Allowed to Drive?

No need for that level of sexism about birds.

Miklosh Posted on 21/3 14:28

re: Should Women Be Allowed to Drive?

Kendal, free choice is good, yes. But it's one of my many pet hates - they should just be honest and cut out the crap and admit it's a status thing. Or better still, walk their kids to school, that way the little chubbers could get some exercise.

bandito Posted on 21/3 14:30

re: Should Women Be Allowed to Drive?

It's pretentious nonsense. Takes me ages to get past the school near my house for all the "competitive mums".

KENDAL Posted on 21/3 14:33

re: Should Women Be Allowed to Drive?

Why buy a BMW when a Ford or Vauxhall would get you where you want to be? Isn't that a status symbol?

TOPIC

MESSAGE

POST

REGISTER

> You can't get a woman to walk past a mirror without spending ten minutes preening at home. Yet put a woman in a car and she will miss all three of them.

colinfearon Posted on 21/3 14:34

re: Should Women Be Allowed to Drive?

I disagree you should buy a Vauxhaull, but Fords, Volvos, Jaguars and Landrovers, Aston Martins and Mazdas are OK.

stretchinnit Posted on 21/3 14:36

re: Should Women Be Allowed to Drive?

You can't get a woman to walk past a mirror without spending ten minutes preening at home. Yet put a woman in a car and she will miss all three of them.

Only jokin', there are some very good women drivers around, and some very bad ones too.

Personally, I think old people are by far the worst drivers, if I were to generalise.

toxic_bob Posted on 21/3 14:36

re: Should Women Be Allowed to Drive?

He heh, you can now have the free choice to pay £300 road tax for your gas-guzzler. Bring it on - shame it's not a grand.

bandito Posted on 21/3 14:38

re: Should Women Be Allowed to Drive?

Let's remind ourselves that the term "gas-guzzler" is awfully American.

KENDAL Posted on 21/3 14:38

re: Should Women Be Allowed to Drive?

Trouble is, to the people who buy the gas-guzzlers, £300 is loose change.

Miklosh Posted on 21/3 14:39

re: Should Women Be Allowed to Drive?

Bandito, I like the way you think.

KENDAL, it's universally acknowledged that most BMW drivers are arsewipes of the highest order.

In terms of premium brands, Audi and Saab drivers tend to be much nicer people.

trodbitch Posted on 21/3 14:39

re: Should Women Be Allowed to Drive?

Cashpoints: are you talking about this?:

* Rummage for 20 minutes for card.
* Put card in.
* Remove Tesco Club Card and put real bank card in.
* Press every button just to see what new options there are for wasting my precious life stood behind you.
* Get a mini-statement.
* Pay a bill.
* Take card out.
* Put same card back in and get a tenner.
* Take ages to put tenner away.
* Insert new card (for 'shoes' account).
* Repeat all above.
* Take 20 minutes to put money away in bag.
* Shout at her kid to "come on!" - who has aged visibly with all the waiting.

KENDAL Posted on 21/3 14:41

re: Should Women Be Allowed to Drive?

That sounds like the queue in Tescos as well.

bandito Posted on 21/3 14:42

re: Should Women Be Allowed to Drive?

Last time I stood behind a woman at a cashpoint I'm sure I grew one of them massive beards like that cricketing fella. The woman turned round and said "Oops, sorry" and I said, "Don't be sorry, just be quick" as I was about to pish myself.

Vinny_Garstroke Posted on 21/3 14:49

re: Should Women Be Allowed to Drive?

It's always like Brands Hatch near the schools at 9 o'clock in the morning. You see the tarty mothers dropping their kids off late, even though they've found time to put a full face of war paint on.

Lennie_Godber Posted on 21/3 14:54

re: Should Women Be Allowed to Drive?

I was thinking of getting a Ford Capri. Sounds like a mighty beast.

Robbo_89 Posted on 21/3 14:54

re: Should Women Be Allowed to Drive?

I'm not a woman, but the point about handling faster cars: I drive a 1L Corsa all week, I'm only 17, but on a weekend I often drive a 2L Saab. I can easily handle it and it is much easier to drive than my Corsa.

DJNOMERCY Posted on 21/3 16:04

re: Should Women Be Allowed to Drive?

Got a Ford Capri for sale, anybody interested?

Lennie_Godber Posted on 21/3 16:05

re: Should Women Be Allowed to Drive?

Really? What state is it in? How much do you want for it?

DJNOMERCY Posted on 21/3 16:34

re: Should Women Be Allowed to Drive?

Michigan, $200.

Lennie_Godber Posted on 21/3 16:38

re: Should Women Be Allowed to Drive?

Cool, my Dad lives in Michigan. I'll send him round.

MarlonD Posted on 22/3 11:52

re: Should Women Be Allowed to Drive?

A slight addition to the original thought. Women should also have to go through another test, which includes moving up the gears quickly to achieve a min speed of 60mph on dual carriageways.

Got stuck behind a Ford Ka doing 50 to pass a wagon this morning.

picknchooser Posted on 22/3 12:01

re: Should Women Be Allowed to Drive?

Do men who had women driving instructors qualify for women's insurance?

Chapter Ten

Should Boro Rename their Stands?

Teesside Urban Legends

TOPIC
MESSAGE
POST
REGISTER

**Handstand,
Bandstand,
Grandstand...**

TOPIC - Should Boro Rename their Stands?

Previous | Next | New Topic | Top Of Board

mitch_mfc Posted on 27/6 15:27

Should Boro Rename their Stands?

If so, what suggestions?

Mattyk50 Posted on 27/6 15:28

re: Should Boro Rename their Stands?

Terraces?

Mattyk50 Posted on 27/6 15:28

re: Should Boro Rename their Stands?

Viewing platforms?

Stepper_T Posted on 27/6 15:28

re: Should Boro Rename their Stands?

Hat Stand.
Coat Stand.
Last Stand.
Long Stand.

mitch_mfc Posted on 27/6 15:29

re: Should Boro Rename their Stands?

Somebody once said a Brian Clough Stand, but don't Forest have that?

branston Posted on 27/6 15:29

re: Should Boro Rename their Stands?

Handstand, Bandstand, Grandstand...

tunstall Posted on 27/6 15:29

re: Should Boro Rename their Stands?

Car Park Stand.
Nearest to the River Stand.
Furthest from the River Stand.
The Other Stand.

Robbo74 Posted on 27/6 15:30

re: Should Boro Rename their Stands?

Yes, Can't be Bothered to Turn Up and Watch Stand, The Desolute Stand, The Kids for a Quid Stand and I'm Five Rows from a Fan Stand.

Tom_Fun Posted on 27/6 15:30

re: Should Boro Rename their Stands?

Gary, Ian, Tobias and Mike.

mitch_mfc Posted on 27/6 15:31

re: Should Boro Rename their Stands?

Seriously, what possibilities?

It's very vague just having North, East, South and West. And it has been 10 years of Gibbo improving the stadium standards. Introducing new names for stands would be a bit more interesting.

longster Posted on 27/6 15:31

re: Should Boro Rename their Stands?

Can't they just be the North, South, East and West, but jumble them up to confuse people?

grantus Posted on 27/6 15:32

re: Should Boro Rename their Stands?

Holgate.
Gibson.
Ayresome.
East.

mitch_mfc Posted on 27/6 15:34

re: Should Boro Rename their Stands?

I was thinking

The Holgate (sick of Ali Brownlee saying "the New Holgate End"!)
Steve Gibson Stand.
The Brian Clough End.
The George Hardwick Stand.

XboroX Posted on 27/6 15:38

re: Should Boro Rename their Stands?

I think it would be a massive insult to great Boro legends like Tim Williamson, Wilf and George Camsell to name a stand after a turncoat like Clough.

jamier86 Posted on 27/6 15:38

re: Should Boro Rename their Stands?

Eston Hills Stand.
Parmo Stand (A MUST).
Transporter Stand.
Ayresome Stand.

CesurYurek Posted on 27/6 15:45

re: Should Boro Rename their Stands?

I think we should name the stands after our old grounds. One called the Ayresome. I don't know the name of the other one, I'm thinking something to do with Linthorpe, but we probably just played in Albert Park or something.

Then one stand called Ken.

boringblock_21 Posted on 27/6 15:45

re: Should Boro Rename their Stands?

Agreed with XboroX. Also, I think that if we were to rename the stands, call the North the Holgate and the other three after players and put statues outside of each stand.

Gillandi Posted on 27/6 15:49

re: Should Boro Rename their Stands?

First name that came to my head was Mary and I think we should all try and be a bit more selfish about this so how's about Mary, Shirley, Audrey and Sylvia? A clutch of Gill-aunties.

Settle down, Catherine, you got Rockliffe, honey.

shortandbald Posted on 27/6 15:50

re: Should Boro Rename their Stands?

CesurYurek, the ground you are on about was called The Old Archery Ground.

How about:

The Mannion Stand.
The Hardwick Stand.
The Maddren Stand.
and, of course, The Gibson Stand.

PV86 Posted on 27/6 15:54

re: Should Boro Rename their Stands?

How about:
Billingham Stand.
Stockton Stand.
Grangetown Stand.
Redcar Stand.

To show a bit of appreciation that Boro support actually doesn't all live in Boro, which is news to some Boro people, ignorant gits that they are.

newyorker Posted on 27/6 16:11

re: Should Boro Rename their Stands?

How about:

Empty Stand.
Not Many in Stand.
Can't Fill It Stand.
Red Seat Stand.

glippy Posted on 27/6 17:00

re: Should Boro Rename their Stands?

The South Stand should be named after Stephen Bell - The Bell End.

sponski2000 Posted on 27/6 17:28

re: Should Boro Rename their Stands?

How's abouts an Alec Smith Sports North West Corner rebrand?

Mat_Evans Posted on 27/6 17:35

re: Should Boro Rename their Stands?

I reckon we should have Holgate/New Holgate. Other end should be the Camsell End and not bothered about the others.

backofthenet_ascl Posted on 27/6 17:39

re: Should Boro Rename their Stands?

The Mannion Stand.
The Hardwick Stand.
The Gibson Stand.
The Holgate.

Max_Headroom Posted on 27/6 17:52

re: Should Boro Rename their Stands?

The Muddy Railway End (South).

The Wobbly Bridge End (North).

Gibson Stand.

For me, ultimately it doesn't matter - you can't superimpose traditions and heritage from Ayresome Park onto a stadium from a different era without it sounding false, so it will always be the N S E and W at the Riverside.

The Stretford End has always been the Stretford End, the Kop has always been the Kop, and their 'aura' is based on years of football played there, not the whim of a marketing exercise.

We should have a standing stand and call it...

The Stand Stand.

whoyadoin Posted on 27/6 18:19

re: Should Boro Rename their Stands?

The New Holgate North.
The Hardwick Stand East.
The Mannion Stand South.
The Maddren Stand West.

I don't think Gibson is vain enough to name a stand after himself.

whoyadoin Posted on 27/6 18:30

re: Should Boro Rename their Stands?

Name what stand what?

Poster adds link to this photograph:

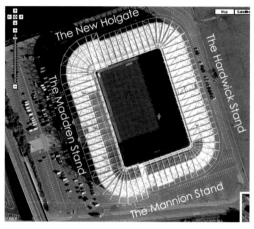

What Do You Think?

Nedkat Posted on 27/6 18:34

re: Should Boro Rename their Stands?

North, South, East and West?

What if I forget to bring me compass?

Mat_Evans Posted on 27/6 18:34

re: Should Boro Rename their Stands?

Max, did you know, Liverpool are naming their home end behind the goal at their new stadium the Kop? What's the difference?

Coluka Posted on 27/6 18:39

re: Should Boro Rename their Stands?

The Gibson Stand.
The Mannion Stand.
The Holgate Stand.
The McClaren Stand (we would need to paint the roof ginger and remove some of the corrugated cladding}.

southwest_corner Posted on 27/6 19:35

re: Should Boro Rename their Stands?

The West Stand should definitely be called the Gibson Stand.

whoyadoin Posted on 27/6 19:50

re: Should Boro Rename their Stands?

Yeah, it should be, but the final decision, I imagine, would be down to Gibson and I can't imagine him going for it.

The West Stand is Gibbo's Stand tho.

boro_ian Posted on 27/6 21:13

re: Should Boro Rename their Stands?

We should have a standing stand and call it...

The Stand Stand.

Along with Mannion, Maddren and New Holgate, because I don't think Gibson would name a stand after himself, like whoyadoin said.

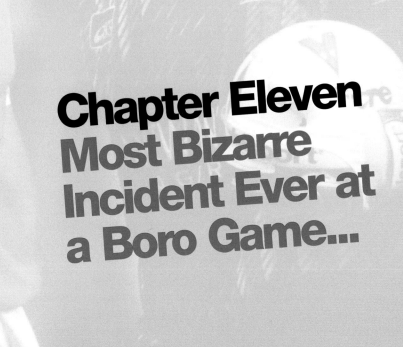

Chapter Eleven
Most Bizarre Incident Ever at a Boro Game...

Teesside Urban Legends

TOPIC - Most Bizarre Incident Ever at a Boro Game...

Previous | Next | New Topic | Top Of Board

CliveRdCorner Posted on 27/3 13:03

Most Bizarre Incident Ever at a Boro Game...

When the lights went out against Leicester in '74/'75 - or Grantham in the cup when someone was swinging on the goal posts as a corner was taken at the other end.

ExiledInStoke Posted on 27/3 13:08

re: Most Bizarre Incident Ever at a Boro Game...

Super Cooper dropping his shorts before he went in goal.

chorleyphil Posted on 27/3 13:09

re: Most Bizarre Incident Ever at a Boro Game...

'Save Redcar baths' for me!

indestructible Posted on 27/3 13:11

re: Most Bizarre Incident Ever at a Boro Game...

When Ravanelli went crazy at the linesman but refrained from headbutting him, merely chesting him instead, and still received his marching orders.

bandito Posted on 27/3 13:11

re: Most Bizarre Incident Ever at a Boro Game...

Season ticket thrower.

Jon2977 Posted on 27/3 13:12

re: Most Bizarre Incident Ever at a Boro Game...

Was it the Chelsea play-off final 1st leg at Ayresome when 3 or 4 people watched the whole game from the top of the Holgate roof?

Moses_Kiptanui Posted on 27/3 13:13

re: Most Bizarre Incident Ever at a Boro Game...

When the pitch was frozen and the opposition all changed into their trainers by the side of the pitch.

Big_Shot Posted on 27/3 13:14

re: Most Bizarre Incident Ever at a Boro Game...

When a programme seller got arrested at Newcastle away. He had walked passed the Boro fans in the Leazes End and tried to take the p*** by pretending to count the crowd. He got loads of abuse. The police obviously saw it and moments later he was arrested and frogmarched back past all the Boro fans. He was only a young lad and looked like he was going to burst into tears. Superb.

Wakey_Boro_Fan Posted on 27/3 13:19

re: Most Bizarre Incident Ever at a Boro Game...

Feb '04 - someone in a shirt much like ours lifted a trophy.

BroughtonLad Posted on 27/3 13:20

re: Most Bizarre Incident Ever at a Boro Game...

That was only a dream.

bandito Posted on 27/3 13:21

re: Most Bizarre Incident Ever at a Boro Game...

The fat Mackem kid who took a penna was funny.

BLUNT_69 Posted on 27/3 13:24

re: Most Bizarre Incident Ever at a Boro Game...

When my friend's dad burst onto the pitch against Manure and kissed Juninho's right boot before he took a corner (which Paul Ince nodded in).

addison_road Posted on 27/3 13:27

re: Most Bizarre Incident Ever at a Boro Game...

The beer belly contest at The Riverside... Sheff Wed fan and Boro lad who ran from the North Stand to the centre circle.

Vinny_Garstroke Posted on 27/3 13:28

re: Most Bizarre Incident Ever at a Boro Game...

The inflatable sumos at our first Premiership game on Sky.

bblf Posted on 27/3 13:28

re: Most Bizarre Incident Ever at a Boro Game...

I was at the game but missed this incident. It was reported in the Evening Gazette that "Whigham launched a long kick into the box which Hickton cacked straight into the net".

heaton_mersey_boro Posted on 27/3 13:30

re: Most Bizarre Incident Ever at a Boro Game...

At Barnsley where they thought they had reached the play-offs by beating us 1-0.

Cue pitch invasion, celebrations... until Brighton scored a late equaliser (even later, as the kick off to their game was delayed).

The look on the chuckle-brother-lookalikes' faces.

Hehehehehehehe.

cheese_shop_john Posted on 27/3 13:30

re: Most Bizarre Incident Ever at a Boro Game...

Half-time keep fit with Jet off Gladiators.

WTF!

YodaTheCoder Posted on 27/3 13:33

re: Most Bizarre Incident Ever at a Boro Game...

I was at that match HMB, it was hilarious.

"Always look on the Brighton side of life..."

Big_Shot Posted on 27/3 13:34

re: Most Bizarre Incident Ever at a Boro Game...

HMB, good shout. However, I think they had just given the wrong final score out. I think they said that Brighton had got beat 2-0, when in fact they'd won 3-1.

YodaTheCoder Posted on 27/3 13:35

re: Most Bizarre Incident Ever at a Boro Game...

Their players and staff were in the directors' box spraying champagne everywhere, players were throwing their shirts and boots to the crowd below. Then the announcer corrected the score.

addison_road Posted on 27/3 13:36

re: Most Bizarre Incident Ever at a Boro Game...

Celtic fans thinking it was a good idea to run round the pitch with a tricolour.

Vinny_Garstroke Posted on 27/3 13:37

re: Most Bizarre Incident Ever at a Boro Game...

Seeing a bloke get out of a minibus at Barnsley and get ran over. His mates waited until the ambulance came, and then left him and went to the match.

Max_Headroom Posted on 27/3 13:40

re: Most Bizarre Incident Ever at a Boro Game...

The two strippers who came on the pitch, took off their Santa coats and gave Gazza a kiss in front of the Newcastle fans (I think?). Christmas of Robbo's last season.

The guy who came out of the Holgate and did a triple somersault back flip thing in front of Jet - at half-time of a 1995 Ayresome Park match.

The safety drills at the Riverside where all the stewards would line the pitch and then, on a signal, walk back to the corners. Why?

sean_boro Posted on 27/3 13:40

re: Most Bizarre Incident Ever at a Boro Game...

I remember Nigel Pearson hoofing it out for a corner then doing a full on Irish jig in front of the South Stand. That was a little strange.

bandito Posted on 27/3 13:41

re: Most Bizarre Incident Ever at a Boro Game...

The "crush" in the Leeds end.

BoroMutt Posted on 27/3 13:42

re: Most Bizarre Incident Ever at a Boro Game...

Jamie Pollock jumping on a defender's back and getting a piggy back off him during an attempted break from his own half. Crowd in hysterics.

heaton_mersey_boro Posted on 27/3 13:42

re: Most Bizarre Incident Ever at a Boro Game...

I'll take your word for it Big_Shot; however to this day I was sure that Dean Wilkins (current Brighton boss and then captain) scored a late goal.

The 4-5 Boro lads who got onto the pitch and legged it into the Barnsley fans were funny. And slightly insane.

Nearly had our car turned over at traffic lights in Barnsley town centre, and had to sneak out of the back door (oo-er) of my uncle's pub, where we stayed the night before, as the regulars were none too happy - ie we were told in no uncertain terms we were going to get the s*** kicked out of us if we appeared back in the pub.

Happy days.

jimmythewondercat Posted on 27/3 13:46

re: Most Bizarre Incident Ever at a Boro Game...

Cardiff - going to a cup final and, instead of the usual sadness and anti-climax, having to deal with winning!

That was a bizarre feeling.

Big_Shot Posted on 27/3 13:52

re: Most Bizarre Incident Ever at a Boro Game...

There was a bloke with a radio stood behind us at Barnsley and he was telling everyone around him that Brighton had actually won and couldn't understand why they got the score so wrong. This was even before the players appeared in the directors' box with the champagne.

TOPIC

MESSAGE

POST

REGISTER

Pollock and a Newcastle player going into a tackle so hard that they popped the ball.

irish_boro_supporter Posted on 27/3 13:53

re: Most Bizarre Incident Ever at a Boro Game...

The lad who threw his ticket at McClown last year. Was my 2nd time at Boro and cost me a fortune to get over. Was the only amusing part of that day.

harry_x Posted on 27/3 13:54

re: Most Bizarre Incident Ever at a Boro Game...

Doncaster away, last day of the season. Five minutes to go, fans were jumping over the fences and nobody was stopping them. With 90 mins on the clock, Boro fans were stood on the touchline on three sides of the ground. People were leaning on the goalposts.

At one point the ball went out for a goal kick, the Donny keeper put it down and retreated, only for one of the lads stood behind him to run up and hoof it up the pitch.

The next time the ball went to the keeper, the ref walked up and just said 'give me the ball'. Cue mass pitch invasion.

flabby66 Posted on 27/3 13:57

re: Most Bizarre Incident Ever at a Boro Game...

The chicken and the witch that ran on the pitch last season. Can't remember the game though.

PhillyMac Posted on 27/3 13:58

re: Most Bizarre Incident Ever at a Boro Game...

How about the mass pitch invasions during the promotion years of 1987/88?

There was one game where there were hundreds of people ringing the outside of the pitch in front of the Holgate. Every time the ref blew in the last five minutes there was a mini-invasion.

I think the ref eventually did that thing where he just happened to be standing by the dugouts when he blew the final whistle.

Jon2977 Posted on 27/3 14:01

re: Most Bizarre Incident Ever at a Boro Game...

The Wolves away game where we won promotion was a pretty bizarre day. Surprised no one has mentioned this already.

Got to the ground to be told that the pitch had been booby-trapped and the old wooden stand set on fire overnight. I was told the game could be off.

Anyway went and had a few drinks, turned out the game was on and we got promoted. Is this the one where Jon Gittens scored a goal? Even more bizarre!

Anyone else there that day?

sponski2000 Posted on 27/3 14:01

re: Most Bizarre Incident Ever at a Boro Game...

Somebody starting a fire in the middle of the Holgate wasn't the most normal thing to do.

Towell Posted on 27/3 14:02

re: Most Bizarre Incident Ever at a Boro Game...

Some time in the '60s my uncle walked on the pitch at Ayresome, told the referee he was bent and then walked off.

Nedkat Posted on 27/3 14:05

re: Most Bizarre Incident Ever at a Boro Game...

I remember the bobbies coming into the crowd when we played away at Deepdale. Loads of people pushing and shoving. I looked up and saw my mate climbing up a stanchion, knocking the bobbies' helmets flying with his shoe! The expression on his face was a picture! He looked like he was really enjoying himself.

Max_Headroom Posted on 27/3 14:06

re: Most Bizarre Incident Ever at a Boro Game...

Were you trying to light one of your roll ups, sponski?

Smogchat Posted on 27/3 14:07

re: Most Bizarre Incident Ever at a Boro Game...

Fjortoft and Tim Flowers kissing!

Ricketts making a run!

Max_Headroom Posted on 27/3 14:10

re: Most Bizarre Incident Ever at a Boro Game...

Two in the 1991 league game with Newcastle where we won 3-0:

O'Brien or Watson doing a flip on the ball before throwing it in the box.

Pollock and a Newcastle player going into a tackle so hard that they popped the ball.

Away fans fighting inside the Riverside is always bizarre. The Coventry fan who hit the policeman after going a goal down, went mental and took a few people with him!

borowally Posted on 27/3 14:11

re: Most Bizarre Incident Ever at a Boro Game...

Can't get much more bizarre than a soldier from The Green Howards blowing a bugle every time we had a corner!

BobUpndown Posted on 27/3 14:15

re: Most Bizarre Incident Ever at a Boro Game...

The Steaua fan running onto the pitch when they went 3-0 up, deciding to feign a heart attack and getting stretchered off. Must have had a real one when he saw the result!

What a night!

Capybara Posted on 27/3 14:16

re: Most Bizarre Incident Ever at a Boro Game...

Inviting Arthur Caiger to the game against Peterborough in 1967. I'm sure it was well intentioned but he hadn't done his research. All was fine when he asked us to sing Song 1 first, but when he then decided to go to Song 6 and the Holgate wanted to sing Song 2 (logically enough), hilarious scenes ensued.

BobUpndown Posted on 27/3 14:19

re: Most Bizarre Incident Ever at a Boro Game...

Charlie Amer turning on the white noise speakers whenever the Boro fans chanted about him. Sounded like someone hadn't tuned the radio in.

mf_c Posted on 27/3 14:21

re: Most Bizarre Incident Ever at a Boro Game...

A few not already mentioned:

Power cut in the North Stand meant the managers had to give the team talks on the pitch like school teams.

Wilkinson's hand ball which neither the ref nor linesman saw and gave as a goal in Lennie's promotion season.

Bristol City (?) home where both Parky and Alan Walsh handled on the line in the last minute with the score at 1-1. Play stopped, waiting for the ref to give the penalty. Phillips hoofed it up to Ripley who scored.

lionrock31 Posted on 27/3 14:34

re: Most Bizarre Incident Ever at a Boro Game...

Some cracking memories amongst that lot!

Got to say we've had some laughs over the years (but many more tears!).

red_rebel2 Posted on 27/3 14:42

re: Most Bizarre Incident Ever at a Boro Game...

The ghostly figures in the fog v Man City at Ayresome and the fans in the East Stand cheering as if there had been a goal.

Bernie and Parky pushing and shoving each other arguing over who should take a penalty v Ipswich. Bernie snatched it, leaving Parky stamping the ground in a meg strop when the legend missed it.

Talking of fires, didn't some Coventry fans torch a few seats when they came in the cup last year?

Bukowski_MFC Posted on 27/3 14:54

re: Most Bizarre Incident Ever at a Boro Game...

I remember when we played Wimbledon in 1988 (?) and Dennis Wise had Gary Parkinson on the floor in a headlock whilst goading the North Stand for about twenty seconds. Neither the ref nor linesmen saw it.

Also can anybody remember the Roary vs Wolfy penalty shoot-out?

Boateng_7 Posted on 27/3 14:58

re: Most Bizarre Incident Ever at a Boro Game...

Juninho scoring a header.

borokaza Posted on 27/3 15:15

re: Most Bizarre Incident Ever at a Boro Game...

Loved the Barnsley away game. Never laughed so much at a match.

Another bizarre incident happened while standing next to Bam Bam in the open stand at Bolton, which was so packed that he decided he couldn't be bothered pushing his way through to get to the loo, so he had a lag where he was. Bloke in front wasn't too chuffed.

Another was when we were away at Sid James' when they wouldn't let us out and there was a real crush in the concourse. I was 6 months' pregnant and my dad was going mental trying to stop me getting crushed against a wall.

holgateoldskool Posted on 27/3 15:40

re: Most Bizarre Incident Ever at a Boro Game...

True story. Was with a group of mates from Guisborough and it was the final match of the season. At the end of the match, there was a pitch invasion. One of our group was determined to get a memento and tried for a player's shirt - failed.

Not to be put off, we walked back towards the Linthorpe Road end and he picked up the corner flag - heavy wooden stake, more like - and walked out of the ground! Carried this down Linny Road and asked the bus driver if he could bring it on to travel to Guisborough with us. He said yes! My mate then placed it in his back garden for years!

AtomicLoonybin Posted on 27/3 16:11

re: Most Bizarre Incident Ever at a Boro Game...

I can remember Sunlun trying to set light to the away terracing at Ayresome - must have been 1982, 1983. Only thing I can remember about a deadly dull 0-0 draw.

The Holgate going 'Uwe, Uwe, give us a wave' at a corner, which he ignored - he didn't understand enough English. One of the opposing players - Charlton? - went over to him and showed him what to do by waving and pointing at us. Cue shy little wave from the Fuchs.

Alex Rae scoring for Millwall, and dancing away while flicking the V's like a ten year old at the Holgate. He'd probably get arrested these days.

The 'nice white trainers' game v Barnsley. Abandoned at half time with us winning 2-1. The replay ended 1-1.

smoggyramone Posted on 27/3 16:31

re: Most Bizarre Incident Ever at a Boro Game...

The lad climbing the floodlight at Notts County in the cup.

The chicken on the pitch at Arsenal.

The dog on the pitch v the Jawdees.

The train getting set on fire on the way back from Darlo.

The fire in the middle of the Holgate and Bubble getting shot out for his method of extinguishing it.

The grey sock that was attached to one of the flagpoles in the Boys' End. It was there for years.

Me trainer coming off in the goal melee in the Boys' End, and 5 minutes later seeing it somersaulting onto the pitch.

shmarry Posted on 27/3 17:12

re: Most Bizarre Incident Ever at a Boro Game...

Stan Bowles reading the match programme before a QPR corner.

addison_road Posted on 27/3 17:21

re: Most Bizarre Incident Ever at a Boro Game...

The Stamford Bridge play-off Chelsea mob pitch invasion.

wilfym Posted on 27/3 18:01

re: Most Bizarre Incident Ever at a Boro Game...

Gary Gill getting injured, trying to play on for ten minutes, then getting carried off with a broken leg!

UCN_BORO Posted on 27/3 18:09

re: Most Bizarre Incident Ever at a Boro Game...

Roary having a half-time fight with the Reading mascot, and them having to be dragged away from each other. Think it was League Cup quarter final in '97?

Classic.

TOPIC

MESSAGE

POST

REGISTER

Two women streakers at the Newcastle game, chasing Gazza around like something on the Benny Hill Show.

tees_tripper Posted on 27/3 18:09

re: Most Bizarre Incident Ever at a Boro Game...

1996/97 season: Clayton Blackmore impressively, but blatantly, making a fingertip save over the bar - cue red card and penalty to Southampton.

Also remember that blatantly biased ref at some Anglo-Italian Cup game where Wilko lost his rag and got sent off. The game was an absolute farce. Turned out the ref was Italian. Robbo wasn't impressed.

CliveRdCorner Posted on 27/3 18:19

re: Most Bizarre Incident Ever at a Boro Game...

I remember me and my brother were walking down Lowfields Road once at a night match in the late '70s when, out of nowhere, a gang of around 30 nutters in balaclavas and carrying sticks charged into the queues and started knocking hell out of anyone in the way.

After Norwich '77 when the players all came back onto the pitch wearing only towels to wave at the Holgate, who refused to leave the ground after we'd gone top of the league because no one else had played a game that day.

shortandbald Posted on 27/3 18:27

re: Most Bizarre Incident Ever at a Boro Game...

Was also at the Barnsley match. Was one of the funniest things ever when the score was corrected.

But one of the most bizarre things I've seen, and I too am surprised it hasn't been mentioned sooner, was in that European game (Banik, I think), when all their fans stood up and turned their backs to the pitch en masse.

CliveRdCorner Posted on 27/3 18:34

re: Most Bizarre Incident Ever at a Boro Game...

I remember at Highbury in the '70s there had been a bit of fighting in the North Bank and there were some lads getting escorted round the track. One of them shouts something to Jack Charlton, who faces up to him and tries to cuff him. Seem to remember it was a little bloke and it all looked hilarious from the clock end.

nicku Posted on 27/3 19:48

re: Most Bizarre Incident Ever at a Boro Game...

Everton away, some time in the '90s - huge Boro lad jumps up and stands on the seat shouting "Live lobster loose in the stand". Never did work that one out.

Man City away, when Festa broke a City player's nose with a punch which everyone in the ground saw, bar the 3 officials.

Norwich at home in the '70s, when their fans started to sing along to The Birdie Song, only to be greeted by thousands of Boro fans singing "You're going to get your f****** heads kicked in". Their naive faces were a picture.

Festa (again) running round like an idiot with his shirt off at Reading, thinking he had scored the winner in a cup match, only to have it disallowed and spend 5 minutes trying to get it back on in the pouring rain. Boro actually did score before he could get it back on.

smoggyramone Posted on 27/3 19:58

re: Most Bizarre Incident Ever at a Boro Game...

From Merson's free kick, I believe. Can't remember much.

robert_hoffman Posted on 27/3 20:01

re: Most Bizarre Incident Ever at a Boro Game...

Two women streakers at the Newcastle game, chasing Gazza around like something on the Benny Hill Show.

They were in the The Daily Sport the next day and lied about their age - but one had a huge pair of jugs...

boros_moggy Posted on 27/3 20:28

re: Most Bizarre Incident Ever at a Boro Game...

Boro v Chesterfield semi-final replay at Hillsborough when everyone around us thought we'd gone 2-0 up (even the giant scoreboard changed) until a minute or two later a debate ensued about whether the goal had been allowed or not. Nobody had seen the restart and we had to ring home on the mobile to find out it was still only 1-0.

jd1973 Posted on 27/3 20:30

re: Most Bizarre Incident Ever at a Boro Game...

The scoreboard at Arsenal when we won 3-0, with the stats showing:

Boro
Shots - 2
Goals - 3

What a day that was!

jofus53 Posted on 27/3 20:45

re: Most Bizarre Incident Ever at a Boro Game...

Bizarre and a little unnerving, when we knocked the Geordies out of the Coca-Cola Cup on the way to Wembley. Beck scores and dives to the ground near the North Stand. Juninho runs to celebrate with him, lies on top of him and stretches his arms out for balance and seemed to stay there for ages. Why?

paulo86 Posted on 27/3 20:52

re: Most Bizarre Incident Ever at a Boro Game...

Standing at the bus stop on Linthorpe Road after we had just beat Newcastle in the cup at Ayresome, night time. Cooper, I think, scored in injury time. The Boro fans trying to rip the doors off any car/taxi that housed a Geordie in it. In hindsight, I think it was probably cars of just Boro fans.

Johnny_Briggs Posted on 27/3 21:45

re: Most Bizarre Incident Ever at a Boro Game...

Timmy Mallett walking around the Riverside, hitting kids on the head with his mallet at half-time when we played Bradford on the first day of the season about seven years ago.

maxter Posted on 27/3 23:38

re: Most Bizarre Incident Ever at a Boro Game...

Barnsley playing in our away shirts at Ayresome because they forgot their own kit.

AtomicLoonybin Posted on 28/3 9:13

re: Most Bizarre Incident Ever at a Boro Game...

Another 'bizarre things on away scoreboards':

Blackburn 0
Middlesbrough 4

Man of the Match: Barry Ferguson.

How we laughed.

Moody41 Posted on 28/3 9:17

re: Most Bizarre Incident Ever at a Boro Game...

Paulo, was that the Zenith Data Systems game? If I remember rightly, Cooper picked the ball up inside our half on the left-wing and ran it down before cutting inside and slotting home. Might have nutmegged the keeper, who I think was Burridge.

dicky_rooks Posted on 28/3 9:18

re: Most Bizarre Incident Ever at a Boro Game...

Two stand out for me. First was Jim Montgomery, famously cock-eyed ex-Mackem keeper. When playing for Birmingham, he tried to take a quick goal kick at the Holgate End and ran backwards into a post.

Second was at a cup match v Everton one evening in the late '70s. We got in late and were crushed at the front of the Holgate near the corner flag. Two coppers on the track were arguing about the name of the Everton goalie, so one of them asks a bloke in the crowd who the Everton goalie was. Quick as a flash comes the response, "He's that fat barsteward in the green jumper."

Moses_Kiptanui Posted on 28/3 9:21

re: Most Bizarre Incident Ever at a Boro Game...

The Blackburn away game a few years ago when Chris Kamara was on the bench and the speaker system with crowd cheering from the construction site behind the goal.

UgoAfro Posted on 28/3 9:38

re: Most Bizarre Incident Ever at a Boro Game...

Anything involving Emerson. More specifically Emerson's cousin playing for the first team and being man of the match and then never playing again.

Was once driving back from a game at Forest and the lights failed on our car. Pulled into a hotel car park to try and sort it out. A car pulled up next to us to see if they could help and it was Steve Cherry (Notts County goalkeeper) and his dad. His dad was very helpful but Steve sloped off. The git!

Chapter Twelve
FMTTM Posts that Never Were

Teesside Urban Legends

Previous | Next | New Topic | Top Of Board

TOPIC - FMTTM Posts that Never Were

BobUpndown Posted on 20/08/2008 09:43

FMTTM Posts that Never Were

Before the internet we used to surf Ceefax to get our fix, but we had to phone or go to the match/pub to talk about the gen we'd heard.

FMTTM Posts that Never Were:

Foggon the Tees is all ours!

Davenport signs, no stopping us now!

ridsdale Posted on 20/08/2008 09:44

FMTTM Posts that Never Were

Beatles or the Stones?

Scrote Posted on 20/08/2008 09:46

FMTTM Posts that Never Were

Captain Cook discovers world's biggest prison.

The_Lizards_Jumpers Posted on 20/08/2008 09:51

FMTTM Posts that Never Were

Where's the money gone?

What are we going to do with the sports hall?

We're doomed!

Receivers move in.

Gates padlocked.

Do they have cash machines in Shrewsbury?

Amer out!

Willie Sacked!

etc etc

Just makes us realise how lucky we are now!

Jerry_Brown Posted on 20/08/2008 09:54

FMTTM Posts that Never Were

Will you boo Alfie Common?

captain5 Posted on 20/08/2008 09:56

FMTTM Posts that Never Were

The Geordies are gonna be on here winding us up about that trophy they've won.

TMG501 Posted on 20/08/2008 09:58

FMTTM Posts that Never Were

Beat me to it, captain!

Capybara Posted on 20/08/2008 10:03

FMTTM Posts that Never Were

It's typical of this club's lack of ambition that we are buying Tottenham reserves. Souness ffs? Never heard of him.

Muttley Posted on 20/08/2008 10:04

FMTTM Posts that Never Were

Judas Clough signs for Mackems!

BobUpndown Posted on 20/08/2008 10:05

FMTTM Posts that Never Were

1973 National - CRISP… it's a sure thing! Rum's got no chance!

toxic_bob Posted on 20/08/2008 10:11

FMTTM Posts that Never Were

Dansette problems - techie help please.

Nolan sister of the day.

Is it gay to use Sun-In?

Capybara Posted on 20/08/2008 10:13

FMTTM Posts that Never Were

Had to pay one and ten a pint in London!

ridsdale Posted on 20/08/2008 10:15

FMTTM Posts that Never Were

Start at I.C.I. Monday!

TMG501 Posted on 20/08/2008 10:20

FMTTM Posts that Never Were

I've just bought a brand new car. What do you think of this?

Link: Poncey Style

toxic_bob Posted on 20/08/2008 10:23

FMTTM Posts that Never Were

Throcking Man, I'll be in Holgate bogs before kick-off on Saturday. Same place every week - Harrington jacket and oxblood DMs. Or will you bottle it again?

Muttley Posted on 20/08/2008 10:24

FMTTM Posts that Never Were

Germans shell Hartlepool, thousands of pounds worth of improvements result.

toxic_bob Posted on 20/08/2008 10:25

FMTTM Posts that Never Were

Deluded Ironopolis fans

Capybara Posted on 20/08/2008 10:26

FMTTM Posts that Never Were

Orient! We're as good as in the semi-final.

toxic_bob Posted on 20/08/2008 10:28

FMTTM Posts that Never Were

Derby away - LMS or LNER?

toxic_bob Posted on 20/08/2008 10:30

FMTTM Posts that Never Were

Friendly vs Hibernian - anybody got Polaroids of the goals?

BobUpndown Posted on 20/08/2008 10:31

FMTTM Posts that Never Were

Best place to get a perm?

What's with the white band, Jack?

bororeddaz Posted on 20/08/2008 10:32

FMTTM Posts that Never Were

Split arses allowed to vote. FFS, they'll let them in the bar next.

Puckoon Posted on 20/08/2008 10:34

FMTTM Posts that Never Were

Rioch FFS! We'll never get anywhere with a bunch of kids.

Jerry_Brown Posted on 20/08/2008 10:37

FMTTM Posts that Never Were

Who's going to Blackburn on Saturday?

The_Lizards_Jumpers Posted on 20/08/2008 10:41

FMTTM Posts that Never Were

Why are we signing Scottish teams' rejects - I mean who the f*** is this Slaven?

Muttley Posted on 20/08/2008 10:42

FMTTM Posts that Never Were

League will be ours this year (that dumb f***er, Hitler, won't dare invade Poland now).

captain5 Posted on 20/08/2008 10:45

FMTTM Posts that Never Were

How come we're always the last match on Shoot?

Capybara Posted on 20/08/2008 10:47

FMTTM Posts that Never Were

The Death Penalty - should it be abolished?

toxic_bob Posted on 20/08/2008 10:50

FMTTM Posts that Never Were

Is Middlesbrough in Cleveland or the Metropolitan Borough of Teesside?

The_Lizards_Jumpers Posted on 20/08/2008 10:51

FMTTM Posts that Never Were

Do they have bank tellers in Doncaster?

London - anyone been?

bororeddaz Posted on 20/08/2008 10:53

FMTTM Posts that Never Were

PP, is it true you wear deodorant? You homo.

number1jonnycash Posted on 20/08/2008 11:00

FMTTM Posts that Never Were

Anyone rented a colour telly yet?

TOPIC

MESSAGE

POST

REGISTER

Stonewashed jeans or spandex pants?

Capybara Posted on 20/08/2008 11:07

FMTTM Posts that Never Were

Hinton's or Pybus?

BobUpndown Posted on 20/08/2008 11:09

FMTTM Posts that Never Were

Anyone post a link to the Pathe highlights?

Chumley Warner on Legends, what a bounder, 1127 LW, at 18:00.

toxic_bob Posted on 20/08/2008 11:11

FMTTM Posts that Never Were

What colour tights do you like on a bird?

How many baths do you have a week - one or two?

ThePrisoner Posted on 20/08/2008 11:20

FMTTM Posts that Never Were

What do you reckon to these floodlight things, then? Playing at night will never catch on.

We've just got an indoor netty!

BobUpndown Posted on 20/08/2008 11:34

FMTTM Posts that Never Were

42,000? Seemed more like 45,000 from where I was stood... be going straight into his pocket!

bororeddaz Posted on 20/08/2008 11:36

FMTTM Posts that Never Were

Are there any coach inns near Accrington?

toxic_bob Posted on 20/08/2008 11:37

FMTTM Posts that Never Were

Stonewashed jeans or spandex pants?

atomicloonybin Posted on 20/08/2008 11:44

FMTTM Posts that Never Were

The wheel - yay or nay?

Would you give Eve one?

PinkPonce Posted on 20/08/2008 11:50

FMTTM Posts that Never Were

Pisa Away Anglo-Italian - Irish bars?

atomicloonybin Posted on 20/08/2008 11:52

FMTTM Posts that Never Were

Shevchenko - is he better than what we've got?

Big_Shot Posted on 20/08/2008 11:53

FMTTM Posts that Never Were

Mariner or Wood?

bernieisgod Posted on 20/08/2008 11:54

FMTTM Posts that Never Were

"The wheel - yay or nay? Would you give Eve one?"

On that theme...

Snakes - can we trust them?

joseph99 Posted on 20/08/2008 11:56

FMTTM Posts that Never Were

When will this recession end?

Why have they stopped 'Love Thy Neighbour'?

Best place to buy a pair of Oxford Bags?

What time does Baums close?

toxic_bob Posted on 20/08/2008 11:58

FMTTM Posts that Never Were

Ena Sharples - would you?

atomicloonybin Posted on 20/08/2008 11:58

FMTTM Posts that Never Were

Working offshore with the Vikings - any tips?

I'm a .com millionaire, and therefore better than you.

red_rebel Posted on 20/08/2008 12:08

FMTTM Posts that Never Were

Thatcher - worse than Heath?

Has anyone seen this new "fanzine?"

Who's going to see Acme Rebel?

Moskovictwz (sp) - anyone used his envelopes?

BobUpndown Posted on 20/08/2008 12:10

FMTTM Posts that Never Were

Guess which player I saw driving his Capri down Linthorpe Road?

Shin pads are for fannies.

red_rebel Posted on 20/08/2008 12:14

FMTTM Posts that Never Were

I've got a VIDEO!!

Players' summer jobs.

New roof on the hospital end?

Ayresome will be World Cup venue - FACT!

TMG501 Posted on 20/08/2008 12:17

FMTTM Posts that Never Were

Been down to the phone box at the end of the road to ring Rediffusion about that channel changer on our windowsill.

Didn't have any 2p pieces though.

BobUpndown Posted on 20/08/2008 12:20

FMTTM Posts that Never Were

I think we should use John Hickton up front... not at the back!

Miklaadt Posted on 20/08/2008 12:42

FMTTM Posts that Never Were

Got to win this weekend... it's a real four-pointer!

Let's all laugh at Bradford Park Avenue.

Teams for cribbage on Wednesday night.

Spurs going to give you chaps a jolly good seeing to.

Middlesbrough: Northumbria or Mercia?

Gillandi Posted on 20/08/2008 12:52

FMTTM Posts that Never Were

Visionary Charlie Amer. Players on the pitch are one thing but no-one loses money on bricks and mortar. Brother-in-law to get building contract too, guaranteeing no cowboy job. Those old wrought iron gates will be first to make way in Boro's bold modernisation plans.

Ayresomes_on_Fire Posted on 20/08/2008 12:57

FMTTM Posts that Never Were

Football at Albert Park - Friday 8:30pm.

As usual, just confirm your availability.

1. Lefty.
2. Twed.
3. BanPowerGame.
4. Baretto.
5. Anyone4aCamerons.
6. Boro is in my blood.
7. ArcheryGrounds_on_Fire.
8. God.
9. Matthew.
10. Barry.
11. Ilie Nastase.
12. Nicholas.
13. Piggy.
14. MFC in Anglo Scottish Cup.

If it gets dark before we finish, PP has said he will drive his Capri over and put the full beam on for floodlights.... not that any of us believe he's actually got one!

sasboro1 Posted on 20/08/2008 12:59

FMTTM Posts that Never Were

"Has anyone been to Boro Fish Bar and what's it like?"

Miklaadt Posted on 20/08/2008 13:00

FMTTM Posts that Never Were

Trilobite of the day.

Holgatewall Posted on 20/08/2008 13:07

FMTTM Posts that Never Were

Anyone on here enrolled at Kirby?

Gillandi Posted on 20/08/2008 13:09

FMTTM Posts that Never Were

Club Doctor prescribes cigarettes ahead of nervy 2nd leg at Maine Road. Charlton to limit alcohol intake on journey down.

Muttley Posted on 20/08/2008 13:13

FMTTM Posts that Never Were

That stupid bridge with the big swing on it - which daft bastadd thought of that?

indestructible_7 Posted on 20/08/2008 13:18

FMTTM Posts that Never Were

GBR win 56th Gold of the Games! - rigged or not rigged?

captain5 Posted on 20/08/2008 13:20

FMTTM Posts that Never Were

What the hell are we putting a white band on our home shirts for?

The main problem in the game is that the players aren't paid enough.

CrazyL Posted on 20/08/2008 13:24

FMTTM Posts that Never Were

Bumming - should it be legalised?

CrazyL Posted on 20/08/2008 13:24

FMTTM Posts that Never Were

Took the kids to see Gary Glitter at The City Hall last night. Great show - good clean family entertainment. Top bloke IMO!

zoec Posted on 20/08/2008 13:42

FMTTM Posts that Never Were

Anyone know the best place to get a Filofax unlocked?

CrazyL Posted on 20/08/2008 13:47

FMTTM Posts that Never Were

Has anybody tried a 'pork parmesan'?

ridsdale Posted on 20/08/2008 13:50

FMTTM Posts that Never Were

Strippers at the Claggy Mat!!!

CrazyL Posted on 20/08/2008 13:52

FMTTM Posts that Never Were

You won't believe this. I'm sending this from HOME!!!

zoec Posted on 20/08/2008 13:55

FMTTM Posts that Never Were

Don't you hate being stuck behind a woman cashing a postal order? A man would just cash his postal order and leave, but a woman has to cash the postal order, buy some stamps and a first day cover and then spend 10 minutes checking the balance on her post office account book before she leaves. Drives me nuts.

atomicloonybin Posted on 20/08/2008 13:58

FMTTM Posts that Never Were

Guess which player I saw on the 37 bus?

England v Ottoman Empire - teams announced.

Ankle of the day.

BobUpndown Posted on 20/08/2008 16:16

FMTTM Posts that Never Were

Anyone listening to the England game tonight?

Does anyone, really, believe we've been to the South Pole?

Piggy Posted on 20/08/2008 16:24

FMTTM Posts that Never Were

Dodo of the Day.

bororeddaz Posted on 20/08/2008 16:25

FMTTM Posts that Never Were

Just got the bus back from that ASDA place. Everything under one roof. Can't see it catching on, me, like. Frankie Dee's won't be losing no sleep.

CrazyL Posted on 20/08/2008 16:39

FMTTM Posts that Never Were

The Sports Gazette just got in. Boro won.

CrazyL Posted on 20/08/2008 16:45

FMTTM Posts that Never Were

I don't care about anybody else but during the season, come 3 o'clock on a Saturday afternoon, I'll be at the match.

Aurora Posted on 20/08/2008 19:21

FMTTM Posts that Never Were

Doodlebug stops match – bugger, just as we were 4-0 up against the mighty Woolwich Arsenal as well.

Ayresomes_on_Fire Posted on 20/08/2008 22:05

FMTTM Posts that Never Were

Saw that Hardwick in town after the match on Saturday, setting fire to half a crown and lighting his cigar with it.

Jonicama Posted on 20/08/2008 22:23

FMTTM Posts that Never Were

Kempes and Houseman - both to sign.

Were you on the League Liner train back from Luton?

Johnny Vincent for England.

Warwick_Hunt Posted on 20/08/2008 23:30

FMTTM Posts that Never Were

Are there any Irish bars/McDonalds in Gainsborough?

Gillandi Posted on 20/08/2008 23:32

FMTTM Posts that Never Were

What a bunch of unhappy scoundrels they are that collect cigarette cards. Like they are going to be worth something one day. I'm happy to say I give mine to the first urchin who asks outside my local tobacconists.

orlando2boro Posted on 20/08/2008 23:43

FMTTM Posts that Never Were

Bloody Yanks ruining Queen's English!

(some things never change)

bear66 Posted on 20/08/2008 23:44

FMTTM Posts that Never Were

And next week we have a local derby against Leeds.

MADMICK Posted on 20/08/2008 23:46

FMTTM Posts that Never Were

Car trouble advice please... I've snapped the crank handle. Anyone know where I can get a replacement?

bear66 Posted on 20/08/2008 23:48

FMTTM Posts that Never Were

When will they stop playing Telstar as the goal music?

How about the POWER GAME?

Gillandi Posted on 20/08/2008 23:49

FMTTM Posts that Never Were

What are we going to do with our horses once these A roads are laid? I'm gonna eat mine and get an auto-mobile. No more 6 ounces of red meat a week for me.

bear66 Posted on 20/08/2008 23:50

FMTTM Posts that Never Were

The clock's been fixed at Ayresome Park.

TOPIC

MESSAGE

POST

REGISTER

Season tickets going up to £50 next season! Scandalous...

bear66 Posted on 20/08/2008 23:51

FMTTM Posts that Never Were

Season tickets going up to £50 next season! Scandalous...

Gillandi Posted on 20/08/2008 23:57

FMTTM Posts that Never Were

Cine-8 porn?

Will we all go blind?

ProudToComeFromTeesside Posted on 20/08/2008 23:57

FMTTM Posts that Never Were

Why do the board always appoint novice managers? First we had Raich Carter, then Stan Anderson. Now they've appointed Jack Charlton. FFS! Amer is clueless.

ThePrisoner Posted on 21/08/2008 00:08

FMTTM Posts that Never Were

Ha ha! Man U relegated. Get the f*** in!

Ha ha ha ha ha ha ha!!!

Gillandi Posted on 21/08/2008 00:10

FMTTM Posts that Never Were

Is it okay to like Germans since last May's FA Cup Final? Despite his heroics, I think I'd still like to see Trautmann face a firing squad. Not least to quell the sudden interest in the game our women-folk are taking. Imagine being crammed onto a terrace next to somebody's wife or daughter.

ProudToComeFromTeesside Posted on 21/08/2008 00:10

FMTTM Posts that Never Were

A shilling a year more for a season ticket!!!

ProudToComeFromTeesside Posted on 21/08/2008 00:12

FMTTM Posts that Never Were

£1000 for a player! Exciting times.

Gillandi Posted on 21/08/2008 00:12

FMTTM Posts that Never Were

Bill Shankly will regret choosing Liverpool over us for the rest of his life.

ProudToComeFromTeesside Posted on 21/08/2008 00:15

FMTTM Posts that Never Were

Archduke Ferdinand assassinated. I reckon it could all kick off.

Gillandi Posted on 21/08/2008 00:17

FMTTM Posts that Never Were

"£1000 for a player! Exciting times."

But why are we signing strikers when we need half-backs?

ProudToComeFromTeesside Posted on 21/08/2008 00:17

FMTTM Posts that Never Were

It'll be good when we go to this new ground, Airsome Park or whatever it's called. Real state-of-the-art stuff, the new place.

byrno Posted on 21/08/2008 00:22

FMTTM Posts that Never Were

Mobile phone advice.

Thinking of getting one of these.

Link: What do you reckon?

red_rebel Posted on 21/08/2008 00:40

FMTTM Posts that Never Were

Coffin protest - cringeworthy?

Access problems in Boot Boy Alley.

What game was Cliff Mitchell watching?

Anyone going to Stockton races?

Gillandi Posted on 21/08/2008 00:43

FMTTM Posts that Never Were

I've heard Blenkinsopp has failed his medical.

Measles, tape-worm and cholera look to have scuppered the deal Boro struck to sign the goalscoring midfielder that we so desperately need.

It seems box-to-box is good, but box-to-box-to-box is bad in the rheumy eyes of our medical staff.

Should we take a chance on the prolific but sickly Blenkers?

If our squad wasn't so young, under-nourished and feebly inoculated, I might have been tempted.

red_rebel Posted on 21/08/2008 00:47

FMTTM Posts that Never Were

Brotton game off - SMALLPOX!

I wouldn't sell Bloomer for £500

Can we win the Northern League?

Gillandi Posted on 21/08/2008 00:54

FMTTM Posts that Never Were

Sod the Northern League, rebel, I hope you are at the Park Hotel on Friday night with your capitalist hat on and ready for a good lashing of tripe and onions as we plot to take Middlesbrough into the 20th century.

Blimey, 20th century? Never thought I'd live to see that when I was up to my eyes in it in the Crimean.

And have you read Uncle Tom's Cabin yet?

CrazyL Posted on 21/08/2008 10:49

FMTTM Posts that Never Were

Saturday's 2-1-7 formation. Are we becoming too defensive minded?

Brazil are s***!

Only 53,274 there Saturday! How can we get the crowds back in?

Camsell has been walking out with Williamson's spouse.

Chuds Posted on 21/08/2008 11:00

FMTTM Posts that Never Were

Anyone rented a TV from Rumbelows?

Betamax or VHS?

speckyget Posted on 21/08/2008 11:30

FMTTM Posts that Never Were

Difference Engine Help Plz.

Wilson, Keppel and Betty RIP.

Bandy Posted on 21/08/2008 11:32

FMTTM Posts that Never Were

How s*** is the club shop! They only have one f***in' till and 20 McLean Homes shirts!

red_rebel Posted on 21/08/2008 11:36

FMTTM Posts that Never Were

Palestine: Balfour's got it wrong!

It all kicked off in Cannon Street last night.

Know anyone who's got a telephone?

Guess which Boro player I saw in the Gaumont.

boro_exile Posted on 21/08/2008 11:42

FMTTM Posts that Never Were

Just bought some class near new gear from Littlewoods - I'll be looking better than PP in the Killy on Saturday.

Annoyed about the sheer volume of traffic on Stockton High St though. Wish it was pedestrianised.

esmond_million's_bungalow Posted on 21/01/1961 00:47

FMTTM Posts that Never Were

Abolition of minimum wage.

What I want to know is, what's the point? What team is realistically ever going to shell out more than £20 a week anyway?

glur Posted on 21/08/2008 12:35

FMTTM Posts that Never Were

Anyone know if training at Tollesby Road is open to the public?

Algarve Posted on 21/08/2008 12:43

FMTTM Posts that Never Were

Assembley Rooms or Astoria?

That Asprilla looks like he could be a good signing for the Mags.

Algarve Posted on 21/08/2008 12:48

FMTTM Posts that Never Were

Easy life, this football stuff, like. Just been down to Hutton Road - Shepherdson had 'em do 10 laps round the pitch, gave them a mug of tea, then they all walked into Doggy to get the bus home. Cloughy didn't run, like. Just kicked a ball about for a bit.

dooderooni Posted on 21/08/2008 12:50

FMTTM Posts that Never Were

Scarves - wool or silk?

Need to re-lace a casey, anyone know if Jack Hatfield's can do it?

glur Posted on 21/08/2008 12:50

FMTTM Posts that Never Were

I was on the pitch at half time during Mogga's testimonial.

[FACT]

TOPIC

MESSAGE

POST

REGISTER

Just got an apprenticeship in the yards... SORTED. They'll always need ships!

atomicloonybin Posted on 21/08/2008 12:51

FMTTM Posts that Never Were

Shin pads are for poofs.

Blokes who go to the ground without a hat on - right or wrong?

ProudToComeFromTeesside Posted on 21/08/2008 12:53

FMTTM Posts that Never Were

"But why are we signing strikers when we need half-backs?"

Agreed. We've never solved that right-half problem.

Ayresomes_on_Fire Posted on 21/08/2008 12:54

FMTTM Posts that Never Were

Hitler has invaded Poland [FACT].

ProudToComeFromTeesside Posted on 21/08/2008 12:55

FMTTM Posts that Never Were

Is it me or are rattles at football matches for ra-ras?

red_rebel Posted on 21/08/2008 13:02

FMTTM Posts that Never Were

Can we ever be bigger than Bishop Auckland?

Only 1,012 at Archery Ground, how the nation laughs.

Lady Gertrude Bell.... would you?

General strike - how long before capitalism crumbles?

ProudToComeFromTeesside Posted on 21/08/2008 13:05

FMTTM Posts that Never Were

2-3-5 formation next season - that's the way forward!

red_rebel Posted on 21/08/2008 13:09

FMTTM Posts that Never Were

RICKETTS. Who suffered as a child?

Been away on National Service. What have I missed?

New signing Delapenha - just been told he is a "colonial".

ProudToComeFromTeesside Posted on 21/08/2008 13:12

FMTTM Posts that Never Were

Transfer rumour - Charlie Wayman seen at Hutton Road.

ProudToComeFromTeesside Posted on 21/08/2008 13:16

FMTTM Posts that Never Were

David Jack – better manager than Wilf Gillow?

Capybara Posted on 21/08/2008 13:16

FMTTM Posts that Never Were

Is the Eleven Plus getting easier?

Chris_From_Pitchside Posted on 21/08/2008 13:18

FMTTM Posts that Never Were

Anyone got the Brian Clough shirt with the white tied collar for sale? I'm going for the retro look.

ProudToComeFromTeesside Posted on 21/08/2008 13:21

FMTTM Posts that Never Were

ST's up by a shilling, matchday prices up by 1d!

red_rebel Posted on 21/08/2008 13:22

FMTTM Posts that Never Were

FFS Igor Cvitanovic! He's brilliant on FM94.

Lawrence sacked. New boss RON ATKINSON, breaking news on Clubcall.

Agiadis. Next big thing?

Anyone been in the 100 Club?

ProudToComeFromTeesside Posted on 21/08/2008 13:24

FMTTM Posts that Never Were

I saw Cloughie out last night with his bird.

ProudToComeFromTeesside Posted on 21/08/2008 13:27

FMTTM Posts that Never Were

This Mannion kid is over-rated.

speckyget Posted on 21/08/2008 13:29

FMTTM Posts that Never Were

Stylophone vs Bontempi

Will you miss school milk?

ProudToComeFromTeesside Posted on 21/08/2008 13:31

FMTTM Posts that Never Were

Why doesn't Anderson pick Downing?

BobUpndown Posted on 21/08/2008 14:53

FMTTM Posts that Never Were

We need another 59 league goals-a-season man… Camsell can't do it all on his own!

Just got an apprenticeship in the yards… SORTED. They'll always need ships!

red_rebel Posted on 21/08/2008 14:58

FMTTM Posts that Never Were

Burnley, Wolves, Blackpool, Huddersfield… can anyone ever catch the Big Four?

BobUpndown Posted on 21/08/2008 15:03

FMTTM Posts that Never Were

Just seen an aeroplane!

A substitute? What is the point of that? Doesn't he know his best 11?

Ayresomes_on_Fire Posted on 21/08/2008 20:14

FMTTM Posts that Never Were

Liverpool on Saturday. Who else is taking bananas to chuck at Barnes?

CrazyL Posted on 21/08/2008 21:22

FMTTM Posts that Never Were

I got one of those cassette recorders today. You can store up to THIRTY songs on a single cassette and then play them back on this tiny machine, which I swear is no bigger than a shoe-box!

mowbrays_number_4 Posted on 21/08/2008 22:15

FMTTM Posts that Never Were

Transit van to Cambridge leaving from the cenotaph Saturday morning - anyone interested?

Should we limit transfers to 2 months a year?

Don Revie - an utter disgrace!

I voted ERIMUS STADIUM - what did you vote for?

ProudToComeFromTeesside Posted on 21/08/2008 23:47

FMTTM Posts that Never Were

Gerrinthere! We've signed Kinnell!

ProudToComeFromTeesside Posted on 22/08/2008 11:20

FMTTM Posts that Never Were

Sweepstake - when will the sports complex finally open?

atomicloonybin Posted on 22/08/2008 11:32

FMTTM Posts that Never Were

Pink Ponce - I'll see you outside YK Chow's. I'll be the one in the twelve button Oxford Bags.

New Light Programme Wireless show announced - the Three Legends: Hughie Gallacher, Micky Fenton and Raich Carter. You can join in by Morse Code.

Dibzzz Posted on 22/08/2008 11:33

FMTTM Posts that Never Were

Eagle Eye Action Man or Stretch Armstrong?

ProudToComeFromTeesside Posted on 22/08/2008 11:44

FMTTM Posts that Never Were

How the hell did Ashcroft miss that?

speckyget Posted on 22/08/2008 11:56

FMTTM Posts that Never Were

Ugo(lini): more clubs than Sam Snead.

Ishmael Posted on 22/08/2008 12:02

FMTTM Posts that Never Were

Fanny at the Olympics.

Link: Cor!! Fanny Blankers-Koen

mowbrays_number_4 Posted on 22/08/2008 12:03

FMTTM Posts that Never Were

Tim Williamson - unsettled at the Boro?

slipshod Posted on 22/08/2008 12:14

FMTTM Posts that Never Were

Is T.R. Wright's the best place in town to buy some slacks?

Capybara Posted on 22/08/2008 13:57

FMTTM Posts that Never Were

Does anyone know what the 'U' in Dr UN Philips stands for?

ProudToComeFromTeesside Posted on 22/08/2008 18:49

FMTTM Posts that Never Were

Missed out on a ticket for the Titanic - gutted!

swindonred Posted on 22/08/2008 21:26

FMTTM Posts that Never Were

Why play Geoff Hurst instead of Greaves for tomorrow's final?

boro74 Posted on 22/08/2008 22:05

FMTTM Posts that Never Were

Brut, Censored or Hai Karate?

bear66 Posted on 22/08/2008 22:11

FMTTM Posts that Never Were

Boro will never win a cup... or have a Brazilian playing for us.

ProudToComeFromTeesside Posted on 23/08/2008 11:48

FMTTM Posts that Never Were

Don't worry, we'll stuff Wolves in the replay.

Renrut Posted on 23/08/2008 12:27

FMTTM Posts that Never Were

Apparently we're keeping an eye on this little French kid called Francois Grenet.

Let's have a card display in the Holgate!

ProudToComeFromTeesside Posted on 23/08/2008 12:54

FMTTM Posts that Never Were

After Wolves defeat, I really hate Andy Gray!

BobUpndown Posted on 23/08/2008 13:07

FMTTM Posts that Never Were

This bloke Hilter (sp?)... Chamberlain had him in his pocket! What's he going to do now we've got his signed 'submission'.. never amount to anything!

"One world war & you shut up! Eio Eio..."

ProudToComeFromTeesside Posted on 23/08/2008 13:12

FMTTM Posts that Never Were

Hodgy's blonde hairdo - WTF?

Chapter Thirteen
Our Holgate
End in the Sky

Teesside Urban Legends

TOPIC - Our Holgate End in the Sky

Previous | Next | New Topic | Top Of Board

TOPIC

MESSAGE

POST

REGISTER

Just above The Riverside there is a massive stand called The Holgate. I am not too sure how many it holds but I know they have just completed filling in the corners to get more in.

BroughtonLad Posted on 6/4 7:57

OUR HOLGATE END IN THE SKY

I woke up this morning thinking about the match tonight. Then I had a thought about my relatives and friends who supported Boro but have sadly passed away.

Just above The Riverside there is a massive stand called The Holgate. I am not too sure how many it holds but I know they have just completed filling in the corners to get more in.

People will be up there tonight, waving their scarves and balloons and shouting the Boro on.

We won't hear them but we all know someone who is up there.

So if you are at the match tonight, shout just a little louder for our relatives and friends up there IN OUR HOLGATE END IN THE SKY

Come on Boro, we can do it!

littledick Posted on 6/4 8:03

re: OUR HOLGATE END IN THE SKY

Spot on, mate, I know quite a few.

chmfc66 Posted on 6/4 8:22

re: OUR HOLGATE END IN THE SKY

Great post, BL. Sent a shiver through me when I read it. You are spot on, mate, and with people with as much passion as you, we deserve to win tonight. I told my ten-year-old son this morning that this is the biggest game in our history and I want him to come home after the match tonight without a voice.

"Sing your heart out for the lads"

BroughtonLad Posted on 6/4 9:08

re: OUR HOLGATE END IN THE SKY

SING YOUR HEART OUT FOR THE LADS!

Bram Posted on 6/4 10:38

re: OUR HOLGATE END IN THE SKY

BL, you got me there! Sat here at work, filling up just thinking about it!

My Dad passed away about six weeks ago - lifelong Boro fan. He even gave me Hickton as a middle name.

My old man always used to say "Typical Boro!" when describing a disappointment and I had thought to myself that it would be typical of the Boro to go and win a European trophy after he had gone BUT he will be watching tonight from above.

I will sing for both of us tonight.

guyb Posted on 6/4 12:22

re: OUR HOLGATE END IN THE SKY

We need all the help we can get tonight, from Teessiders past and present.

COME ON BORO!

HOWWAAAAAAAAYYYYYYYYYYYYY!!!

Smifter Posted on 6/4 12:24

re: OUR HOLGATE END IN THE SKY

I totally filled up then. I'm way too emotional today! Great post, BL. I particularly liked how they all had their balloons

C'mon Boro!

Marlon_D Posted on 6/4 12:35

re: OUR HOLGATE END IN THE SKY

One of my close workmates died over three years ago. Massive Boro fan.

This link is spooky as I was sat thinking last night how much he would have enjoyed the Euro experience and he would have been like a kid at Crimbo today.

COME ON BORO!

junior17_1985 Posted on 6/4 12:48

re: OUR HOLGATE END IN THE SKY

BL. I am quite spiritual... thanks, that was a great post... and he is right, we all know someone. And I know what it's like thinking I could have done this and that... so let's not walk away with anything to regret, even if we go out. Let's be able to say to ourselves 'I gave everything'. I would do anything to progress in this comp and win it.

Red_Clowne Posted on 6/4 12:51

Re: OUR HOLGATE END IN THE SKY

My mate's up there waiting for kick-off but some tall bastud has just gone and stood smack in front of him!

holgate_rochey Posted on 6/4 13:33

Re: OUR HOLGATE END IN THE SKY

It's quite emotional today, like.

holuc Posted on 6/4 13:35

re: OUR HOLGATE END IN THE SKY

Whatever happened to that bloke who collapsed at the Bolton match?

Nedkat Posted on 6/4 13:37

re: OUR HOLGATE END IN THE SKY

That's probably me Dad, Red Clowne. He was a big bugger, 6'5" and built like a proverbial brick shithouse. Nice fella though, quiet, wouldn't hurt a fly type. I wonder what he'd think about all of this Europe shenanigans?

BroughtonLad Posted on 6/4 13:37

re: OUR HOLGATE END IN THE SKY

I must admit when I was typing it, I had a tear in my eye.

Let's give it rock all tonight as you do not know what is round that corner. I have a good feeling about tonight. Not to be missed.

I am sure OUR HOLGATE will be watching over us.

On a brighter note: Up there they won't have to pay £20+ to watch tonight.

Zamboni80 Posted on 6/4 14:54

re: OUR HOLGATE END IN THE SKY

That gave me a lump in my throat, quite stirring stuff. I know my nanna will be there shouting us on from the heavenly Holgate.

COME ON BORO!

northeastcorner Posted on 6/4 17:17

re: OUR HOLGATE END IN THE SKY

I'm not generally into all that stuff, but that was quality, BL. Really got to me. I'm even more fired up to sing my heart out tonight.

COME ON BORO! Do it for Teesside, past, present and future!!

ayresome_82 Posted on 6/4 17:29

re: OUR HOLGATE END IN THE SKY

Great post, BL!!

I know a few people who will be congregating in the 'Holgate' tonight.

I WANNA BE IN THAT NUMBER WHEN THE REDS GO MARCHING IN!

BroughtonLad Posted on 6/4 17:59

re: OUR HOLGATE END IN THE SKY

COME ON BORO!
GIVE IT ROCK ALL!
SING YOUR HEARTS OUT FOR THE LADS!

RedWurzel Posted on 6/4 18:01

re: OUR HOLGATE END IN THE SKY

Nice one - I had similar thoughts at Cardiff, especially when you see pictures of the gap in the roof and the sunbeams coming in from the sky above, sort of old guys "getting a squeeze" through a turnstile in the sky.

I think a Boro qualification tonight should also be dedicated to the guy who didn't make it back from Amsterdam. I think he should have a spiritual word in the ear of fans on Teesside who think it's too expensive to go tonight.

holuc Posted on 6/4 18:06

re: OUR HOLGATE END IN THE SKY

There are too many to mention. They'll all be watching, maybe putting a balloon in the keeper's eyeline on a shot!

newholgate Posted on 6/4 22:54

re: OUR HOLGATE END IN THE SKY

I think they must have all been there tonight, cheering us on! And they would be proud to be Boro tonight.

MysticMogga Posted on 6/4 22:56

re: OUR HOLGATE END IN THE SKY

Top post... shivers up my spine.

Boro1961 Posted on 6/4 22:58

re: OUR HOLGATE END IN THE SKY

Good post. Kenny L**** in Stockton was one of the biggest fans in the town - he died four years ago and every time we get to a final or go further in the cups, I think of Kenny - top lad and Boro nut.

Tonight was for you, Ken.

helie Posted on 7/4 0:07

re: OUR HOLGATE END IN THE SKY

I knew you were all watching down tonight.

Boro Forever.

TOPIC

MESSAGE

POST

REGISTER

> I had a word or two with my Dad tonight in my thoughts. He died 25 years ago, a couple of hours before the Wolves game in the quarter-finals of the FA Cup in 1981.

lawnranger Posted on 7/4 0:13

re: OUR HOLGATE END IN THE SKY

Superb post!

Sat there, I had a word or two with my Dad tonight in my thoughts. He died 25 years ago, a couple of hours before the Wolves game in the quarter-finals of the FA Cup in 1981. We were supposed to go to the game that day as well, which is why I have probably been as passionate about the Boro as I am.

But no matter what you believe, something shone down on us tonight. I am just so glad my Dad made me a Boro fan.

BroughtonLad Posted on 7/4 0:21

re: OUR HOLGATE END IN THE SKY

Not long back from the match. Considering there was only 25,000 there tonight, what an atmosphere.

THE HOLGATE IN THE SKY WAS ROCKING!

It was what dreams are made of. You could not write the script any better.

THERE IS A HEAVEN!

jamesuk001 Posted on 7/4 0:28

re: OUR HOLGATE END IN THE SKY

My thoughts are with you, Danny.

My old workmate died suddenly at the weekend. His story is on the front page of the Gazette.

Sorry I didn't see more of you, mate.

theboydom Posted on 7/4 0:46

re: OUR HOLGATE END IN THE SKY

Top thread, BL.

When we got to the ZDS Final, my Grandad wouldn't go. He had been a season ticket holder on the South Terrace from age six in 1922 and had given up going when he came out after we played West Ham one day and all the fences and dogs and treatment of the fans reminded him too much of what he'd seen after WW2. He knew there would be bother v Chelsea at Wembley, and we couldn't really tell him otherwise.

As it was, on the way out, we saw an old lady pushed down the steps of Wembley Way going into the tube station by a load of Boro trying to get at some Chelsea over the fence in the car park. We picked her up and dusted her down, but our apologies weren't really enough. It would have broken our Grandad's heart to see it so our Dad was glad he never went in the end.

By the time we got to the first League Cup Final, football was a friendlier game but the change came too late for our Grandad. He had passed away, heartbroken at his wife's passing. He only lasted a couple of months longer than her. He always used to say to me, "I am a football fan, not a Middlesbrough fan, because fan means fanatic, and I am not as fanatical about the Boro as you," but he was always as excited as me when Boro won.

When I went to that game against Leicester, all I could think about was Grandad as I went up Wembley Way with the fans being so friendly to each other. This was just the occasion he and all the Boro fans who had gone before him were yearning for during their long years of support. The result would have mattered, but not as much as being there.

I had to split off from my mates, who I had followed the Boro with all over the country and known in some cases since I was a bairn, because I knew I would cry as I went through the turnstile for Grandad and the fans like him who had passed away before such a great occasion.

The same feeling followed me to Cardiff. I, along with a lot of fans, knew it was going to be our day. I was crying or fighting back tears from the moment we scored our first and by the time I left the ground I was spent, like most people I knew.

Tonight was another highlight, an even higher high tidemark for my club. I can remember reading a book on European football as a kid and, as I would always do, I turned to the index to look to see if the Boro were in the book. They were! One entry! We were in the long list of clubs who had finished in European qualifying positions in their league history. I was a walking, talking statto about the Boro at this age so I knew only too well we had never graced the top European table with our presence, but look, there we were in 267th place out of 268! Then, I noticed the footnotes to the table. We were in because they included finishes in the top three even during years before there were no European competitions to qualify for, 1913-14 we finished 3rd.

Well, tonight we properly re-wrote the book. A comeback that exemplified Teesside steel and determination, with no little style. Semi-finalists in a UEFA competition. Grandad, and all those up there with him, would have been bursting with pride.

proud Posted on 7/4 0:51

re: OUR HOLGATE END IN THE SKY

BL, you normally talk a lot of sense but that statement there sums you up mate. But obviously I have read this thread after the game so will give my thoughts on them when we lift the trophy in the final, mate. SUPER BORO!

beera Posted on 7/4 1:19

re: A hoof from the heart!

A night for celebration and also a night to remember family and friends who have passed on, but who loved the Boro as much as any of us. This night was for them.

grainger1981 Posted on 7/4 1:56

re: A hoof from the heart!

Another would have been up there tonight. He was only 23 when he passed away nearly two weeks ago and was buried today. That's for him.

RIP Ste.

kerro1959 Posted on 7/4 2:35

re: A hoof from the heart!

RIP Dennis and Peter Pan Rowe. Tonight was for U. RIP U beautiful Reds.

BroughtonLad Posted on 7/4 8:18

re: A hoof from the heart!

DEEP IN MY HEART...

So proud.

Bram Posted on 7/4 10:51

re: A hoof from the heart!

I had always thought that people wanting "help from above" were a little bit desperate but last night something helped to create a phenomenal atmosphere and something helped us score 4 times in an hour in a cup quarter-final.

"Our name's on the cup" is another cliché but now it doesn't seem so ridiculous.

After celebrating Maccarone's goal, the first thing I thought of was my Dad. I could imagine him shouting (as he always did) "Blow the f***ing whistle, ref!!" so I shouted it on his behalf.

BoroMutt Posted on 7/4 10:54

re: A hoof from the heart!

Got home, took the dog out, looked up at the stars and told me Mam about it. Bless her.

BoroMutt Posted on 7/4 10:54

re: A hoof from the heart!

sniff

OnAMission5 Posted on 7/4 10:59

re: A hoof from the heart!

Don't forget Brendan O'Connor who was out in Amsterdam.

BroughtonLad Posted on 7/4 14:21

re: A hoof from the heart! Please read the post...

We are the Ayresome Angels and we never miss a match

We will follow THE BORO.

penry1 Posted on 8/4 1:04

OUR HOLGATE END IN THE SKY

I think it would be a great idea to have the paragraph painted somewhere in the concourse for all to see. Maybe on the wall before you go up to your seat. I think it could be inspirational to the fans in a similar way that the Liverpool badge is to the players before they run out. Maybe a bit of poetry around the ground. It would be a shame to lose these words as it seems to have made a lot of people remember a lot of people.

AyresomeMark Posted on 8/4 14:29

OUR HOLGATE END IN THE SKY

Top idea that, P. Come on, Rob, wheels in motion stuff.

Gains Posted on 8/4 15:12

OUR HOLGATE END IN THE SKY

Excellent words. I thought of my Dad on Thursday night after the game. Bucharest away will be 5 years to the day since he passed away and I'll think of him then too. I know he'll be watching.

BroughtonLad Posted on 8/4 18:28

OUR HOLGATE END IN THE SKY

The Dream will go on I am sure and OUR HOLGATE IN THE SKY will be full to the rafters again tomorrow.

B_Hills Posted on 8/4 19:52

OUR HOLGATE END IN THE SKY

I dedicated the win to my Grandfather and my father (RIP) who rarely missed a game since 1947, and who took me to my first ever game. How proud you lads must have been looking down on Thursday night.

BroughtonLad Posted on 21/4 7:58

OUR HOLGATE END IN THE SKY

Well, the Dream goes on.

The Ayresome Angels are still singing.

Someone up there is looking down on us (1-0 but could have been much worse).

COME ON BORO!

junior17_1985 Posted on 21/4 8:18

OUR HOLGATE END IN THE SKY

Yes, they are still singing and they will carry our lads to a cup this year... if we all believe, it will happen. 2-0 Thursday. Come on!

OverTheTopAussie Posted on 21/4 8:53

OUR HOLGATE END IN THE SKY

(To the tune "Spirit In The Sky")

Cheering us on from The Holgate In The Sky.
That's where I'm gonna go when I die.
But before they lay me to rest,
Boro will show we're the best.

Too corny? Needs a little work.
Would love to get something about a "Cup Double" in there.

junior17_1985 Posted on 21/4 9:06

OUR HOLGATE END IN THE SKY

I don't think you are too far off...

Cheer us on from The Holgate In The Sky,
Take me there when I die,
They always told us it can't be done,
The Boro will prove you wrong.

Tweek Posted on 27/4 13:02

OUR HOLGATE END IN THE SKY

The biggest day ever seen on Teesside. Let's do it for all those who have watched and worn that red shirt, who sadly are no longer with us, but they will all be there tonight.

Smifter Posted on 27/4 13:05

OUR HOLGATE END IN THE SKY

Made me sad when I saw flowers at the scene of an accident in Park End yesterday and saw the MFC flowers.

C'mon Boro!

grantus Posted on 27/4 13:17

OUR HOLGATE END IN THE SKY

Good thread, BroughtonLad. Great post, theboydom. Almost shed a tear there, fella.

Cheering us on from The Holgate In The Sky,
That's where we're gonna go, when we die.
When we die and they lay us to rest,
We'll still be cheering the team we love the best.

BORO!!!!
BORO!!!!

Nedkat Posted on 27/4 13:40

OUR HOLGATE END IN THE SKY

And did those feet in ancient times
Walk upon Ayresome's Holgate end?
And was the holy Lamb of God
On Holgate's pleasant terrace seen?

And if yer did, mate, do us a favour, make it happen tonight. Not just 'happen' happen... let the Boro rise above the rest and give the supporters and the town a mighty rapturous evening. Let us be victorious!

Oh, and a bit of a hand in the Final wouldn't go amiss either.

OK, OK, I'll be in church on Sunday... Jeeeeeesh...!!

Red_Clowne Posted on 27/4 14:56

OUR HOLGATE END IN THE SKY

As I tread the verge of Ayresome
Bid my anxious fears subside
Death of death and their destruction
Land me safe on Teesside
Boro Boro,
Boro Boro,
We'll support you ever more!
We'll support you ever more!

Boro_lyzzy Posted on 27/4 15:06

OUR HOLGATE END IN THE SKY

I'll be thinking about my Mum who passed away 7 years ago. She was the first person to show me that it's fine for women to be interested in football, even though she always missed a goal when she had gone to the loo or to make a cup of tea. And ALWAYS when things were looking dodgy for us, or there were a few minutes left for us to win the match, she'd leave her seat in the front room next to the TV or radio and go and pace around in the kitchen, jumping back into the living room when the whistle had gone.

I'd like to think that my Mum would be pacing around the kitchen all tonight, and that she won't miss a single thing.

RIP Cathy x

boredreceptionist Posted on 27/4 15:08

OUR HOLGATE END IN THE SKY

Almost moved to tears reading this. My grandad would be so proud of Boro coming so far. Don't let him down!

keelo Posted on 27/4 15:15

OUR HOLGATE END IN THE SKY

If me Dad's looking down tonight, he wouldn't believe it for a minute. "Boro in a UEFA Cup semi-final... naaaaaahhh!"

Well, this is for you, Jack.

bigwheater Posted on 27/4 15:16

OUR HOLGATE END IN THE SKY

Yeah, he would be proud. Mine and Bored's Grandad was really ill when we won the Carling Cup. He died 2 weeks later. He bought me my first season ticket when I was a nipper and his love for Boro rubbed off on his 5 kids and 20+ grandkids.

Also, a few other family members who didn't get chance to enjoy the good times will always be deep in our hearts. God bless and Come on Boro!

dan_boro Posted on 27/4 16:23

OUR HOLGATE END IN THE SKY

Come on Boro...

Win it for those who cannot be there tonight in person, those who are there, and for those who are not yet born!

COME ON BORO!
COME ON BORO!
COME ON BORO!

guyb Posted on 27/4 16:46

OUR HOLGATE END IN THE SKY

Some events are so laced with emotion and meaning that they leave an imprint behind in collective memory.

Basel was one. We'll have another tonight as the ghosts of Teesside bear witness with 34,000 lucky ones.

One Last Chance
One Last Effort
One Last Time

COME ON BORO!

Nedkat Posted on 27/4 17:06

OUR HOLGATE END IN THE SKY

I hope Big Paddy's got his beer sorted out up there.

Kick back on that cloud and enjoy every minute, Dad! I know you don't believe it, but it's true!! We're in the UEFA Cup semi-final!!

COME ON BORO!

BroughtonLad Posted on 27/4 17:16

OUR HOLGATE END IN THE SKY

Come on, you Ayresome Angels.

libertine Posted on 27/4 17:29

OUR HOLGATE END IN THE SKY

Wow... what a great post, mate. Both of my grandmas recently passed away. One was a Boro supporter for 95 years, the other was Scottish and hated the English (lol) but always followed the mighty MFC and I'm sure she will be willing them to win tonight, along with myself and my family.

COME ON BORO!

James x

ross_94 Posted on 27/4 17:31

OUR HOLGATE END IN THE SKY

Spot on, m8.

Come on the Boro!

Sing your hearts out for the lads!

The_Commisar Posted on 27/4 17:42

OUR HOLGATE END IN THE SKY

It's not just for us, it's for each and every one of 'em who followed through thick and thin and thinner still and saw nothing. Count your blessings, friends, these are magical times.

Cheers, our Ian. Cheers, Mam.

COME ON BORO!

amelvg1 Posted on 27/4 17:58

OUR HOLGATE END IN THE SKY

Crazy Dave, RIP mate, u would have loved tonight.

Come on Boro!

TOPIC

MESSAGE

POST

REGISTER

I don't know how angels fly but I suspect God's going to have a lot of travel problems on 10.5.06.

borobuddah Posted on 27/4 22:31

OUR HOLGATE END IN THE SKY

Me Dad just said, "Yes but don't expect 'em to win in the Final."

guyb Posted on 28/4 0:51

OUR HOLGATE END IN THE SKY

I don't know how angels fly but I suspect God's going to have a lot of travel problems on 10.5.06.

BOOOOOOOOOOOOOOOOORRRRRRRRRRRRRAAAAAAAAAAAAAAAAAAAAAAAAAAAA!!!!!

boro_spike Posted on 28/4 0:56

OUR HOLGATE END IN THE SKY

They must be Ayresome Angels and I hope they are enjoying every minute of it. I know I am!

penry1 Posted on 28/4 0:57

OUR HOLGATE END IN THE SKY

Get that verse painted in the concourse of the North Stand.

Nedkat Posted on 28/4 1:01

OUR HOLGATE END IN THE SKY

Ammm sat 'ere on me back porch thinkin', "Oh, fook! We've bloody done it" and to be fookin' obvious, I would have to say we have!

flabby66 Posted on 28/4 1:02

OUR HOLGATE END IN THE SKY

My husband's grandfather was a massive fan. He died before the Riverside was built and his father died in November just gone now. My husband and son carry the baton well and are truly "Boro till I die" people.

BroughtonLad Posted on 28/4 1:39

OUR HOLGATE END IN THE SKY

There is someone up there looking after us.

GET IN, YOU BEAUTIES!

guyr Posted on 28/4 1:46

OUR HOLGATE END IN THE SKY

Still well fired up. My son's 12 today message was on the electronic board in the ground. It took forever to get home due to the singing in the North Stand at the end.

Came out and my eldest son was saying that it was the first time he has ever experienced the crowd singing outside as we walk away. I have hooked my two boys on the club. I was stood there tonight and thought how proud I am that my two little ones were shouting their heads off for Boro. We even started some chants in the North Stand. I never managed that in The Holgate.

YES! YES! YES!

WHAT A DAY.

Fingers crossed for Eindhoven and tickets.

skeelo Posted on 28/4 1:46

OUR HOLGATE END IN THE SKY

Top post. Pass the Kleenex, kidder.

boroboy87 Posted on 28/4 1:50

OUR HOLGATE END IN THE SKY

Luckily so far in life I haven't lost anyone that close to me, Boro fan or otherwise. But reading thru sum of these made me realise that it's wot this club's all about, the ppl, past and present. We have one hell of a club and ppl shouldn't worry whichever Holgate end their loved ones watched it in, up there or down here, they will be proud of the team and proud of u all 4 the support u gave the lads! My thoughts and prayers are with everyone who has lost someone close to them.

Arctic_Mongoose Posted on 28/4 1:50

OUR HOLGATE END IN THE SKY

I remember playing Sensible Soccer when I was younger... Boro v some Yugoslavia team in the 2nd round. My Grandad burst out laughing as he walked past... "It will never happen!"

If only, hey Grandad?

skeelo Posted on 28/4 2:05

OUR HOLGATE END IN THE SKY

I'm sure those of us who knew Fred Appleton will imagine him with a big smile on his face tonight as he watched the game from up above. God rest his soul.

Valer Posted on 28/4 2:08

OUR HOLGATE END IN THE SKY

April 27th 2000 - docs told us my mum had a brain tumour and had a month to 6 weeks to live - devastated. She held out for nearly 6 months.

Couldn't believe it when I found out that the second leg was on the anniversary of the worst day of my life. Prayed to her all day today and truly believe that her wings were on Massimo's foot - from that Holgate End In The Sky.

boroboy87 Posted on 28/4 2:10

OUR HOLGATE END IN THE SKY

Valer, she was there, they all were!

Valer Posted on 28/4 2:28

OUR HOLGATE END IN THE SKY

I sooo hope so - tears are dripping off the end of my chin now!

Lost my Dad too last year. I am officially an orphan!

Heard myself shouting "Come on, son" to Downing et al tonight - Dad's vocabulary, not mine!
Resigned myself to very little sleep tonight (the Basel game taught me there is no point in even trying) so I will spend an evening on the sofa with JD instead!

Bet Mum and Dad are tucked up happy as Larry with the Philadelphia girl!

boromagic Posted on 28/4 2:31

OUR HOLGATE END IN THE SKY

I have to say I didn't see this thread before the match but at 3-2 and 4-2, I started to think of my Dad who passed away 2 years ago and did wish that he'd been there to see this moment. So thank you for the balloons for those who are sadly no longer on this earth but who are the Ayresome Angels xx

Valer Posted on 28/4 2:45

OUR HOLGATE END IN THE SKY

The chap who sat directly behind me in the East Stand was a MASSIVE Boro fan - he ran the Middlesbrough Supporters Club for years and was always on the telly. He died just before our Carling Cup victory. Think he deserves a mention on this thread - I think of him often and many times tonight.

Night, God bless x

j_orourke Posted on 28/4 5:47

OUR HOLGATE END IN THE SKY

Our kid would have watched it, some piss up on his cloud!

Boro_lyzzy Posted on 28/4 6:53

OUR HOLGATE END IN THE SKY

My Mum had an old navy polo shirt with the Boro badge on. It was one of the very few things that I kept after her death. I decided to wear it to the match last night.

Thanks, Mum.

Valer Posted on 28/4 20:22

OUR HOLGATE END IN THE SKY

At least those we are remembering here won't have difficulty getting tickets/flights/hotels for Eindhoven - the big fella is laying on first class travel and accommodation and comfy cloud seating!

Trinity Church Eindhoven is a multi-denominational church, serving English-speaking people in the Eindhoven area. Suggest we all light a candle there on 10th May and have a big show for all those Boro fans we have loved and who can only be with us in spirit.

chris1976 Posted on 28/4 20:25

OUR HOLGATE END IN THE SKY

Let's do it for the other Ayresome Angels.

God bless, Grandad xxx

---

chorleygeorge Posted on 30/4 11:01

OUR HOLGATE END IN THE SKY

Bloody hell. My brother, David, died of a cancerous brain tumour the night we beat Spurs on the way to the Carling Cup.

I shared my sadness on this very forum and the wonderful fmttm people were a fantastic tonic. One comment said: "Let's go and win it for your brother," a comment that will live with me forever.

Let's hope we can dedicate a UEFA win to our loved ones on those sky terraces.

FunkyPotatoe Posted on 30/4 12:24

OUR HOLGATE END IN THE SKY

Grandad, my fave person in the world to talk about the Boro to. I used to give Beck some stick and when walking back from the Riverside after one game, I popped in to see him in Pally Park. He looked me straight in the eye after Beck had scored the winner and said, "Who's Mickel Shyyyte now?" Classic!

My father-in-law, the best man I have ever known. Died last November after a battle with lung cancer - converted him to a Boro fan and prayed to him on Thursday night when my prayers were answered!

God bless you both! x

---

bodysausage Posted on 30/4 14:51

OUR HOLGATE END IN THE SKY

A mighty Mick Baxter HOOF,
A mazy Mannion dribble,
A chip to the back post.

Maddren!
4-3!
Get in!

---

dan_boro Posted on 30/4 23:38

OUR HOLGATE END IN THE SKY

I'm sure the likes of Mannion, Clough, Maddren, to name only a few, were kicking every ball up there on Thursday with the rest of the Ayresome Angels...

Now let's win the Final for them all. A lot of the 'old timers' never thought we'd ever win a cup, Boro just don't do that. We proved them wrong in Cardiff!

All aboard for Eindhoven - let's do it again!

---

bodysausage Posted on 30/4 23:50

OUR HOLGATE END IN THE SKY

You'll never take the Holgate!

BoroMod Posted on 30/4 23:58

OUR HOLGATE END IN THE SKY

What a brilliant thread.

My Grandad was a true Boro cynic, always bringing me back down to earth when I got a bit carried away. Not because he was a miserable git, just because he was battle weary from the countless false dawns he had seen over 70 years. He loved this club though, from the very bottom of his heart.

He died just before the '97 dramas - that would have added more fuel to the fire. He would have loved Cardiff though. That was the day he longed for.

Eindhoven, he'd never believe! I read this thread before the game and thought of him after the game. He'd have given his right arm to be in Eindhoven. Hopefully he will be, following from above.

---

collo1875 Posted on 1/5 0:19

OUR HOLGATE END IN THE SKY

Can't read this. It is too upsetting. But it has got to be the best post I've seen on fmttm. I'll read it in a couple of weeks.

This must be the best thread I have ever seen on here, even though I can hardly see my screen for tears.

kazzaxxx Posted on 1/5 0:51

OUR HOLGATE END IN THE SKY

Well, this post has been amazing. Lost my Nana 18 months ago and she loved the Boro.

God bless, everyone.

RIP.

Scrote Posted on 1/5 3:39

OUR HOLGATE END IN THE SKY

What a beautiful thread.

There must be so many stories and it is humbling to read just the few that are here.

Thank you all for sharing.

mboroboy Posted on 1/5 8:00

OUR HOLGATE END IN THE SKY

Just thought of my Grandad and a friend called Fiona who both passed on a couple of years ago. I wish they could have been here now.

God bless.

BroughtonLad Posted on 1/5 9:48

OUR HOLGATE END IN THE SKY

We are the Ayresome Angels and never miss a match, we will follow the Boro.

OUR NAME IS ON THAT CUP! BELIEVE IT!

rozi Posted on 1/5 9:58

OUR HOLGATE END IN THE SKY

This must be the best thread I have ever seen on here, even though I can hardly see my screen for tears. Well done, Broughton Lad, for being brave enough to put it on in the first place. Wonderful words which I agree should be somewhere at the ground for everyone to see. Don't think there will be many fans who have never said, "If only xxx had lived to see this". Thanks, BL.

craigyboro4eva Posted on 1/5 10:10

OUR HOLGATE END IN THE SKY

Me brother will have been sat on his cloud having a pot with Gabriel telling him he watched us when we were s***e. RIP Wilf, lad.

speckyget Posted on 1/5 19:28

OUR HOLGATE END IN THE SKY

My Dad died on Saturday night.

RIP Tommy. You were a great Dad, a great Boro fan and a great man. I'm privileged that you were my father. You were straight as an arrow and as strong as Teesside steel.

I'll love you and miss you until the day I die.

Goal_Scrounger Posted on 1/5 19:33

OUR HOLGATE END IN THE SKY

Specky, I don't know what to say.

Sincere condolences, my friend.

twoshots Posted on 1/5 19:36

OUR HOLGATE END IN THE SKY

Specky, I thought you might show up on this thread. Really sorry.

Nedkat Posted on 1/5 19:37

OUR HOLGATE END IN THE SKY

Spec, so sorry to hear that... please accept my sincere condolences. I hope your family will get through this and manage to keep each other in their hearts. It's tough, but there is a light at the end.

holgate69 Posted on 1/5 19:37

OUR HOLGATE END IN THE SKY

I lost my mother coming up to two years ago now. I remember phoning her on the way out of Cardiff. She was crying her eyes out that the Boro had finally won a cup. She told me she had watched it with my dad and they were both in sheds of tears.

My Dad still listens to Boro games but does not go any more. He used to years ago but is one of the old buggers who always tell us, "Boro always let you down, son."

I still miss her so much and think of her every day. I am sure she is in The Holgate In The Sky cheering us on and loving our recent adventures.

The_Commisar Posted on 1/5 19:38

OUR HOLGATE END IN THE SKY

Specky, sorry to hear that. Chin up, mate.

BroughtonLad Posted on 1/5 19:44

OUR HOLGATE END IN THE SKY

So sorry, Specky. One thing is that he will be with good company in OUR HOLGATE IN THE SKY.

holgate69 Posted on 1/5 19:48

OUR HOLGATE END IN THE SKY

Thoughts with you and your family, Specky.

Valer Posted on 1/5 22:32

OUR HOLGATE END IN THE SKY

Let's go and lift the cup for him, Specky. Sincere condolences.

twoshots Posted on 5/5 10:18

OUR HOLGATE END IN THE SKY

Speckyget has asked me to give this a quick hoist this morning as it's his Dad's funeral at 10.30. He also wanted to say "thank you" to those who posted condolences on this thread.

South_Stand_Steward Posted on 5/5 11:35

OUR HOLGATE END IN THE SKY

Thoughts with Speckyget and his family on their sad occasion. Deepest sympathy from me.

BroughtonLad Posted on 9/5 7:58

OUR HOLGATE END IN THE SKY

Well, not long to go now. Tomorrow our thoughts again will be with our Ayresome Angels. I doubt if any of our family and friends up there in OUR HOLGATE IN THE SKY will be worried about getting to Eindhoven. They will be up there, shouting the lads on.

Make sure we all give that extra cheer when Gareth Southgate lifts that cup tomorrow night.

MIDDLESBROUGH FOOTBALL CLUB - UEFA CUP WINNERS 2006.

Come On Boro!!!

ray192 Posted on 9/5 8:09

OUR HOLGATE END IN THE SKY

Come on, Dad and the rest of the Earls, we really need you. I know all of you dreamt of this happening, well now it's here, the UEFA CUP FINAL.

COME ON BORO.

BroughtonLad Posted on 9/5 8:17

OUR HOLGATE END IN THE SKY

Hoof for:

Ernie 'Ragbo' Robinson
Trigg Deaves
Alfie Thomas Harburn
RIP

They will be up there tonight with their flags waving.

MickDude Posted on 9/5 9:18

OUR HOLGATE END IN THE SKY

Going on up to The Holgate In The Sky,
That's where I'm gonna go when I die.
When I die and they lay me to rest
I'm still supporting the team that's the best...

BORO... BORO...

Come ON!!!

wool_skull Posted on 9/5 16:23

OUR HOLGATE END IN THE SKY

I've got a couple of Grandads up there who'll no doubt be watching, having a pint with all the rest of our Ayresome Angels!

C'MON THE BORO!

teessider11 Posted on 9/5 17:05

OUR HOLGATE END IN THE SKY

Love you, Mam, always will.

COME ON BORO!

gargle1 Posted on 9/5 22:40

OUR HOLGATE END IN THE SKY

Great post! I'm sat in a hotel in Eindhoven with my wee boy (conked after travelling all day from Ireland). My dad passed away in February this year and I have felt he's helping us all the way! He had 78 years of basically fekk all... we got the Carling Cup when he could barely notice! I have those Boro doubts tonight... I'm preparing wee boy for dejection but secretly praying we can do it. We have come so far and travelled so much for those not here. Deliver please, boys!

Andy.

borobuddah Posted on 9/5 23:12

OUR HOLGATE END IN THE SKY

Dad, Aunty Audrey, "Are you watching up above?"

(They'll be back tomorrow saying "Told you".)

Anyway, getting there is a dream and we're all in it.

onthemap Posted on 10/5 0:23

OUR HOLGATE END IN THE SKY

Only one thing to do - we need to get this thread to the players. I have no idea how but surely it can be done. It would certainly motivate me if I was a player and my Grandad would agree. So how?

Grumpy_Paul Posted on 10/5 0:42

OUR HOLGATE END IN THE SKY

Les Mann - Boro daft and yet another early exit from this earth.
RIP Les, I'm sure you'll be watching.

Commiserations to Speckyget.

borodownunda Posted on 10/5 1:32

OUR HOLGATE END IN THE SKY

My Dad left the Boro to come to Australia over 50 years ago. As a kid, he would talk to me about the Boro with love and despair - love of the town and the team, despair of his desire for a better life that meant leaving his home. His legacy was to leave me a lifelong love of the Boro and everything that is part of it. He taught me to understand the people of the North-East, he taught me to value being Australian, he taught me the joy and value of being true to your past, no matter how hard the lows and how wonderful the highs.

He will be in The Holgate In The Sky tonight. He left to get his seat 15 years ago. Every day I miss him and thank him. Tonight is for the true believers, I know deep in my heart.

YearbyRed Posted on 10/5 5:30

OUR HOLGATE END IN THE SKY

I'm just about to set off. Let's win it for every Boro fan, past and present, who can't be there.

Tears streaming down my face. Thanks for taking me to the Boro, Dad.

To all Boro fans who have passed away over the years and look down on us from above:

"YOU ARE OUR AYRESOME ANGELS"

Evanzio Posted on 10/5 7:46

OUR HOLGATE END IN THE SKY

Charlie Wayman... Boro legend... RIP.

For you, Charlie, and everyone else who has pulled on a red shirt and fought for the cause, the boys will do you proud tonight.

cmagpie9 Posted on 10/5 8:01

OUR HOLGATE END IN THE SKY

From a Mag, I just want to mention a great Redcar lad.

Andrew "Fred" Flynn died 17 years ago. He was a good mate and a top Boro fan.

wolver Posted on 10/5 8:07

OUR HOLGATE END IN THE SKY

Eddie Thompson, first match v Everton 1938, died April 2005.

For you, Dad.

ray192 Posted on 10/5 8:27

OUR HOLGATE END IN THE SKY

Specky, deepest sympathy from the Derbyshire Reds.

AyresomeMark Posted on 10/5 9:42

OUR HOLGATE END IN THE SKY

Grans, Grandads Shirley and Aud.

Shirl - Boro has a special place for you. Your flowers were red and white. I know you've been keeping this UEFA Cup run going. One more night. I love and miss you. Hope you lot are playing cards and watching the Boro.

the_righteous_one Posted on 10/5 10:12

OUR HOLGATE END IN THE SKY

To all Boro fans who have passed away over the years and look down on us from above:

"YOU ARE OUR AYRESOME ANGELS"

Simon1 Posted on 10/5 11:20

OUR HOLGATE END IN THE SKY

My little sister was too young to follow football but I'm sure if she was around today she would have supported the lads tonight (she would have if I had my bloody way!)

tony_block19 Posted on 10/5 11:33

OUR HOLGATE END IN THE SKY

I haven't really got any close family who loved the Boro and are deceased, but I'll still say thank you to my Dad who took me to that first game back in 1993, who got me hooked on something that no drug in the world comes close to beating! He gave his Season Ticket up in 2000, when we (as a family) were really struggling financially and couldn't afford the prices every year. He never really got back into the groove of it as he lost touch with his mates, but I carried on the baton and now I'm doing the same to my younger brother, teaching him the ways of Middlesbrough Football Club. I think he's getting the hang of it.

But I do have a story about a great uncle who passed away about a month ago. He was a big Boro fan and like many others, lived to see the day when the Boro would reach the dizzy heights we're at now! Anyway, whilst watching the Bucharest home leg, as soon as the fourth goal went in, my Great Aunty stood up and shouted "RAY, WE'VE DONE IT!" Then, to her surprise, the dog came running in as he heard my Great Uncle's name!

God bless the Boro fans who laid the foundations for what we have today, for inspiring your sons, daughters and grandchildren to follow the Boro through thick and thin, knowing that all those 1-0 defeats on a cold, wet, windy January afternoon are all made up by massive, euphoric occasions like tonight.

Boro Til I Die!

redcarbob Posted on 10/5 11:39

OUR HOLGATE END IN THE SKY

I will never forget the smile on Mam's face when I came home after a Boro win, or the sympathy she used to offer after a defeat, especially those '90s cup finals.

Hope you are up there smiling tonight, Mam. Love and miss you x

newholgate Posted on 10/5 13:26

OUR HOLGATE END IN THE SKY

Today, on the most historic day in the life of our club, I am not only carrying in my heart and mind my loved ones who have gone, but all Boro fans who would have loved to share this day with us. I'm particularly thinking of all those who started this season's European campaign with us, but died before the end of it, especially Brendan O'Connor.

TODAY IS FOR ALL BORO FANS, PAST, PRESENT AND FUTURE.

starbecksmoggy2 Posted on 10/5 13:44

OUR HOLGATE END IN THE SKY

Arthur, I know you will be up there, sat with Wilf and George (your heroes), supping a couple and cheering the lads on. Well, sing louder, sing your hearts out for the lads as you always did.

RIP Da.

Rozi Posted on 10/5 14:01

OUR HOLGATE END IN THE SKY

Specky, our sincere condolences to you and your family on your loss.

I stayed away from this thread until today because it makes me blub every time. I just thought it was the thing to do on this most important day in our history, to read all the messages and remember how lucky I am to still be around to see a day like today. Still blubbing all the way through, though.

Love_Me_Love_My_Smog Posted on 10/5 14:15

OUR HOLGATE END IN THE SKY

Dad, you never saw us win anything (we don't count the Anglo-Scottish) and you died the season before the Carling win. Have a pint up there, tell everyone how this lot aren't fit to lace Wilf's boots and watch us win our FIRST European trophy.

spanboro Posted on 10/5 14:20

OUR HOLGATE END IN THE SKY

My Grandad, Norman Brakewell, died on 28th March this year after falling outside the Boro ground at the Blackburn Carling Cup game. He was 83 years old. He absolutely worshipped the Boro and everything about them and went to every single home game. Last year, he even had to get a passport as he made it to the Graz game. I know he is watching as the day after his funeral, we beat Basel 4-2 and I'm sure he had something to do with it.

Come on Boro! Do it for my Grandad!

Boro_Forever Posted on 10/5 16:22

OUR HOLGATE END IN THE SKY

When I was younger, I was very close to my great gran. She was as big a Boro fan as anyone I have ever met. After going to the match with my Dad, I'd go round my gran's house to talk about the game with her.

She sadly passed away five years ago and reading this made me think of her. If she was alive today I think she'd die of sheer amazement.

RIP Irene Gray. Gone but never forgotten.

Nedkat Posted on 10/5 16:25

OUR HOLGATE END IN THE SKY

Dad, I miss you even more on days like this. I just want you to know we're all going to enjoy this day, whatever the result. The lads have done us proud just getting to the Final.

We were all together for the ZDS and those Wembley finals. You missed out on Cardiff, but you get yerself a good spot to watch this one. Look after Span's Grandad, have a word with the Big Yun for a Boro victory and remember how much we all mean to each other... All those glorious years!

Ned.

the_righteous_one Posted on 10/5 16:43

OUR HOLGATE END IN THE SKY

Some of these stories about loved ones who have passed away really are heart wrenching. Makes me proud to be a Boro lad.

Arthur, I know you will be up there, sat with Wilf and George (your heroes), supping a couple and cheering the lads on. Well, sing louder, sing your hearts out for the lads as you always did.

wobschall Posted on 10/5 16:57

OUR HOLGATE END IN THE SKY

My Grandad, Millwall fan by birth, lived in South Bank for 50 odd years after meeting my Nana up here in the war whilst stationed at Saltburn.

The stubborn old bugger stopped watching Boro when Cloughie was sold to the Mackems... my family and I had to carry things on...

He used to always moan about the Boro letting you down, but secretly he kept the faith I think - just.

I'm sure he was looking down on us against Basel and Bucharest.

expat_boro Posted on 10/5 17:10

OUR HOLGATE END IN THE SKY

Dad, I know that you are here in this room in spirit with me. I just wish that I could wrap my arms around you and thank you for making me a Boro fan. I am so proud of that and so proud that you were my Dad. Bring it on home, lads, especially for my Dad.

ian1969uk Posted on 10/5 17:11

OUR HOLGATE END IN THE SKY

Before every European game this year, I've had a little word with my Mam who died a couple of years ago, asking her to bring us some luck. Will be doing the same tonight.

One last time, Mam, you can do it!

chrissy2002 Posted on 10/5 18:05

OUR HOLGATE END IN THE SKY

Dad, I know you're watching and I'm so glad you got me involved at the age of 10 when I used to stand outside the gates watching the players come in whilst you worked on the turnstiles and did for 30 years before you became ill.

I know you've been gone now for 1yr 5mths but I still miss you more than ever. Please give a cheer from Heaven cos I'll always remember you always moaned after every match, no matter what the score, but that was a big part of you. Please let us win tonight and put your magic touch on the Boro.

Always remembered by your ever Boro-loving daughter, Christine xx

donnysmoggie Posted on 10/5 18:42

OUR HOLGATE END IN THE SKY

My Grandad passed away in 1995. He never saw the Riverside but I am sure he is stood on The Holgate End In The Sky. If he could only see that the team he followed for almost 70 years are playing in Europe, never mind a European Cup Final, he would be on cloud nine. This night is for you, Grandad, and all lost Boro fans, whoever they might be.

COME ON BORO!

MontagueWithnail Posted on 11/5 0:54

OUR HOLGATE END IN THE SKY

We did our best, Mam. One day we will do even better x

ian1969uk Posted on 11/5 1:04

OUR HOLGATE END IN THE SKY

Yeah, thanks for trying again tonight, Mam. We'll be back.

Love you and miss you loads xxx

rozi Posted on 11/5 9:31

OUR HOLGATE END IN THE SKY

There'd be as many tears in Heaven last night as there were down here I'm sure.

AyresomeMark Posted on 12/5 10:21

OUR HOLGATE END IN THE SKY

One day everyone, one day.

Thanks to everyone for this life affirming, inspiring post. The Boro family is a strong bond that will NEVER be broken.

BroughtonLad Posted on 25/8 10:08

OUR HOLGATE END IN THE SKY

Such a shame for someone so young.
23 years old with so much to look forward to.
Deepest sympathy to all family and friends.

RIP.

We will be thinking of you when we play Portsmouth. God Bless.

rozi Posted on 25/8 10:36

OUR HOLGATE END IN THE SKY

Sincere condolences to all of his family and friends. It's hard to imagine a young lad going out to watch a game of football and something like this happening. (Thanks, BL, for giving us the chance to read this again).

craigyboro4eva Posted on 25/8 10:49

OUR HOLGATE END IN THE SKY

Deepest sympathy to the young lad's family, thoughts with you all season.

hells_bells83 Posted on 25/8 10:58

OUR HOLGATE END IN THE SKY

What an amazing thread. I didn't see this first time round and I didn't think anything I would read on here could get me crying like this.

We are one, come on Boro!

newholgate Posted on 25/8 11:03

OUR HOLGATE END IN THE SKY

I have just been reading back over this thread and it got me thinking:

Wouldn't it be nice to have a long banner hanging from the top of the North Stand saying, "OUR HOLGATE END IN THE SKY" in memory of every Boro fan we have lost. I think it would be a lovely tribute and good to know that when our time is up, it serves in our memory too.

Or maybe add a bit on so it says, "OUR HOLGATE END IN THE SKY - With Us In Spirit".

Just a thought.

grantus Posted on 25/8 11:25

OUR HOLGATE END IN THE SKY

Yeah, a beautiful thread. Couldn't read it just now, I nearly lost it reading a few posts. Can't have a bloke shedding tears in the office.

Very emotional indeed.

The blood of the Boro runs deep.

Noj1 Posted on 25/8 11:41

OUR HOLGATE END IN THE SKY

I very rarely post anything on here but often read what you lot have to say in the office while at work. This is an amazing post. I missed it first time round. I've only managed to read a few responses to this and am really struggling to read on. Great idea about the banner, newholgate.

dan_boro Posted on 25/8 12:20

OUR HOLGATE END IN THE SKY

Yeah, definitely a good idea about the banner - maybe something to think about organising and raising cash for.

This post should be permanently added as a link on the website, as a sort of condolence/inspirational book for the fans to remember those who are no longer with us.

Sad news about the young lad who died on Wednesday. I saw the paramedics etc below me (I sit in SW Upper) and was wondering what happened. RIP - I'm sure he's in The Holgate In The Sky and will be there cheering the lads on Monday night with the rest of the Boro faithful.

B_Hills Posted on 25/8 13:47

OUR HOLGATE END IN THE SKY

I'd be happy to contribute to that banner in memory of Boro fans I have known and lost!!